ADVANCE PRAISE FOR *Their* **Highest** VOCATION

"This book...should be mandatory reading for anyone serious about the role of and opportunities confronting higher education today. I hope all of us will consider the deeper educational questions Helen Fox raises in relationship to serving the intellectual and moral development needs of the Millennial generation. I come away from her text with a much clearer understanding of this generation of students and what I can do as an educator to support their growth and development. Further, I'm filled with a greater optimism that the world will benefit from this generation of leaders.

Fox has written with great insight and clarity about questions that my colleagues and I wrestle with every day: how do we support students' growth and development as they consider their role in making the world a better place? We toss around words like 'justice, inclusion, mattering, non-violence' as desired outcomes of higher education and the development of an educated person—but what educational structures are necessary to support students' own discovery of the meaning of justice and role in bringing that about? I look forward to the many important conversations this book will inevitably stimulate!"

—*Susan A. Wilson, Associate Dean for Community Life,*
Academic Dean's Office, Goddard College

"This short, radiant, radical book is several things at once. It is a critical but loving assessment of the strengths and weaknesses of the Millennial generation of undergraduates admitted to the elite American public universities. It is a wise and practical reflection on what faculty can do to encourage their students' flourishing, both as subjects who arrive at university constrained by unexamined assumptions..., and as agents who are already gifted and passionate about making a positive difference in the world, but too often lack the self-understanding and the insight into others very different from themselves necessary to realize this aspiration. The book is enlivened by the kind of moral passion we find in Jonathan Kozol, and tempered by the grace and wisdom that comes from many years of practicing the pedagogical principles of Myles Horton and Paulo Freire. Consistent with those principles, many of the insights in this book emerge as meditations on respectful but challenging dialogues with undergraduates and colleagues with whom Fox has worked. From these diverse voices, Fox weaves an inspiring, multi-colored vision of higher education as a vital force for building what Freire called 'a world in which it will be easier to love.' This is a book to be read, re-read, cherished, and shared by all who care about higher education and its relationship to human development and social justice."

—*Ian Robinson, Lecturer and Research Scientist,*
Department of Sociology and Residential College, University of Michigan-Ann Arbor

"Helen Fox...first offers a careful look behind the usual broad-brush characterizations of the Millennials, which, as a parent of a Millennial child just starting college, I found engaging, provocative, and full of ideas to help me understand and support my daughter. Fox then successfully dares to construct a conversation between Paulo Freire and her students in a way that deeply explores the dilemmas of social justice in this generation. The lively dialogues between her and her student respondents give real examples of how Millennial students feel as they face the contradictions and injustices of our times, and of the kinds of conversations that can lead them into growth and change. By intertwining the lessons of her extensive personal experience with the viewpoints of other practiced educators and the perspectives of students, she subtly constructs a menu of new ideas, options, tools, and strategies for social justice education. I learned so much that I will use to develop my teaching and to continue to struggle to help myself and others 'become fully human' in the Millennial world."

—*Marla Solomon, Professor,*
Department of Intercultural Service, Leadership, and Management, SIT Graduate Institute

Their **Highest** VOCATION

This book is part of the Peter Lang Education list.
Every volume is peer reviewed and meets
the highest quality standards for content and production.

PETER LANG
New York • Washington, D.C./Baltimore • Bern
Frankfurt • Berlin • Brussels • Vienna • Oxford

HELEN FOX

Their **Highest** VOCATION

Social Justice and the Millennial Generation

PETER LANG
New York • Washington, D.C./Baltimore • Bern
Frankfurt • Berlin • Brussels • Vienna • Oxford

Library of Congress Cataloging-in-Publication Data

Fox, Helen.
Their highest vocation : social justice
and the millennial generation / Helen Fox.
p. cm.
Includes bibliographical references.
1. Generation Y—United States. 2. College teaching—United States.
3. Social justice—United States. 4. United States—Race relations. I. Title.
HQ799.7.F69   303.3'7208350973—dc23   2011031683
ISBN 978-1-4331-1276-8 (hardcover)
ISBN 978-1-4331-1275-1 (paperback)
ISBN 978-1-4539-0184-7 (e-book)

Bibliographic information published by **Die Deutsche Nationalbibliothek**.
Die Deutsche Nationalbibliothek lists this publication in the "Deutsche
Nationalbibliografie"; detailed bibliographic data is available
on the Internet at http://dnb.d-nb.de/.

Cover art by Leisa Thompson.

The paper in this book meets the guidelines for permanence and durability
of the Committee on Production Guidelines for Book Longevity
of the Council of Library Resources.

© 2012 Peter Lang Publishing, Inc., New York
29 Broadway, 18th floor, New York, NY 10006
www.peterlang.com

All rights reserved.
Reprint or reproduction, even partially, in all forms such as microfilm,
xerography, microfiche, microcard, and offset strictly prohibited.

Printed in the United States of America

Contents

	Introduction	1
1.	Who Are the Millennials?	7
2.	Critical Education	26
3.	Knowing Where You're From	42
4.	Connecting in a Digital Age	60
5.	Lighting the Fire	77
6.	Radical Equality	99
7.	Millennial Leadership	119
8.	Teaching Peace	141
9.	Visions of the Future	165
10.	The Soul of a Great University	188
	References	209

Introduction

Dear Ms. Fox,

I am a fan of your work. I grew up an avid activist and have always been very passionate about making a difference within my community. The past few years, I have been focused on prisoner rights, mostly juvenile prisoners. As I'm sure you know, in the United States, and especially in the State of Michigan, putting juveniles in adult prisons for life without the option of parole is a very big problem. I would like to do an independent study/anthropological research project on the issue in hopes I can show people that locking these kids up for life and not giving them the opportunities that can help them lead a better life and make a difference in their community is wrong. I have made a connection to the prisons and am waiting to hear back to see if I can plan a timeline of dates for interviewing, observing, studying, etc.

What I need now is an adviser to help me with this. I cannot do it alone, it is too big a project and to be honest, it's not about getting credit for me. This is more to me than school—this is what I want to do with my life and I want to do it now. When I find an issue I believe in, I will do anything to make sure that I can help and follow through. I want to make a difference and I want to prove that I can be a good anthropologist.

I know you're not a professor of anthropology, but you are someone who teaches about making a difference in the world and about peace, and someone who I look up to for that. I am asking you for help; if you know of anybody who would advise me, or if you could even be my adviser, or even give me pointers, I would appreciate it sincerely.

This e-mail arrived while I was immersed in my own research project on social justice education and the Millennial generation. I was touched by this student's energy, her intense desire to "make a difference," her willingness to contact a faculty member she had only read about online, and her youthful sense of urgency—*this is what I want to do with my life and I want to do it now*—all of which, I thought, was emblematic of the Millennial students I was reading about—and whom I had taught for the last ten years at the University of Michigan.

Shortly after the turn of the century, some of the long-time faculty started noticing something different about the students showing up in our classes and coming to us for advice. While my courses in human rights, race and racism, nonviolence, and development in the Global South had attracted many outstanding students in the past, these young people were particularly bold in their belief that they could plunge right in and solve the world's problems. Some of them had impressive résumés right out of high school: internships abroad and community service at home, perhaps starting a chapter of Amnesty International, or organizing a concert to raise money for cancer research or a children's hospital. By their third or fourth year in college, many of these students had been involved in a dizzying array of social justice activities on and off campus, often in leadership roles, while still maintaining a high grade point average. One of my advisees, for example, was double majoring in Creative Writing and Social Theory and Practice (writing an honors thesis for each) and, in her spare time, had planned and facilitated weekly writing workshops for Michigan prisoners, coordinated campus conferences on immigration rights, organized Latina workers fighting labor abuses, tutored low-income Spanish-speaking women, and organized volunteers and participants in an after-school tutoring program for socioeconomically disadvantaged youth. And that was only the beginning. She had also organized a grief support network for students, given public lectures on prison reform, and, at graduation, she was working on an entirely new project: a prison museum, "conceptually analogous to the Holocaust Museum," she told me. Visitors would be assigned the identity of an actual inmate and walked through that individual's life and prison experience in order to give the public a fuller sense of their humanity and the complexity of their situations. She is twenty-two years old.

No longer is it unusual to hear of an undergraduate who has raised thousands of dollars to build a school in a Kenyan slum where she had worked over her summer vacation—right after she completed an internship with the United Nations. Nor is it surprising that a couple of undergrads would team up to organize and staff a program in Ecuador, complete with courses, readings, home stays, and field trips, so their fellow students could learn about global poverty firsthand. I even had a sophomore who led a team of physicians and graduate students to Vietnam, his parents' home country, to research health problems and advise the Vietnamese government on best hospital practices. Clearly, this kind of student engagement was different from my own experience in the 1960s, when as one of the early Peace Corps Volunteers I had embarked on an adventure to a remote corner of India with a vague notion of helping out. It was different, too, from the single-minded determination of the students who had marched in Selma, or had massed by the hundreds of thousands to protest the Vietnam War. This new kind of student activism seemed to be built on brash individual initiative, the confidence to pick up the phone and make things happen, an entrepreneurship for the good of others that valued immediate action over words, or context, or history.

As Millennial students started arriving in our social justice courses with their grand plans to change the world, instructors were also noticing, somewhat paradoxically, that they seemed to have a greater need for structure, an insistence on detailed explanations of the assignments and exactly how their work would be evaluated. Faculty who preferred a looser, more reflective classroom, with discussion rather than lecture and questions to which there were no right answers, were met with student frustration and, at times, a troubling insistence that teachers should present more facts and examples leading to definite conclusions that they could reproduce on papers and tests, rather than asking them to consider for themselves what those facts might mean. They were good workers: quick, efficient learners, polite, and willing. Yet they seemed reluctant to express points of view that might differ from those of their peers, or stray very far from their idea of "what the teacher wants." Many of them were energized by calls for swift, immediate action: Stop the genocide in Darfur! Fund earthquake relief in Haiti! Go Green! Yet they became discouraged when we asked them to investigate the complex interconnections of social problems, their multiple, inconclusive causes, the pitfalls of quick solutions. Where did such determined energy and, at the same time, such anxious conformity, such "intellectual timidity," as one of my colleagues put it, come from? And how should progressive educators respond to it?

As I embarked on my project to understand our work with this new generation, I reflected on my own development as an educator. Hired by the writing program in the early 1990s to work with U-M's increasingly multicultural population, I had quickly found ways to get students thinking about the values I cared most about: equality, inclusion, and peace with justice. My classroom style had been influenced by many progressive educators including Paulo Freire and Myles Horton[1]—both of whom I had met in graduate school—as well as John Holt, whose gentle voice had critiqued the rigid teaching style common in U.S. schools in the 1960s,[2] and Jonathan Kozol, who had worked in the Boston ghetto at around the same time I had, and whose moral outrage in *Death at an Early Age*[3] paralleled my own indignation at a racist school system that destroyed children's humanity through a lethal combination of arrogance, incompetence, prejudice, and fear. I came to college teaching rather late in life—I was almost fifty when I joined Michigan's faculty—hoping to "make a difference" in my own way by teaching students at an elite university to question standard assumptions about race, culture, poverty, and the inevitability of war.

I started my research for this book by rereading Freire and contemporary commentators on his work. Invoking Tolstoy,[4] Freire reminds us that man's highest vocation is to become more fully human, that is, to live to one's fullest potential by working in "dialogue, hope, humility and sympathy"[5] for a world of greater equality between peoples, a more just order among nations, "a world in which it will be easier to love."[6] This, indeed, is a goal that progressive educators and their students have always shared. But students' longing for a better world must be shaped and nurtured, informed and interrogated by facts, analysis, reflection, experience, and opportunities for leadership.

How, then, should progressive educators address this particular generation's desire to serve humanity? What do these students, especially the relatively privileged students at elite universities, need to know? How can more of them be drawn into significant social justice work? What skills and whose knowledge should the college experience provide? How can we nourish the mental and spiritual stamina these young people will need as they confront injustice? What unique strengths do they bring that educators can build on? What weaknesses should we address? In what ways should the university's overall mission change to help the Millennial generation make effective contributions to the social good?

Those were some of the questions that came to mind as I read and reflected on the characteristics of this generation and the history of progressive education. Soon I realized I needed to talk to other faculty who teach U-M's social justice courses, counsel Millennial students, and direct programs that reach these students through experiential learning, reflection, dialogue, and service. I also needed to hear from students themselves, both current undergraduates whom I knew to be social justice leaders and recent graduates who are taking their Michigan education into the world. In the end, I recorded, transcribed, and analyzed thirty-two, one- to two-hour interviews—or, in most cases, "collaborative conversations"—with twelve progressive U-M faculty and staff, seven program heads (who are also faculty or staff), eight student leaders, four recent U-M graduates working in social justice fields, and a community storyteller, who, as an intellectual and an elder "telling history" in impoverished local schools, offers insight into what educators should be doing at the college level. I made no attempt to choose my conversation partners randomly; I knew them all through various collegial relationships. They had been students in my classes, or my advisees, or respected colleagues, or simply people I knew to be doing good work. For chapter 7, "Teaching Peace," I drew on my previous research on college students' attitudes toward war and peace, where my undergraduate research assistants and I had talked to eighty U-M undergraduates, about a quarter of whom had taken my class on nonviolence. All these stimulating interviews were extremely helpful to my thinking. They built on and challenged my ideas and those of the authors I was reading; they added new questions and some wonderful stories and often led the conversation in unexpected directions. I highlight my informants' voices throughout this book in order to reproduce as accurately as possible their thoughts and convictions, their contemplative moments, their uncertainties, frustrations, passion, and insights.

I would like to express my deep appreciation to the students and colleagues who engaged me in these long, intense conversations, read my drafts, and trusted me to tell their stories. Many thanks also to my daughter Cybelle Fox and my step-daughter, Sara Koopman, who supported and challenged my thinking in most productive ways, and to my husband Jim Koopman, whose generous spirit offers me the space and time to do this work.

This book is dedicated to my grandchildren, Sarah, Devyn, Kendall, and Aidan, who, at twelve, seven, four, and four months, will soon inherit a world shaped by the dreams and foibles of today's college students—the Millennial generation.

Notes

1. Especially Horton's autobiography, *The Long Haul* (1999).
2. Holt, 1994.
3. Kozol, 1967.
4. Tolstoy, 1914. "The highest vocation in the world is that of those who live in order to serve God by bringing good into the world and who have joined together for that very purpose" p. 51.
5. Freire, 1986, 21.
6. Ibid., 24.

Chapter 1

Who Are the Millennials?

> Yes, there's a revolution under way among today's kids—a *good news revolution*. This generation is going to rebel by behaving not worse, but *better*. Their life mission will not be to tear down old institutions that don't work, but to build up new ones that do. . . .Today's kids are on track to become a powerhouse generation, full of technology planners, community shapers, institution builders, and world leaders, perhaps destined to dominate the twenty-first century like today's fading and ennobled G.I. Generation dominated the twentieth.[1]

It was Neil Howe and William Strauss who named the Millennial Generation and popularized their attributes in *Millennials Rising: The Next Great Generation*. Between them, the authors have been policy advisors, journalists, magazine editors, directors of teen musicals, political satirists, think-tank pundits, and "fathers with a pro-kid bias."[2] They have written widely about previous generations, and clearly, they are crazy about this one.

Howe and Strauss seem relieved that Millennials, whose first members were born in 1982 and began pouring into college around 2000, are, as a whole, model citizens. These young people "manifest a wide array of positive social habits that older Americans no longer associate with youth, including a new focus on teamwork, achievement, modesty, and good conduct."[3] Millennials are optimists: happy, confident, ever-positive.[4] They look to authorities for guidance and are strongly connected to their parents, who have regarded them as "special" since birth and obsessed over them at every age.[5] They have been successful rule-followers since childhood; cooperative and compliant, they have responded to the high expectations of parents and teachers with a string of achievements. Perhaps because of their warm relationships with adults, Millennials tend to trust the government and believe it should be more actively involved in taking care of its citizens. Yet their approval of older generations is contingent on adults' good behavior: Millennials are dismayed by squabbling politicians and misbehaving celebrities, considering them "vastly more spoiled and unethical than their own generation."[6]

Despite their tendency to conform to the expectations of their Generation X parents—whose profile is one of cynicism and disengagement—Millennials show a "team player" ethic and a social conscience that has not been seen in U.S. politics for a long time. They are strongly progressive, voting Democratic in large numbers, and showing a "deep concern for today's income inequalities and social stratification,"[7] a desire for a more multilateral foreign policy, and an "overwhelming" belief that "the country should do 'whatever it takes' to protect the environment."[8] On social issues, too, Millennials are much more liberal than previous generations. On survey questions about interracial dating, women's leadership, and the rights of gays and lesbians, the majority of Millennials respond positively. According to the polls, at least, race, gender, and sexual orientation are "no big deal."[9]

Ethnic and racial diversity is a hallmark of this generation, both because of the group's sheer size[10] and because of the impressive number of immigrants arriving in the United States since the 1990s. Forty percent of Millennial adults are people of color.[11] Because of the increasing mix of ethnicities and the explosion of the Internet, Millennials are "the world's first generation to grow up thinking of itself as global."[12] And of course, they are deeply attached to the new technologies that, perhaps more than anything, characterize their era; electronic toys and workplace tools are their entertainment, their connection to friends and family, their source of information, their school essentials, their window on the world.

Most college-age Millennials grew up at a time of unprecedented affluence, which has deeply affected their outlook on life. The students surveyed by Howe and Strauss lived "in houses that contain 50 percent more things (measured by the pound)"[13] than houses did in 1990. Before the stock market crash of 2008, it could be said that Millennials had "never known a year in which America doesn't get richer."[14] This has surely contributed to both their sense of confidence about the future and to their parents' ability to chauffeur them to after-school activities and send them around the world on programs that might improve their chance of admission to a competitive college.

"*Everyone* is high achieving now," an international program head told me. "So how is your kid going to look distinctive in this crowd? Parents are determined their kid will make it. And the way they're going to make it is by having the most unbelievable set of experiences on their resume: 'I worked on the pampas of Argentina!' 'I learned Swahili in Mozambique!'" Even for students growing up in less affluent areas, the pressure to pack their high school résumés is intense. "There's a kind of insane competition to get into universities now," says a Detroit-based instructor of color. "You know, there's a list of stuff that you have to do. You have to be practically a Rhodes Scholar to even get in anywhere. So you have to do music, you have to do activism of some sort, volunteer in some way. You have to do athletics, plus excel in everything. Regardless of whether the university is top tier or not, everybody is caught up in a crazy scramble."

In this struggle for survival, one also can get ahead by sheer gall. "What are the characteristics of this generation that stand out in my mind?" laughs an academic counselor. "They're incredibly self-absorbed. A lot of them have been very indulged by their parents, and their life has been all about them. They're—I don't want to say spoiled and bratty, but there's a sense of entitlement that's very different from students in the past. There's an edge to it, a sense that they're owed something." This isn't entirely negative, the counselor adds, although it can try her patience. "I think a lot of parents have instilled in their kids that if they feel strongly about something they should push, they should fight, they should agitate for what they feel is rightfully theirs. At whatever cost. Don't take no for an answer!" Of course, agitating for what you feel is right can be admirable, she continues, but sometimes it's simply not warranted. "I've had students make comments that the teacher had no right to criticize them. I've even had students who say their *parents* said that nobody has a right to criticize them. That is such a ludicrous idea to me—but I do understand where it's coming from. They're pushing because they want the 'A,' because they want the best possible record, so that the future choices they might make are not limited. So if they want to go to medical school or law school, as so many of our students do, then their record will show them in the best possible light so they'll look better than the other candidates and get in."

These comments highlight a striking contradiction in these students' lives. They may have been pampered by their parents, but they've also been pushed to the limit to excel. "We have students who are emotionally fragile—a *lot* at this institution," says a program director. "It's disturbing when you realize how many students here are sort of on edge. I think many students feel that to make it you have to show you can make it. You have to be tough, you can't crack. That push to be 'the leaders and the best,' is all about smiling, not giving the impression that you're struggling. And that makes it very hard on the student who *is* struggling. You just struggle *way more* because there are all kinds of things you never talk about, because they would reveal you're not as strong as you say you are, or that you don't really fit in."[15]

A writing instructor agrees. "I see a lot more anxiety among college students these days. They come in to see me more frequently because they want to know where they stand in the class, or where they stand with me, or if they're doing a good job on their projects, or how their writing measures up. I think a lot of them have anxiety disorders. And they're coming in already a little freaked out about the education process. Several of my students have told me they are on medication to help relieve their anxiety, or they need to take time off from school, that they didn't do really well the first time around. And in class, you can see them sort of looking around the room, comparing themselves to each other. They feel that already, their status and career are at stake."[16]

"You know, the whole stress thing is interesting," says the academic counselor. "It certainly *seems* as if they're under stress: 'Oh! I have so many things to do! Oh, I'm so busy! Oh, I'm involved in this and I've got to do that.' It's a sense of busyness that they give off. Yet they live in a time when so much has been made possible for stress-free living. They have the conveniences of life—word processing as opposed to having to type papers, information on line rather than having to go to the library. You'd think that things being readily available would ease the stress. But it doesn't seem to."

Of course, she adds, not all students are overwhelmed—most seem to manage their myriad activities and deadlines pretty well. "When they come in to talk about their schedules, I see the way they've organized their daily planners. They've color-coded them! They're impeccably organized. It's amazing!" she says. But these students are used to tight programming and back-to-back activities. "Today's kids may comprise the most supervised and scheduled child generation ever," say Howe and Strauss. "For most, hardly an hour goes by in which they are not within sight of a parent, a teacher, a coach, a relative, or a child-care provider (with Mom and Dad occasionally peeking in via their internet 'kiddiecam')—or, strapped into a minivan, in supervised transit between various adult-watched activities."[17]

"I think there's a hunger to get out into the world because they've been locked indoors," adds a program director. "They're so determined to get out there! And I think it's because they've been spending so much time looking at screens, or being chauffeured around." Indeed, parents have been hyper-alert to their Millennial children's safety, with government and corporations following suit. Citywide curfews, new consumer protection laws, the policing of schools, the heightened fear of predators and drastic illnesses—cancer, autism, global epidemics—have both increased Millennials' physical well-being and hemmed them in. When they get to college, their parents are still overly cautious, calling their cell phones often, and hovering over their daily affairs. But students don't seem to mind. They may text or phone Mom several times a day, yet they seize the opportunity to strike out on their own.

"They're fearless!" exclaims the counselor. "They're not afraid to get out there, they're not afraid to make connections, they're not afraid to go into foreign lands, different places, different situations. And parents, to their credit, are saying, 'Go ahead, figure it out, I trust you.' There's an openness of allowing their children to go forth, conquer, experiment, explore. Find your way! Find your path! That's there, in a huge way. And once they graduate," she adds, "it astounds me, the number of young people who start businesses with no background at all, but they're willing to get out there and risk it! It's a kind of weird irony, that innovation and forward movement is coming out of somebody who has been locked into a little box. But that's the thing about this generation. They have been coddled and over-scheduled. Their lives have been scripted. Their parents are protective and always in touch. But then there's that fearlessness!"

This contradiction between students' comfort with the constraints of authority and their desire for challenge and independence appears in other forms as well. "I find that my first-year students are more obedient," says a psychologist. "And that makes me concerned. Like if we're watching a film and someone raises their hand to ask if they can go to the bathroom. My god, you're in college, you don't have to ask that question! And there have been times when I've seen a certain level of intellectual timidity on the part of some of our students. If something isn't part of the curriculum in an official way, students don't seem to want to break out of that."

A writing instructor adds, "They want things to be very organized. When I was in college, classes were more about [the professor saying], 'I don't know what we'll do today. Let's see, here's a question! Let's talk about this.' And that struck me as great! I loved it! We were told, 'Don't expect any special attention; we're not going to take time with you to spell anything out.' But now, students get frustrated if you change something in the syllabus mid-semester or get off the daily schedule. This is totally upsetting to otherwise mature students. They're like, 'Oh my God, he just turned everything around! What am I going to do?' It's like I've totally upset their life. And they're the center of it! They seem not to have any benevolence in thinking that I'm trying to approach the topic in a way that would make more sense, or that I can make it work. It's just, 'No! You've changed things! You've betrayed me!' This group that is so generous and so wanting to make the world better also seems to be very tied to being told *how* to make it better. So to help them break out of that focus on 'what the teacher wants,' I just continue to give them my open-ended prompts: 'Do something that's improbable for you and then write a first-person account of what happened.' It's a kind of assignment where they have to examine themselves—What sort of person am I? What is something that's improbable for me? But you know, Helen, it's very strange. They will pin me down on every detail of that assignment as though they can't think for themselves—and then they'll turn around and do a pretty darn good job, and break some rules, and write with a kind of command that I never would have expected."

Most Millennials have learned to be good rule-followers in their K–12 education. "Enter a classroom today and you might hear an entire class reciting facts and tables in unison," say Howe and Strauss. "Why? Because these questions are starting to appear on 'high stakes' tests that can spell the difference between success and failure for students, teachers, schools, even governors. Such is the power of the new 'standards' movement in public schools."[18] In both struggling and high-performing schools, multiple-choice tests, back-to-basics curricula, and fast-paced, scripted, "teacher-proof" lessons have assumed more importance than family conversations or trips to the museum, as business models, often designed by policy makers with no education background, have replaced traditional public school education.[19] Across the nation, more homework is being assigned to younger and younger children. Class periods are longer, summer vacations shorter. And students are responding by digesting more and more information and acing the exams. While progressive faculty at all levels are alarmed at the increased emphasis on "banking education,"[20] as Paulo Freire termed top-down learning, Howe and Strauss believe that the mastery of facts and tougher standards are making students smarter. "During the 1990s, aptitude test scores have risen within every racial and ethnic group, especially in elementary schools. Eight in ten teenagers say it's 'cool to be smart,' while a record share of teenagers are taking AP tests, say they 'look forward to school,' and plan to attend college."[21]

If the profile as described by Howe and Strauss doesn't quite fit the Millennials you know, you're not alone. Many of my informants expressed surprise at some of these characteristics, and questioned whether the polling data adequately captured all segments of society—young people who join the military, or get married, or take a dead-end job right out of high school; students at historically black colleges; new immigrants; Evangelical Christians; Native children growing up on tribal lands; first-generation college students; or even young people in whole regions of the country: Hawaiians or Californians, for example, who live in a much more ethnically diverse environment than, say, Millennials from upper Michigan.

I agree that these reservations are important to note, especially when we look at our particular schools, our classrooms, or the young people we happen to know through the blunt instrument of survey research. Surveys measure trends rather than describe individuals, and unless they are designed to capture specific regional, ethnic, religious, and/or income differences, they can only say what is true of the nation as a whole. It is indisputable, for example, that the United States is becoming more progressive because of the liberal attitudes of this generation, but as individuals, or even as groups of individuals, many of these young people are decidedly old-school. On some questions, progressive attitudes outweigh more conservative ones by only slight (though measurable) margins. The up-beat, smiley-faced Boy and Girl Scout persona that Howe and Strauss describe as typically Millennial does not represent countless young people who are more individualistic and creative, or less compliant, or more disaffected, or, occasionally, downright mean.[22]

Second, survey research asks respondents what they think, without differentiating their immediate reactions from what they might *like* to think about themselves or their society. When Millennials say, for example, that "race is no big deal," they may never have thought about their own contributions to the racist atmosphere that persists in so many communities, much less question why their high schools were so divided along racial lines (or so unique in their open and accepting atmosphere), or why their circles of friends are mono-cultural, even though they may be visually diverse. When Millennials say they take women's leadership as a given, they may not recognize how deeply sexism is still embedded in U.S. society or see their vulgar endearments ("Hey, bitches!") as perpetuating gender inequalities. Surveys also miss motivations and actions that reveal one's character: questions that measure high schoolers' civic responsibility do not ask if they do community service primarily as a résumé-builder, nor can they discern whether that service has taught them to interact respectfully with people in difficult circumstances.

Howe and Strauss's glowing profile of the Millennial generation was gleaned in large part from two surveys of their own design, a teachers survey of two hundred K–12 teachers in twelve public schools in Fairfax County, Virginia, and a class of 2000 survey, which asked 660 high school seniors in four public high schools in that county about their opinions, preferences, and activities, as well as those of their peers, younger siblings, parents, and teachers. While the students who participated in these surveys were comparatively diverse in terms of ethnicity—13 percent Asian, 10 percent Latino, 8 percent African American, and 3 percent "other"—they were less representative of their entire generation in terms of socioeconomic class. As the authors admit, the median income in Fairfax County is nearly twice the national average.[23] And since the low-income families who do reside in Fairfax County's upper-middle-class environment are able to take advantage of the well-funded schools, after-school activities, safe neighborhoods, state-of-the-art hospitals, and grocery stores filled with healthy food choices, their Millennial children have had different experiences growing up than most impoverished families in the United States and, more than likely, different interpretations of their life experiences and future prospects.

At the University of Michigan, as at many elite colleges, impoverished but talented urban students have lived with crumbling infrastructure, burned-out buildings, irregular or nonexistent public transportation, and few ordinary services like restaurants, pharmacies, health clinics, coin laundries, playgrounds, movie theaters, or any place to buy something to cook for dinner but the poorly stocked corner store. Other low-income students who live in somewhat less drastic circumstances may still have been raised quite differently from the "typical Millennial": some have been strongly pressured to achieve, but because of grim economic realities, family size, and/or cultural values they have never felt particularly "special" or sheltered. Some were brought up to feel uniquely loved and cared for but feel out of place in a high-stakes college environment surrounded by peers whose sense of entitlement is palpable.

Although all Millennials live in the historical era that has shaped their generation, with the same national priorities, the same events and trends dominating the news, the same alarming media exposés of dangers to children, the same misbehaving celebrities, and the same abundance—at least in stores—of fashionable clothing and clever technology, their access to the fruits of the era has been quite different. So when low-income students do make it to colleges like Michigan, they also have a different attitude toward service. As an academic counselor working primarily with students of color reminded me, these students are more likely to talk about their desire for a better world in terms of "giving back" to their communities, acting as role models for younger cousins and siblings, or fulfilling their parents' hopes and dreams as the first person in the family to finish college than about something as nebulous and high-minded as "social justice." Helping a little boy learn to read in an underfunded, chaotic Detroit classroom has quite a different meaning for a student who came from an impoverished area himself, or who is just one generation away from the experience of stark oppression.

Nevertheless, Howe and Strauss's research does capture some important characteristics of this generation, especially those who attend elite colleges and are best positioned to become our nation's future leaders. In fact, the typical Millennial persona describes most University of Michigan students quite accurately. The majority of our students have indeed lived comfortable lives: 70 percent of first-year students report parental incomes equal to or exceeding $60,000 a year, and one-fifth report incomes of $150,000 or higher, nearly double what students report at other top public institutions.[24] The majority of their parents have at least one college degree. The percentage of students of color at Michigan is fairly similar to that in Fairfax County; the 2008 entering class was 6 percent African American, 4 percent Hispanic American, 12 percent Asian American, 1 percent Native American, 8 percent "unknown"—which means they declined to check the box—and 5 percent international.[25] Like many of our white students, many of these students of color have come from upper-middle-class or elite families. They are all, for the most part, "special, sheltered, confident, team-oriented, achieving, pressured, and conventional."[26] And some, to be sure, are simply spoiled, or as Howe and Strauss say of the generation as a whole—with a hint of approval—"brash and bold, given to unseemly bursts of temper and cockiness and ambition, as though the world is being handed to them and all they have to do is grab it."[27]

How sincere are Millennial college students in their quest to make a difference? When activist instructors compare students today to their own involvement as young people, they may shrug or roll their eyes in disbelief. "I don't know, I don't see much action on campus, compared to the '60s and '70s, when I was a student," says an instructor of color who worked for thirty years in a Detroit auto plant. "That's when campuses were really jumping. Even though there are things to do in terms of community work and wrongs to be fixed, you're not immediately facing a draft, like we were; you're not immediately on the heels of the Civil Rights Movement, watching Bull Connor with his fire hoses and attack dogs on TV. What are students doing now? They don't show up at rallies—all I see are the old, gray-haired activists and a smattering of young people. They're saddled with all these courses. They've got to maintain grades, because mommy and daddy are paying their tuition and they want to see some action. And so far, the sky hasn't entirely fallen. Look, it's a beautiful day! And if there's global warming, well, they might just think there's an upside to that. We had a mild winter!"

This perception, that despite their progressive profile and community service credentials, most young Millennials are not seriously engaged—or even interested—in social change, is shared to a greater or lesser degree by many of the student activists I talked to. I am more sanguine than they are about the potential of our students, as upcoming chapters will show. But it's important to hear the concerns of the most seriously committed students, who are in a unique position to know what their peers really say and do, and how student culture affects their own spirit and heart.

"I came to college expecting a lot of exciting political action," says Abby,[28] a third-year student. "Ann Arbor is known for being a liberal town, so I had images of students discussing and getting really riled about social problems—I had a really 1970s Berkeley image of the place," she laughs. But it wasn't like that at all. Not only are there few large rallies for political causes, students are so over-scheduled they have little time to engage in discussions that would help them think their ideas through. "At this point in my life I'm not very sure about what I believe or what I want to do," Abby continues. "Most people my age are like that. And I think talking about these things is so important. But we have no time. And our education has been so goal-oriented. Most of my peers would be upset about the way the world works if they stopped to think about it for ten minutes. But we're so busy, we don't have a chance to stop and think. If I try to talk about some current event with a friend, she'll say, 'I'm really upset, but I have to study.'"

Student organizations have disappointed Abby as well. Even though Michigan supports a great variety of clubs that sponsor service projects of some kind, "their meetings are so agenda driven," she tells me. "When I first came to campus I joined Amnesty International. But all we did at meetings was, we sat down, did an icebreaker, then we wrote two letters for a letter writing campaign without any discussion of the problems we were addressing. Like, we passed around the form that Amnesty gave us that said, 'Please release this political prisoner, blah blah blah.' And we'd transcribe it word for word, and then put stamps on it, seal it up and then talk about having an event or a conference so we could get a bunch of other people to do that. Sure, it's better to support Amnesty in some way than not at all," Abby sighs, "but there was no climate that encouraged us to stop and think, what does this mean, why is this happening? The ultimate goal should not be to release this one political prisoner. That would be wonderful, of course, but we need to think about why this problem exists at all."

Siobhan, a senior who has taken a leadership role in a student organization called "Human Rights Through Education," sees several groups of students on campus: the activists like herself, who tend to learn about many of the causes of injustice through their classes and political discussions with like-minded students, and a much larger group, who are motivated by sympathy, but not much else. "There are people at the core—the activists—and people in the periphery—the ones who do charity and volunteering," says Siobhan. "The periphery people obviously care about humans in some greater sense, but they don't understand the theoretical or structural things behind injustice. I think what they're working against is not really 'injustice' but 'things that are bad' and 'things that are sad.' Like going to Children's Hospital and seeing kids in pediatric care—that is really sad and it pulls on a lot of real, human emotions. And a lot of student organizations do good, charitable things—like knitting and donating what they make to homeless shelters. But there's no discussion within their organizations about *why* they need to donate stuff all the time. Those students have the caring about humans, but they need to peel back one more layer and figure out why homelessness or whatever is an issue."

"Some students don't even seem to care," adds Abby. "But when they stop and think, their compassion and concern comes out. I brought one of my friends to a campus event a few weeks ago. She only came because this rapper, M1, was speaking. M1? He was in this group, Dead Prez, who we love! And his message, essentially, was about people of color throughout the world opposing imperialism in all its forms. He had just come back from Egypt where he had gone with a group of internationals who were attempting to break the siege on Gaza. My friend doesn't have a lot of social justice background of any kind. She was just like, 'This famous person is coming here and Abby's been talking to me about it for two months, so I have to go.' And I mean she left that presentation *sobbing*. Just like *bawling*. And she was like, 'I didn't know any of this stuff was going on!' She was bawling so much she had to sit down. And—well, I didn't want her to cry, but it made me so happy because that shows that people can care! I felt so inspired by how upset she was. She was like, 'I want to do something—NOW! This is so stupid! We're just helping to oppress people!' And I was like, 'YEAH!' And she was like, 'So what do we do?' And I was like, 'I—I don't know!!'"

Some students are critical of the shallowness of their peers' knowledge about political issues—even when they do seem to care. Sanjeet, whose intense interest in politics led him to publish a journal of student and faculty writing, the "Michigan Journal of International Affairs," expressed his annoyance with the lack of meaningful political discussion among his classmates. "The Ann Arbor campus has this reputation of being really liberal, so everyone wants to be perceived as socially aware, even if they aren't. So they just sort of agree with a liberal take on whatever issue comes up. They don't really delve into the issues or know any interesting arguments that might counter that point of view. Even in the seriously progressive classes I tend to take, there's pressure to be sort of alternative, and reject mainstream political wisdom and mainstream economics. Which is fine, but I think sometimes people who don't really believe it just say these things because they feel they have to. That's why it's hard to get any real dialogue on the issues. Like in class today we were talking about the protests around the World Trade Organization, and everyone said they were opposed to the WTO. Or at least no one was ready to argue in favor of it. Even though our instructor does throw the counter arguments out there, no one will support them seriously, or even take a devil's advocate position. It makes a lot of discussion of social issues on campus seem a bit contrived."

Other activist students see their peers as irredeemably apathetic. "A lot of my friends ask why I care about social problems. And I don't know what to tell them!" Talia laughs in exasperation. "Like, how can you *not* care that people are starving everywhere and you're sitting there eating *far* more than you need to be eating, and you're not even hungry! And there are a lot of people starving to death. I don't understand why people don't care. And if so many people don't care, then how is it going to help when there's just a small number of people who do? Because it sometimes feels like there are only a few other people that actually care and actually want to do something."

The pervasiveness of detachment from human suffering can be discouraging to young idealists, especially those who take on the most controversial issues. As an Israeli American who has long dreamed of helping to solve the Israel Palestine conflict, Talia is majoring in Middle Eastern studies and has been learning Arabic to prepare herself for a career in peace building. But now, three years into her program, she's feeling lost and disheartened. "Maybe that's still the direction I want to go but it's just—I don't know. I guess being told you're naïve has an effect after you've heard it one too many times," Talia confides, holding back tears. "I've heard it a lot from my peers: 'Oh, you think you can help solve the problem, but you can't, because there's always going to be a problem and there's no resolution to it.' It's hard to be optimistic and hope for the best when so many people are so negative."

Caitlin, a third year student who works as a resident advisor in one of U-M's largest dormitories,[29] agrees that students are apathetic, or, as she says, "pretty selfish." "Most of the people in my hall are looking to socialize or do some kind of service that's immediately beneficial to *them*," she says. "They're not looking for a community partnership that has to be built slowly, over time; they're not looking to invest themselves in a working group that takes on a complex issue, or in doing coalition work. And they *definitely* don't want to come out for a cause that someone might disagree with them about. I think the real issues—the ones that are complicated and political—threaten their ability to belong. Standing up for a controversial issue means that people might not like you."

"So why are they into community service at all?" I wonder.

"Most students care about their image," Caitlin replies. "They do community service because they've been told all their lives that it's the right thing to do, the honorable thing to do." Polls of Millennial students indicate that, indeed, volunteerism is spiking. An astonishing 94.2 percent of students entering U-M in 2009 reported they had done community service in high school.[30] These numbers drop off sharply once they get to campus, but still, more than half of entering female students and over a quarter of entering male students said they plan to volunteer or engage in community service during college.[31] And many more get pulled in to a particular event—especially when it's one of the biggest social functions of the year.

"For example, Dance Marathon," says Caitlin with a laugh. Many activists and instructors invoked this popular campuswide event when talking about the charity model of service. "DM is definitely a conversation piece. It has a ton of funding for advertising, so when you join you get a sign on your door that says, 'Welcome to DMUM.' And people get t-shirts that say 'Marathon Bound.' So it's like this advertisement: 'I belong!' And since the money you raise is going to a cause that no one can fault, like children with disabilities, it's an easy one to join because you don't have to think very hard about it to decide that you support it."

I look up the Dance Marathon Web site:

> Imagine running with hundreds of other students under the 'Go Blue' banner to take on a challenge that will be exciting, fun, and inspirational. The Dance Marathon features these students standing valiantly for 30 hours to symbolize the difficulties that the DMUM children cope with every day. However, these 30 hours are so much more than standing. These 30 hours feature DJs, cultural shows, local performers, games, food, crafts, and dancing that combines into one giant party. However, the real stars of the show are our families and children, who take the stage to share their inspirational stories, cheer on the teams, and do a little dancing along with our dancers.[32]

Despite its appeal to fun and sociability, DM participants—hard-working Millennials that they are—put an amazing amount of energy into this event. Dance Marathon volunteers have spent the previous year raising money under the leadership of fellow students who have motivated and inspired them, organized them into teams, taught them how to ask for donations, and kept them focused on the final event, when they'll be able to show their stamina and heart with the others who have worked so hard all year. A photo posted after the event shows cheering, clapping DMUM organizers in their identical blue shirts and khaki pants, holding up huge numbers that announce the final tally of the money the students raised.[33]

"Even if the event is one big party—which it is—I wouldn't fault the organization," says Katie, a former Dance Marathon organizer who just returned from India on a post-graduation internship. "They've been incredibly effective at raising funds for a good cause. They raised almost half a million dollars this year for pediatric rehabilitation! And they're entirely student-run! Imagine the organizing ability, the communication skills, the talent that it takes to pull off something like this! And they know how to appeal to students' sense of competition and fun. Take a look at the prize for the top fund raiser this year:

- 3 nights hostel in London
- Chunnel ticket to Paris, 3 nights

- Fat Bike tour in Paris
- 3 nights in Amsterdam
- Red light district tour
- International Cell Phone
- International Student ID Card
- France and Benelux rail pass"[34]

Not surprisingly, most of the activists I talked to are less than enthusiastic about such events. "I never felt that great about Dance Marathon," says Mark, a graduate student who during his undergraduate years had committed himself to life-long activism. "I had a good friend who was doing really great social justice work, and had decided he would always make that kind of work part of his life. But he was also a Dance Marathon organizer. I couldn't quite figure that out. I always was like, 'So wait. You get a bunch of people together, you dance, and you make a bunch of money and you give it to the hospital?' There are lots of people with lots of money that are already giving to hospitals. Of course, I'm glad they're doing that. But there are so many other problems in the world that get neglected because people are fixated on health issues in affluent and privileged countries like ours. And students spend so much time running marathons and organizing these huge social events for causes that are already amply funded. If they'd just put that time into doing more of what I think of as justice-related work in terms of trying to un-do inequality, the world would be *such* a better place!"

Notes

1. Howe & Strauss, 2000, 7 and 4–5.
2. Ibid. "About the Authors" (frontpiece) and 369.
3. Ibid., 4. Also see Pew Research Center (2010, February) for these and other characteristics and attitudes of Millennials.
4. Ibid., 7.
5. Ibid., 13.
6. Ibid., 18.
7. New Politics Institute, 2007.
8. Ibid.
9. Ibid.
10. "Between now and 2018, the number of Millennials of voting age will increase by

about four and a half million a year." (Madland & Teixeira, May 2009).
11. 18 percent Hispanic, 14 percent black, 5 percent Asian, and 3 percent other (Madland & Teixeira, May 2009).
12. Howe & Strauss, 16.
13. Ibid., 20.
14. Ibid., 21.
15. According to a survey of more than 200,000 freshman at 279 colleges and universities, "fewer students than ever are reporting above-average mental health" (Pryor et al., 2010). The *New York Times* reports that "44 percent [of college students] in counseling have severe psychological disorders, up from 16 percent in 2000, and 24 percent are on psychiatric medication, up from 17 percent a decade ago" (Gabriel, December 2010).
16. Students are not only prescribed more anxiety-relieving drugs these days, says a psychologist I interviewed, but they are also using amphetamines illicitly to gain a "competitive advantage" over their peers in studying for their exams. "One student's mother sent her a 'care package' including cookies, Margarita mix, and a bag of Adderall [an amphetamine used to treat narcolepsy and attention deficit disorder]. So one must ask—which generation are we actually talking about?" See also the *60 Minutes* broadcast on elite students' use of drugs to enhance mental performance (Schorn, 2010, April) http://www.cbsnews.com/stories/2010/04/22/60minutes/main6422159.shtml
17. Howe & Strauss, 134.
18. Ibid., 157.
19. Ravitch, 2010.
20. Banking education, in which teachers make "deposits" of knowledge in students' heads and "withdraw" them on examinations, is described in Freire's *Pedagogy of the Oppressed* (1986).
21. Howe & Strauss, 9.
22. Bullying, out-casting, and school shootings shocked the nation during this period, and negative attitudes toward gays became more open. As Howe and Strauss (2000) report, "A 1998 Primedia/Roper survey revealed that thirty-one percent of seventh through twelfth grade boys identified 'gays and lesbians' as one of the groups 'most responsible for problems at my school'" p. 228.
23. Howe & Strauss, 376–77.
24. Fenty, 1997.
25. University of Michigan. 2009b.
26. Howe & Strauss, 43–44
27. Ibid., 23–24.
28. All student names have been changed, either by the students themselves or by the author. Pseudonyms reflect the gender and, usually, the ethnic heritage of the student informants.
29. A resident advisor helps build a well-functioning community in a university res-

idence hall, and is responsible for the safety and well-being of the students who live there.
30. University of Michigan, 2009a.
31. University Record, 2010.
32. http://dmum.org/marathon.html
33. http://www.dmum.org/index.html
34. http://dmum.donordrive.com/index.cfm?fuseaction=donorDrive.home

Chapter 2

Critical Education

What would Paulo Freire have thought of the Millennial Generation had he lived long enough to see them come to maturity?[1] Surely, he would have been delighted to talk with them, regardless of their motivations for supporting good causes, or whether their work was truly progressive, or whether or not they looked deeply into the roots of the problems they were trying to solve. He knew that the world these young people had inherited was increasingly complex, deeply divided by race and class, closer to ecological disaster, still sullied by war. He knew that the world needs the energy and will of the Millennial Generation, and he would have seen their potential to meet the challenge.

Freire enjoyed talking with North American students, just as he did with impoverished farmers in Brazil, literacy workers in Guinea Bissau, educators at the World Council of Churches in Geneva, or intellectuals, like himself, in exile.[2] His gentle personality and his ability to listen with curiosity and kindness put everyone at ease. His wise advice to slow down, reflect deeply, question standard notions of authority, develop a comprehensive vision of a more livable world, and enter into education with the goal of "becoming more fully human" was inspiring to countless audiences during his lifetime.

But what if we had told him that this generation was different? What if we had said that according to polls and surveys, at least, the Millennial Generation was more progressive, more energetic, more civic minded, and more connected to the world than any U.S. generation in memory—despite their "banking education"? What if we told him this generation of young adults, especially those at elite colleges like Michigan, felt "special," even entitled to the best the world has to offer: travel abroad, high-paying careers, luxurious homes, and constant electronic entertainment? Yet they were reaching out in impressive numbers to do something, in Siobhan's words, about "things that are bad" and "things that are sad." And if he sat down with the progressive Millennial students we met in the last chapter—Abby and Talia, Caitlin, Siobhan, Sanjeet, Katie and Mark—and listened to their disappointments with their peers, whose focus on their image and grades and careers, whose need to belong, and whose reluctance to question the social order seems so shallow and self-serving, what would he have counseled them?

Freire enjoyed doing what he called "spoken books," edited conversations on social problems with other progressive educators and activists.[3] He believed in the power of dialogue to illuminate complex questions and to clarify the abstractions that sometimes deterred students from understanding his texts. So he might be amused and pleased at the idea of talking with Millennial students from the world beyond. Here they are, sitting in a circle, as Freire would have wanted, so that all are on the same level, teacher and students alike.

"Everyone has something to contribute," Freire says, "and everyone, including me, has something to learn. Who has a question we can discuss deeply?"

"I've been told on many occasions that I have an attitude," begins Abby. "So I am perhaps more dismissive of my peers than I should be. But I have had a progressive education since I was very young, and I think that's made me more politically aware than most other students I know. I'm even more progressive than my parents! It's just been instilled in me, ever since I was a little kid: 'Your actions affect other people. People should be equal. You should love everyone.' And I think I really took this seriously! I mean, lots of people say these things, and maybe even believe these things, but they don't think about how to practice them in ways that will actually make a difference. So my question for us is, 'How can we get other students to act on their so-called progressive values?' That's what frustrates me the most. They seem so apathetic, or resistant, or—something!"

"Well," says Paulo. "Let's look at their education. I have heard that most U.S. schools are more focused than ever on basic skills—like reading and mathematics, geography, history, science—and that these subjects are drilled into students, just like they were when I was a boy in Brazil. Students learn procedures, they memorize facts, and they take tests where they regurgitate these facts without exploring any deeper meaning: 'Four times four is sixteen. The capital of Michigan is Lansing.' The student records, memorizes, and repeats these phrases without perceiving what four times four really means, or realizing the true significance of 'capital' in the affirmation, 'the capital of Michigan is Lansing,' that is, what Lansing means for Michigan and what Michigan means for the United States."[4]

"That is so true," says Caitlin. "But I think the focus on the basics has a good reason behind it. There are an unacceptable number of youth in poor communities who haven't mastered those elementary skills. They read way below grade level, they hate math and are convinced they'll never be good at it. And they don't even know Lansing exists, or if they do, it's just not part of their world, it's not important to them. The idea of 'skill and drill,' as much as I disagree with it, is supposed to ensure these kids get up to speed."

"Also, I wonder if it's possible to get urban youth to reflect on something so deep as what Michigan means for the United States," adds Siobhan. "They are so caught up in the problems in their immediate environment, they have no knowledge—or even interest—in anything outside of it. And even if they cared, discovering the meaning of something means they have to know how to analyze, and, when they can't even read—I don't know. I don't want to sound politically incorrect, but it seems to me that they need to start with the basics and then go on to critical thinking later."

"Well, even if I agreed with that—which I don't," Abby interjects, "that doesn't explain why they're doing more banking education than ever in suburban schools, where most kids already do well. And even here at the university, most of our classes are large lectures. Students themselves insist on the banking format! Like my sociology professor says, students even want the power point slides in advance, so they can fill in the little blanks during the lecture! What's the excuse for that? And although I've had some small classes, they are typically more like lectures delivered by a seated professor who knows my first name. Sure there are discussions, but professors' questions are usually met by five seconds of silence and somebody uttering a less-than-insightful comment."

"Let me add something from my experience in Brazil," says Paulo. "In the 1950s, we worked with extremely impoverished, illiterate adults in the rural areas, people who were convinced they didn't know anything, they couldn't contribute anything, and that they were condemned by fate to remain poor and ignorant. Yet when we used a particular form of education where we encouraged people to discuss social problems that they were actually dealing with in their homes and communities, and where the first words they read related to these problems, they became extremely engaged. Not only did they learn to read rapidly, but they began to analyze these problems and see that they were not responsible for their impoverished condition.[5] Regardless of whether we're talking about campesinos or urban slum dwellers or wealthy students in North America, everyone is oppressed by a social and economic system that crushes the poor; and everyone is capable of analyzing their situation, as long as their education promotes it."

"You know, this discussion reminds me—I remember seeing a set of graphics in one of my classes, I think it was from a book called *Helping Health Workers Learn*,[6] that showed really clearly what you, Paulo, call levels or stages of consciousness," says Caitlin. "The first one shows a group of village people, maybe in Africa, standing in front of a white man who is obviously their boss. He's smoking a cigarette, pointing at them aggressively, and he carries a paper in his hand that reads, 'Title.' The people are barefoot, dressed traditionally. A woman is nursing a baby at her bare breast. They're all bowing their heads in submission. One of the men is saying, 'Anything you say, wise master.' This is the 'magical' level of awareness, where the people believe they are nothing, and they can easily be bullied into accepting terms that are obviously not good for them.

"In the next frame, two of the villagers are now dressed in Western clothes. The woman is no longer nursing her baby—she's giving it a bottle. Her hair has been straightened, and she wears high heels. She's standing behind a man, perhaps her husband, who has now taken over the role of the white boss. Now *he's* the one who is smoking the cigarette, pointing at his former friends and neighbors, and saying imperiously, 'Your ignorance and customs disgust me!' The people are still bowing their heads in shame and resignation. The white boss stands to the side, smiling a little. This is the 'naïve level of consciousness,' the level of 'reforming or adapting,' where some of the oppressed take on the values and attitudes of the oppressor—to the delight of the boss, who no longer needs to play the heavy.

"But in the final frame, all the people are standing together—except the boss, who has dropped both his cigarette and the title deed in surprise. The people look strikingly different now. Their heads are raised confidently, they look the boss in the eye, and their leader is saying, 'Don't you think it's about time we talk things over as equals?' This is the stage of 'critical awareness' that transforms the relationship between the exploiter and the exploited into one of equality."

"I could not have said this more clearly myself," says Paulo.

"So, wait," says Talia. "Are we saying this describes the condition of the average student on this campus as well as poor people in an exploited country?"

"I'm not so sure about that," says Katie. "I mean, I can see it applying to some people in this country—like if they've been racially oppressed, or if they've grown up really poor. Maybe they've internalized society's racism and have stopped believing in themselves. Maybe they've become convinced that in order to get ahead they need to conform to a system that oppresses their own people—that would be the 'anything you say wise master' stage. And then they might go on to become heads of companies or members of government or doctors or police officers or anyone who carries out policies that are good for the rich and oppress the poor still further. That would be the naïve level of consciousness, right, Paulo?"

"Yes, something like that," says Paulo. "And once they understand, through critical education, or education for the practice of freedom, as I've sometimes called it, that they can and must speak to the oppressors as equals, even if that is more dangerous than these graphics you speak of imply, then they have achieved critical consciousness."

"But I still don't get how all this applies to my friends who grew up middle class," says Katie. "I don't see how they're oppressed. And they're not oppressors, either, at least not like the boss that Caitlin was describing. They're not trying to cheat people out of their land, or keep people poor so they'll be forced to work for nothing. They're good people! They give their time and money to charitable organizations. They go over to third world countries to help. Some of them will even devote their lives to this work."

"I think Paulo would call that an example of false generosity," says Mark.

"Yes, exactly," says Paulo. "People who give out of a sense of duty, or because they want to be perceived as good or worthy, or who try to solve other people's problems for them, or even those who want to work in partnership with people to come up with ways to make them a little more comfortable, a little healthier, a little more 'developed,' all of these people are, in a way, perpetuating an unjust social order. They can afford to be 'generous' because they will never have to give up the privileges that keep them comfortable at the expense of other people. World systems that perpetuate inequality will not be significantly changed because of their activism."[7]

"I agree," says Mark. "Unless we work to dismantle a system in which some people profit at the horrible expense of others, we're not really helping. Our race and class privilege, our access to goods made by cheap labor in impoverished countries, our huge array of supermarket choices that are made possible by migrant laborers here in Michigan—none of that will be changed by a fundraiser, or a program to help migrant kids finish their education, or even by immigration reform, as long as it keeps unfair trade agreements in place."

"Well I agree with all that," says Talia. "But I don't really see that my peers are oppressed by a system that ignores or deliberately exploits the poor. How can they be, if they're the ones profiting from it?"

"Haven't they been telling you how stressed they are, how they have no time to reflect, or discuss important issues with friends?" asks Paulo. "Aren't they saying they're overloaded with a barrage of information that they can't possibly interrogate in depth? Haven't they been pushed to their limits to excel, which, for some, has resulted in crippling anxiety?"

"And for what?" asks Mark. "Would they describe their lives as meaningful? Or even think of themselves as happy?"[8]

"I see your point," says Talia. "But still, compared to the most exploited, impoverished people that you can see every day on TV or the Internet, the problems of college students are trivial! Just think of the daily reality for the little girls sold into sexual slavery in Thailand, or laborers in the ruby mines of Burma, or child soldiers!"

"That's true," says Caitlin. "We can hardly call our lives miserable compared to the most debased and exploited people on earth!"

"But what if we were really aware of what we were doing to other people, just by living our ordinary lives?" asks Siobhan. "And that no matter how much we cared, or how much we learned about the causes of all these problems, or regardless, even, of how much we worked on campaigns to challenge the rules of the unjust order, we are *still* oppressing the most vulnerable people?"

"That would be profoundly depressing," says Talia.

"Scary," says Katie.

"No wonder our peers don't really want to delve into these issues," says Caitlin.

"Right," says Katie. "Most people in our generation really do care about equality. Their progressivism may be shallow, as I'm beginning to understand, but I don't think anyone I know wants people to suffer, or believes that some people are inherently better than others."

"And everyone wants to think of themselves as good people. So it's hard to get them to look at ways they aren't," Caitlin adds. "And when they do, they just feel so guilty."

"I think guilt is sometimes useful," says Mark. "At least you're facing the situation honestly. It only becomes problematic when you get overwhelmed by it and can't move beyond it."

"So back to my original question," says Abby, "how *can* we get more people involved in critical education that would really get them thinking and questioning, despite the disturbing nature of what they'll find?"

"What do you advocate, Paulo?" asks Mark.

"I see education—critical education—as a form of intervention in the world,"[9] says Paulo. "And as part of that education I want students to think about who and what they are for, and who and what they are against. Because education is not neutral. And neither are world systems. When students are treated as fixed observers of facts and happenings, without any analysis, without any understanding of who benefits and who suffers, this is not true education."

"But aren't education and political activism inherently at odds with each other?" asks Siobhan. "Aren't professors supposed to be unbiased? I mean, I know it's probably impossible to be completely objective, but aren't students supposed to hear both sides of the story?"

"I make no pretense of impartiality," says Paulo quietly. "Everyone has a point of view. My point of view is that of the 'wretched of the earth, of the excluded.'[10] So I believe that professors have a duty to talk about people and systems that oppress human beings. Of course everyone's point of view must be respected and allowed to emerge in discussion. But we should not obscure the fact that the world is unjust by design. So I, for one, am clear that I abhor neoliberalism."[11]

"I'm glad you mentioned neoliberalism, Paulo," says Sanjeet, "because that brings up a pet peeve of mine. Students at this university are always throwing around terms like 'social justice' or 'neoliberalism' without really knowing what they mean. I don't want to sound like I'm putting myself above others, or that I always know what these terms mean either. But I think there's this focus on using certain words that make you seem socially aware and interested in social justice, even to the point of saying something like 'neoliberalism' when it's not even relevant."

"No way!" says Caitlin, laughing.

"Well, you'll have to admit, neoliberalism is a bit hard to define," says Mark.

"Neoliberalism is an economic system imposed on the world by institutions in wealthy countries for the benefit of a small, elite minority," says Paulo. "It is a philosophy that objectifies everything: the earth, property, production, the creations of men, men themselves, time—everything is reduced to the status of objects at its disposal."[12]

"In practical terms," explains Mark, "neoliberal trade agreements force struggling countries to open their doors to a flood of cheap goods from wealthy countries, whose farms and industries are economically supported by their own governments. The poor countries are forced to privatize their industries and public services, which clears the way for foreign capital. In order to continue to get vital loans for development, the world's most impoverished countries have been forced to close health clinics and make families pay for their children's education, even at the primary school level. Necessities like bread, rice, fertilizer, and even water are no longer subsidized or available for free. And a village water source can be tapped by a multinational to bring you that bottle of water you're drinking that you probably paid a dollar fifty for, while the farmers' fields go dry."

"Oops," says Abby, capping her water bottle and putting it in her backpack.

"This is what's happening in so many developing countries," says Siobhan. "And then we wonder why development aid doesn't change people's lives fast enough."

"Even if farmers do have enough water," Mark continues, "they can no longer just save a bit of grain from the harvest to plant the following year. No matter how poor they are, farmers have to buy new seed every year from the multinational, which gets richer and richer at the expense of people who have nothing. The result is that small farming has become completely unsustainable, so families are forced to migrate to the cities where they end up in slums."

"Neoliberalism dehumanizes everything it touches," says Paulo. "It is a philosophy founded on cynical fatalism and an inflexible negation of the right to dream differently, to dream of utopia."[13]

"Wow, that's intense," Talia says.

"But wait a moment. I don't know if I agree with that," says Katie. "I mean, neoliberal reforms do sound bad, but can they be *all* bad? I've heard that sometimes those state-run services are really disorganized."

"Totally useless," agrees Sanjeet. "Case in point, telephone services. In India, where my parents are from, the state bureaucracy is so slow it can take months, even years, to get a phone installed in some areas. That's why people in developing countries all over the world are buying cell phones to get around these immensely wasteful government-run systems that don't serve the public."

"That's a good point," says Katie.

"But I don't want to say that forced reforms are a good idea, or even that global capitalism in its present form is a fair or principled system," Sanjeet adds. "Just look at its effects in our own country. Banks that make huge profits off people who lose their homes and family farms. Industrial jobs that used to pay a living wage, outsourced to countries that persecute people who try to organize unions. The obscene divide between rich and poor in this country that's growing year by year."

"Those are all good examples of dehumanization caused by exploitative power relations," says Paulo. "The poor are dehumanized by their abject poverty. And the rich are dehumanized by their desire to accumulate more and more until they suffocate in their own possessions."[14]

"The way you put it, Paulo, it all seems like a huge moral struggle," says Katie. "And I agree that sometimes it really seems like it might be that way. But even if neoliberalism *is* absolutely, unconditionally bad, does that mean that the wealthy elite who make these policies are doing it on purpose to make everyone else suffer? With all due respect, Paulo, yours is such an 'us and them' view of the world. Don't all people contain elements of good and evil? Don't all systems that have ever been devised benefit some more than others? Can't we work toward greater equality and justice without attacking people? It seems like such a negative view of the world."

"I know that my dualisms can make people uncomfortable," says Paulo. "Maybe the way I put them, they sound a bit old fashioned. But I've always believed that human existence is, in fact, a radical and profound tension between good and evil, between dignity and indignity, between decency and indecency, between the beauty and the ugliness of the world. And, therefore, it is impossible to humanly exist without assuming the right and the duty to opt, to decide, to struggle, to be political."[15]

"That's inspiring," says Mark. "I'm going to remember that."

"I'm still sitting here thinking that the problem must be more complex than 'Whose side are you on?'" says Caitlin, doubtfully. "I think I agree with Katie. I'm not comfortable blaming one side or the other."

"These things are perhaps more clear to people who have experienced them personally," Paulo says gently. "I grew up in a rural area of northeast Brazil, where almost everyone was desperately poor. The region had the highest birthrate, the shortest life expectancy, the most severe malnutrition, the lowest literacy rates, and higher levels of unemployment and underemployment than anyplace in the country.[16] My parents were both teachers, so we had a little more stability than most people, but my father lost his job during the Depression, and we had to move, and I had the possibility to experience hunger."[17]

"The possibility?" asks Abby.

"Yes. Looking back, I think it was an opportunity. Because it made it easier to see what other people were going through. And not only could I see and experience the condition of the poorest people in my country, I could also see some of the larger forces that caused these problems. You see, the Northeast had been dominated by huge sugar estates that depended on slave and peasant labor—not that much different from the plantation system in the U.S. South. When multinationals brought industrialization and so-called development to the Northeast, these impoverished, illiterate people had nowhere else to turn. So they migrated to the cities, just like so many rural people do today under the unfair trade policies and development aid requirements of the rich countries. As you can imagine, this created a huge gap in Brazil between rich and poor, powerful and powerless."

"Which is even worse today," adds Mark.

"At that time," continues Paulo, "—this was before the coup that sent me into exile—there was a populist, reformist government in the Northeast which encouraged the formation of rural trade unions, called Peasant Leagues. By 1960 they had 80,000 members! They quickly formulated progressive demands: land reform and the right to vote, which illiterate people weren't allowed at that time. And so we were able to build on those goals through a program of grassroots education, adult literacy, and the development of the critical consciousness of the masses.[18] In this way, I could not only see and experience the desperate conditions under which so many people must live, I also was able to understand the potential for radical transformation of the society through popular participation. This participation is realized through the pedagogy of the oppressed, an educational practice that simultaneously creates a new society and involves the people themselves in the creation of their own knowledge."[19]

"That gives me so much to think about," says Caitlin. "First, that I might really have to choose sides, and second, that critical education for everyone might be the way to achieve a saner world."

"Keep thinking," says Paulo. "Keep questioning. Observe carefully how oppressive systems are constructed and perpetuated. As you work to transform the world, dialogue with people, even those you find the most despicable. Look deeply into the lives of the poorest of the poor. And keep revisiting your ideas and questions. This is praxis: reflection and action upon the world in order to transform it."[20]

"Thank you, Paulo," say the students.

"I will leave you with one last thought," says Paulo. "Humanization is man's true vocation. It is thwarted by injustice, exploitation, oppression, and the violence of the oppressors; it is affirmed by the yearning of the oppressed for freedom and justice, and by their struggle to recover their lost humanity.[21] Of all my writings, all my teaching, this is what I hope will endure: 'my trust and faith in the people, and in the creation of a world in which it will be easier to love.'"[22]

*****

We will leave the quietly departing students to their own thoughts as we return to our consideration of critical education and its relevance to the Millennial Generation.

What can we glean from this conversation and the comments of the students in the previous chapter that might suggest a way to approach Abby's questions: How can we get more students thinking about issues of social justice? How can we help them break out of their apathy, their resistance, their self-centeredness? How can we encourage them to act on their values of equality and community and draw them in to more meaningful engagement with the world?

It is clear that Millennial students need more opportunities to "stop and think for ten minutes about the way the world works," as Abby says about her busy peers, and to let themselves become upset about real-world contradictions to their progressive values of equality, freedom, justice, and integrity. They need more authentic discussion, as these students have tried to model in their conversation with the spirit of Paulo Freire, discussion that challenges Millennial students' intellectual timidity, that encourages them to define their terms rather than glibly throwing them into the mix to appear politically acceptable to their peers; discussion that allows them to express their doubts and questions, to disagree respectfully, to listen deeply to each other. This, of course, means breaking out of the banking education model that characterizes both large lectures[23] and small "discussion sections" where, as Freire notes, "the teacher teaches and the students are taught; the teacher knows everything and the students know nothing; the teacher thinks and the students are thought about; the teacher talks and the students listen—meekly."[24]

Millennial students also need help distinguishing between their charity work—which legitimately helps people meet immediate needs—and solidarity, which involves a deeper and more intimate understanding of the lives of the people they want to help, as well as a political stance, a decision about "who and what they are for, and who and what they are against." They need a kind of education that attempts something larger and more meaningful than personal advancement or technical competence, that pushes the comfortable boundaries of a traditional liberal education: the love of learning, a deeper understanding of the human condition, and the production of well-rounded citizens who can intelligently engage in conversation, cast an informed ballot for the candidate of their choice, and appreciate a variety of points of view. They need a kind of education that sharpens their understanding of global and local power relations, that takes the side of people whose rights have been violated and that humanizes their struggle for physical and spiritual survival.

But critical education for the Millennial Generation must be more than "being involved in creating their own knowledge," as Freire advocated in his literacy program for impoverished adults and, later, for middle-class students as well. In their race to accumulate honors and exotic experiences, to ace the exams and position themselves for high-profile careers,[25] Millennial students have not been provided with the facts and examples that help explain the disparities in the world around them. They need exposure to knowledge created both by scholars and by the people most affected by unjust systems: the suppressed histories, the alternative analyses, the visions and dreams of idealists, the stories of ordinary people. They need ideas to play with, theories to attempt to apply to real-world problems, and models of deeply informed practice. They need opportunities to connect with the invisible people in their neighborhoods—the immigrants scrubbing pots in the back of the upscale restaurants, the teens languishing in juvenile detention, the migrant workers who seize the opportunity to learn English after their ten-hour day in the fields; the homeless families in the tent village just outside of town—and to experience these people as their equals. They need to be inspired by grassroots activists: the "organic intellectuals," the energized youth, and the elders who have spent their lives "giving back" to their communities.

Millennial students need to be separated for a time from their electronic connections with friends and family in order to reflect on what they really want to do with their lives rather than rushing into the prestigious careers they were groomed for. And when they are moved to act, Millennial students need to discover the complexity of the abuses that cry out for their immediate attention, and to be dissuaded from plunging too quickly into their own hastily considered solutions.

But perhaps more than anything, the Millennial Generation needs to learn to ask, "Why?" It's not enough for students to be able to explain how imperialism, racism, sexism, global capitalism, and the war system prevent us all from becoming "more fully human," as Freire puts it. It's not even enough that they learn arguments from all sides of the political spectrum and become proficient at defending their own point of view with lawyerly arguments and counterarguments, fact-based evidence and examples. All these are good, scholarly skills that of course should not be neglected. But asking "why" is a habit of mind that can lead these smart, well-intentioned students into new territory. "Why is this raggedy, filthy man holding up a cardboard sign at the freeway exit? Why does it say, 'Iraq war vet will work for food?' What is this man's state of mind? What have been his life experiences? If we hand him five dollars, quickly, before the light turns green, will he spend it on drink? If he does, why is that? What does it mean? Who suffers because of this man's condition? Who benefits?" Learning to question, as Freire titled one of his "spoken books,"[26] is a first step in creating a society in which a minority does not exploit the majority; a society where asking such questions would be a common, daily activity;[27] a society where the Millennial Generation might reach their full potential.

Notes

1. Paulo Freire died in 1997.
2. Freire was exiled from Brazil in 1964 because his literacy campaign, which would have brought millions of new voters into the system, threatened the military junta that had come to power. Freire was able to return to Brazil in 1980.
3. Horton & Freire, 1990, preface.
4. This and other comments made by Freire in this imaginary conversation are summarized, adapted, and/or quoted verbatim from his written work. This one is from *Pedagogy of the Oppressed* (1986), 57–58.
5. Freire, 1981.
6. Werner & Bower, 1982, 26–13.
7. Freire, 1986, 29.
8. Public health experts point out that as affluent societies grow richer and income differences become more pronounced, levels of depression and anxiety rise. In unequal societies, people are more worried about their self-image and tend to shore up their confidence through defensive self-promotion and an unhealthy focus on the self. This "insecure narcissism" reduces trust, increases aggression, and contributes to declines in health and longevity across the society. In 2006, two-thirds of American college students scored above what had been the average narcissism score in 1982 (Wilkinson & Pickett, 2009, p. 37).
9. Freire, 1998, 90.
10. Ibid., 22.
11. For a complete discussion of the meaning of "neoliberalism," see Harvey, 2005.
12. Freire, 1986, 44.
13. Freire, 1998, 22.
14. Freire, 1986, 45.

15. Freire, 1998, 53.
16. Horton & Freire, 1990, xviii.
17. Ibid., xix.
18. Ibid., xxvi.
19. Ibid., xxx.
20. Freire, 1986, 36.
21. Ibid., 28.
22. Ibid., 24.
23. Even Derek Bok, past president of Harvard, decries the lecture format that is standard at his university and so many others. "By some calculations," says Bok, "the average student will be unable to recall most of the factual content of a typical lecture within fifteen minutes after the end of class" (Bok, 2007, 48).
24. Freire, 1986, 59.
25. According to UCLA's annual survey of first-year students at U.S. colleges and universities, 72.7 percent said that "the chief benefit of college is that it increases one's earning power" (Pryor et al., 2010).
26. *Learning to Question* (Freire, 1989) is a conversation between Freire and the Chilean intellectual, Antonio Faundez, who shared Freire's experience of being exiled for his political activity.
27. Freire, 1989, 61–62.

Chapter 3

Knowing Where You're From

"I know I've been sheltered," Sanjeet tells me. "I grew up in a suburb where everybody was pretty wealthy, and I always had basically anything I wanted. I never saw people who were struggling. So when I came to Ann Arbor and found homeless people asking for money around campus, that was quite a shock."

"But you're so knowledgeable about global poverty, Sanjeet. How did you miss the local?"

"I think most people never notice the inequality in this country," Sanjeet replies. "I guess it's because the rich and the poor are so geographically separated here that it's easy to believe that everyone lives the same way we do. But it's not true. I went to visit my friend in Ypsilanti a few weeks ago, and I had to take the bus to get there. I guess the bus is mostly used by low-income people and more of them live over there. Because I saw them on the bus! And I saw a lot more of them when I got there. Just five miles away and no one sees them or thinks about them ever."

"So you had your eyes opened to this just recently?" I ask, trying to hide my astonishment.

"Yeah," Sanjeet replies, a bit sheepishly.

How could this be? I wondered. Sanjeet was a top student in my international development class, an economics major, a graduating senior. His career goal—after he completes two advanced degrees in Medicine and International Relations—is to work in a high-profile position at the World Health Organization.

"You didn't hear about poor people in your own community in your economics classes?"

"I think the problem with economics courses is that they're really, really theoretical," Sanjeet says. "You're just learning mathematical models and reproducing them. You're not talking about real things that happen in the world. You're just talking about what the model shows and how to manipulate it."

"How about your friends, would you say they are as sheltered as you?"

"Some are. Others are more aware of the gap between the rich and poor—or they're aware of it in theory. But I don't think many of them have seen actual poor people. The other country I'm familiar with is India, and over there, poor people are impossible to miss. But here, poverty is hidden. So it's easy to get the idea that our country has the highest standard of living and the best health care system in the world, which just isn't true. I mean, with the health care debate on TV all the time, everyone knows, at some level of consciousness, about the 48 million people in this country who don't have health insurance. But they don't actually see that many of them. So they're not aware of the contradiction between what they believe about this country and the actual facts."

From the way Sanjeet tells his own story it seems as if he was hit by a revelation that day on the bus, but in fact, as he later explains, he has learned about structural inequality in the United States gradually over his years in college by extrapolating from his experiences visiting relatives in India and by analyzing various approaches to economic and social development in the Global South. More than most students in my international development course, Sanjeet has an intimate knowledge of the global neighborhood, yet his awareness of the local environment has come through independent reading, conversations with friends, and chance encounters with "actual poor people," as he puts it. While he was never advised to take any courses on U.S. poverty to complement his economics training, he did shadow a doctor in a low-income community once, following him on his rounds as he tried to persuade patients to take medicines they couldn't afford. As he was applying to medical school, sending off hundreds of dollars in fees, he heard about another young man, the son of his mother's co-worker, who had to delay his applications for a year while he worked to get up the money—"and that was just for the applications, not even for medical school," Sanjeet adds. Small incidents like these made him realize how much he hadn't known about his own country, and that without the opportunity to connect economic theories to people's life experiences, one could come to some faulty conclusions.

"I argued with one of my friends about this a few days ago," Sanjeet explains. "Actually our debate was about capitalism and socialism. I don't really like either of them in their pure form. But my friend was arguing that people should just pull themselves out of poverty and that capitalism encourages achievement. This is someone who grew up with me in the suburbs. And if you grew up in a rich town like we did, you can believe that people who live there got where they are through capitalism. But there are other people who didn't, who were completely left behind by capitalism. And I found it was really hard to drive that point home, because if you haven't seen people who didn't make it, if you think everyone in America lives like you do, then that's a problem."

A problem, indeed. Residential segregation of the affluent has grown since the end of the last century,[1] when income inequalities rose sharply and higher-status families began buying the large homes that increasingly dominated the new housing market.[2] In Michigan, these homes, with their extensive lawns and gardens, grand entryways, and elaborate kitchens, are built on formerly productive small farms that ring the urban areas. As the new neighborhoods grow, they attract high-quality services and schools, both public and private, as well as access to affluent social networks, jobs, and political power, all of which increase economic inequality still further.[3] Millennials who grow up in such neighborhoods, as well as in the older, more established suburbs, may be politically progressive, and may even be more concerned about societal inequalities than generations past, but despite their best intentions, it is difficult for them to see these disparities when they so rarely interact with anyone unlike themselves. In their neighborhoods, ordinary working people are visible only as service providers. As Sanjeet says, "nobody has to see poor people if they don't want to."

While the community service they do in high school could potentially provide a link between affluent Millennials and the working class, students like Sanjeet and his friends remain surprisingly naïve. How can they have so little personal knowledge of inequality when volunteering has become such a central part of preparation for college? I wondered. "Well, yes, I did community service in high school," Sanjeet says in answer to my question. "But there weren't any poor areas near where we lived. So I guess the kind of service I did was raising money for things, it wasn't actually interacting with poor people. And even when we could have taken a service trip, we didn't. When Hurricane Katrina came along, we just raised money for the people who were flooded out. We didn't go to New Orleans to really see what happened. I still haven't been there."

Sanjeet believes that he is more sheltered than most Americans his age, though he knows that many of his friends have had similar experiences growing up. But even when Millennial students go on community service trips before they get to college, they rarely see beyond the superficial. "Parents of Millennials buy nice, safe experiences for their kids," a program director tells me, "and these visits to poor communities put students into situations that are very predictable. So when their bus arrives in that town in Appalachia, the local children are already assembled in the gymnasium, ready for the volunteers to teach them a little lesson. Or they are given a hammer and a paintbrush and they help build a school. These experiences are very scripted; they're constructed so the students never see backstage. Their group just comes in and—'Wow, we built a school!' The whole experience is sanitized. Students are never purposely confronted with their privilege. They come away feeling they've done something wonderful out of their own enthusiasm, their own desire to make a difference, when actually, that hammer and nailing, that painting, could have easily been done by the local people—once the resources were in place." If students are not asked to think about the fact that household tools may be out of economic reach of the family that lives in that quaint little roadside shack with the hole in the roof they can be left with the uneasy impression that the people are incapable of helping themselves. Despite their progressive desire for greater equality, Millennial students whose view of the poor is shaped by experiences like these cannot help but suspect that their own comfortable position in life is the result of their family's work ethic and virtuous living.

Of course, the reaffirmation of class privilege is not the conscious intent of these service trips, which are now such a central part of elite students' preparation for college. The opportunities are there; the parents believe they will do their children good—not to mention make them more marketable—and the students are willing, even eager, to participate. If the destination is somewhere abroad, so much the better. As the demand for new service experiences grows, some communities in the Global South have become quite savvy to the benefits that young U.S. volunteers can provide. "There are so many groups selling community service experiences internationally," the program director tells me. "For a lot of money! 'Come and work for three weeks building a health clinic in Guatemala!' It's not necessarily a rip off. It's a local community that's figured out, 'Here's how we'll get our clinic built! Invite those crazy Americans who'll pay $6,000 a pop to come visit us. Host them at your house. Be nice to them. They're not going to do much. But then we'll have our clinic!' And they do sincerely show the volunteers a good time. They get together a local dance, they take them around the neighborhood—it's an authentic thing. But they realize there's money in doing this. The volunteers get the experience—which then 'adds value' to their list of accomplishments—and the community gets the development.

"This is not to criticize the communities, or even the idealistic people who run the organizations that arrange these trips," the program head continues. "But it gives Millennial students another naïve experience: 'I've made a difference in the world!' Actually, no. You were just the cog that made the real development happen. You contributed something to it, but the main thing you contributed was paying $6,000 for three weeks." This price tag, however, is reserved for the more exotic locales; when they embark on an "inner-city experience" in their own country, Millennial volunteers who scrub graffiti from a storefront or plant trees in a local park on their "day of service" don't pay the community a dime, which leaves neighborhood activists with scant resources for more substantial improvement. And more often than not, students who go on any of these trips aren't asked to reflect on the implications of their contribution or how their work might be made more useful. Their service ends when the bus pulls away or the plane takes off, leaving the community behind.

Millennial students who arrive at elite colleges with résumés full of such experiences need to begin their critical education with a deeper awareness of the world they inhabit. "It's a question of knowing where you're from," says a Spanish teacher. "And understanding where you're from means knowing who lives near you, in both the local and global sense. It means knowing who supports your lifestyle, who makes your day possible." Knowing where you're from means understanding how the community functions. Who are the prominent people, the ordinary people, the invisible people? Why are we so separated from each other? What kinds of relationships bind us all together? On whose terms are these relationships forged? How did this all come to pass?

Millennial students' lack of familiarity with their local and global neighborhood might seem incongruous in the age of the World Wide Web. It was the Internet, after all, that ignited the intense interest of many in this generation to devote themselves to righting human wrongs. Online photos of victims of AIDS and human trafficking, YouTube videos of stranded polar bears in the Arctic and the disappearing rain forest in the Amazon—not to mention the ease of online chatting, photo sharing, and blogging with people from every corner of the world—have made this generation the first to think of itself as global. Yet elite Millennials remain oddly disconnected from the suffering they want so much to eliminate. Though the most dedicated students take full advantage of electronic news sources, setting the *New York Times* or the BBC as their home page, and keeping up with their own particular causes through Web sites, e-mail newsletters, blogs and tweets, the majority are hazy about the details.

"My students truly want to help," says a director of a community outreach program on campus, "but they can be quite vague about what's happening in the world. They might be aware that some horrible thing happened in Haiti. But they think it's a tidal wave or something, when it was actually an earthquake. Or they're aware there's an economic crisis, especially if it affects their ability to pay tuition. But they don't know what's behind it. They didn't take the time to read it on the news flash on their iPhone!" Obliviousness can be a way of dealing with so much suffering. But the tendency to gloss over painful details is exacerbated by the sheer volume of information and the speed at which it arrives. When information is limitless and instantaneous, the viewer not only can be overwhelmed with the number of abuses crying out for attention but the bad news also can easily be skimmed, or ignored, or reduced to the trivial.

Of course, the rapid pace of life can also be pure pleasure. "For this generation," says an instructor, "it's no big deal to glance at their portable media player and say, 'Oh, I want that song! Beep! I just bought it!'" Within a matter of minutes, Millennial students can skim their text messages, transfer a bit of virtual cash from savings to checking, buy a couple of tickets for a show, find a cool restaurant, and announce their upcoming date to 1,348 friends on Facebook. When what's happening is what's happening *now*, their connections with the past become more tenuous. Time and space become irrelevant, and students can be left with the impression that they exist outside of history.[4] And history—the connections between events past and present, the stories of how wrongs were initiated and magnified over time, the ways that the economic and psychological effects of those wrongs have been passed down through generations—could help progressive Millennials make more sense of the world they have inherited and to know more intimately "where they're from." But invoking that history can be easier said than done.

"My acting class was looking at a play called *Roots in Water*,"[5] a drama instructor tells me as illustration. "It's actually a series of short plays about the '60s generation becoming Yuppies. So all the plays are set in the late '70s to the early '80s. Each of the plays focuses on characters who felt they had a passionate connection to America's political past, and now are consumed with bourgeois issues. Of course, the students have very little connection to events that were galvanizing the country a generation ago. All these political events—whether it's Watergate, or the Iran Contra Affair, or the Vietnam War, none of these things are familiar to them. So I tell them, okay, everyone in the cast has to research one of the events in the play, and then we'll talk about it. And then I have them make a scrapbook for their character about their life in the '60s, so they have to really think about what it meant to live in a commune, what it meant to be marching on Washington. They have to find pictures, they have to come up with text. And they do that, dutifully, most of them, but I wonder, do they care? Do they really want to be part of it?

"Of course in any generation, there were students who didn't care much about history," the drama teacher continues. "But Millennials are different, I think, because for them, the past is not so much about what actually happened. Their point of connection is television, it's YouTube, it's movies. So I'm noticing that when I mention some historical event in class they go, 'Oh, that's just like *Pocahantas!*' or 'Oh, that's like *Inglourious Basterds.*' It's their whole orientation. So when something came up in *Roots in Water* about the Iran Contra hearings none of my students knew what that was. And then someone said, 'Oh, Contras! Isn't there a video game . . . ?' And everyone got very excited: 'Yeah, there are these people attacking you in the jungle and you're shooting 'em down!'"

"Maybe that game was actually modeled on the rebels in Nicaragua," I suggest lamely.

"I think it was!" says the drama instructor. "But the students' reference point was a computer game, rather than the real, CIA-funded coup that involved all sorts of illegal activities that were hidden from the American people.[6] And students don't know or even care to know the difference!"

"It's not only the influence of the media that keeps students ignorant of history," adds the community storyteller. "Our generation dropped the ball. From kindergarten all the way up through high school, we put a big smiley face on U.S. history. And that means we leave out anything that has to do with struggle, why the struggles happened, who struggled, and who benefited. We don't teach history as cause and effect. So students have no context. We just assumed that after the massive social movements that characterized the '50s and '60s we wouldn't have to keep talking about why social change was necessary in the first place. We stopped talking about why all those events happened, what came out if it, what it was all about. We dropped the ball on keeping alive the *pathos* of those events. The result is that even most high school history teachers don't know anything more than what's in the textbook. So if the conversation turns to the reasons behind those events—the story behind the story—teachers can't handle it. As I see it, the teachers themselves don't really know history. Because the history in the textbooks doesn't talk about reasons either. It's our responsibility as educators, as parents, as elders, to provide some sort of historical rootage so young people have a sense of what their antecedents were. Telling these stories as fully and as often as possible—that's what I do. I get invited into schools to tell the stories of my generation, and my parents' generation, and their parents' generation, which has now passed away. So often I tell students, 'This isn't just something I learned in a book. I *lived* this. My *family* lived this.' And then I put those life experiences in the context of history. Not the sanitized version. Real history.

"One of my stories is about being slapped in the face and called a nigger by a white boy when I was seven years old," the storyteller continues. "Now, if you only heard about this kid slapping me in the face without any of the antecedents, you'd probably conclude that he was just a nasty little racist, or maybe that he just didn't know any better. But there's a lot more to it that today's students need to know. Around the time of World War II, whites were going off to fight, and blacks were not going into the military in the same numbers, because, remember, the military was still segregated at that time—there was no serious attempt at equal treatment or opportunity until 1948, at the end of the war. So factory owners brought in blacks and women to the factories to take those jobs that white soldiers were vacating. And at the same time, real estate owners were realizing that with all this influx of black people working in the factories, they would make a mint if they created a scare among the whites who owned the homes, and got them to move. Whites sold quickly at low prices, and then the real estate companies turned around and sold those houses to blacks at a huge profit.

"So to lead up to that incident between the two boys on the street, I talk about the dynamics that changed the 'complexion' of the neighborhood, if you will. I talk about block-busting as an actual practice. I talk about restrictive covenants that prevented African Americans from moving anywhere they wanted in the city. I talk about where the jobs were and how the factory owners played one race against another to keep wages down. So here's this little white kid, who lives in his white enclave, and he's hearing this story about black people: 'They've taken our jobs! They've taken our homes! They're this, they're that.' Constantly! His mom or dad may have been laid off and replaced by a black worker. Their neighborhood had become unfamiliar to them. And it's all the fault of the black man. So then the kid sees me, and, whack! Hits me in the face. I'd never seen him before in my life! But that was the social norm back then. That child's feeling, though he was too young to understand it, was that he had the right to hit me. And that 'norm,' that idea that his behavior was neutral or harmless, came about through all these historical events—and many others that preceded them—that are left out of history books, and that almost no student, black or white, rich or poor, knows about today."

It's true, I reflected—every U.S.-born student in my courses on racism and nonviolence has studied African American history (in fact, many say that they're tired of it, they feel they know it and don't need to rehash it) yet they rarely have looked at the civil rights struggles in detail or connected the segregation of the Jim Crow era with the dire economic predicament many blacks experience today. Nor do most Millennial students appreciate the emotional weight of the past, the "pathos" that the storyteller mentions. They aren't led to understand how traumatic events are passed down through impoverished families, sometimes through stories, but more often through silences. "The oppressed grandchild repeats the suffering of their grandparent," says Freire. "Almost always, concrete situations of oppression reduce the oppressed's historical time to an everlasting present of hopelessness and resignation."[7] History has disappeared, both for the impoverished and for the privileged Millennials who skim the details of their suffering.

To add to their sense of disconnection from the history of their own country, few of my elite Millennial students are aware of how common it used to be for politicians, educators, news media, and ordinary people to speak in blatantly racist terms, to publish racist cartoons in mainstream newspapers, to display racially offensive figurines on their lawns, or to depict people of color as subservient, infantile, stupid, clownish, and aggressive in popular films and stage productions.[8] With scant knowledge of either this history or how the experience of exclusion and humiliation, generation after generation, affects the racial climate today, privileged Millennials have difficulty making sense of the "touchiness" of contemporary race-baiting, the offensiveness of fraternity pranks and insults that recall this earlier era,[9] or the racist violence lurking just beneath the surface at political rallies that denounce our first "post-racial" president.[10] Without either a sense of history or an understanding of how racism shapes and permeates institutions, it is easy for Millennials to believe in the fundamental soundness of the system, to see race as "no big deal," and thus remain profoundly disconnected from their environment.

Of course, the racial "norm" of the storyteller's childhood is hardly a thing of the past. While its form has changed and much of its personal nastiness has gone underground, the idea that there is something natural about the confluence of poverty and race is so pervasive that altruistic Millennial students can have difficulty seeing it when it stares them in the face. Honest and introspective as he is, Sanjeet admits that it's not quite true that he had never seen poor people before that day when he went down to Ypsilanti on the bus.

"I think I always *did* know about inequalities in the U.S.," he says reflectively, "but I thought about them in racial terms, maybe. As a child, I had seen homeless people in Detroit, but growing up in the suburbs you come to expect that homeless people live in Detroit. My family actually lived in Detroit for a couple of years when I was too young to remember, and my parents still have all these horror stories of Detroit that sort of shaped my view of it. Like my dad's car got stolen once—someone just came and sort of hijacked it and drove off. This wasn't exactly a common occurrence, but my parents kept talking about it when I was growing up. So I came to believe that's just the way it is: the city is a violent place where poor people live, where black people live."

Like so many other Millennial students at elite colleges, Sanjeet has learned to see racialized poverty as normal. And what is normal is, in a sense, invisible: seen, but at the same time, unseen. Driving through the city, suburban students notice the broken-down buildings, the dejected communities, the men in shabby coats wandering the streets late at night in the dead of winter, but the "normalcy" of it all stifles their sense of outrage. And if they are drawn to study issues of poverty in their own country, their tacit acceptance of racial stereotypes quickly begins to surface.

An instructor who engages student interns with homeless, runaway, and at-risk youth remarks that most of her students are unaware of the racialized assumptions they bring to the work they so passionately believe in. "Suppose we're introducing a role-play to the youth, or maybe we're asking them to write on some topic that is deep and meaningful to them," says the instructor. "I model these kinds of lessons at the beginning of the semester, so my student interns can watch me in action. That way, they get a sense of the range of issues the kids will come up with, the language they might use (almost nothing is taboo in my classroom), and the tone and quality of the interaction that they should be aiming for. The interns have to observe all this in minute detail and then we debrief extensively, so they are really trained to listen and observe before they take over as group leaders. And what comes out in the debriefing sessions is their surprise that the homeless youth—who are mostly youth of color—are taking these activities so seriously. You know, this sounds really brutal, but it's like they feel they're coming into this zoo, and they're taken aback when one of the animals acts like a civilized human being. I don't know, that's really kind of raw. But there's that feeling of, 'Wow, I expected these kids to be wild and disruptive, and here they are actually writing and listening to each other and making insightful comments about the work.'"

"So how do you get your interns to think more deeply about their racial assumptions?" I ask.

"Well, we talk about them," the instructor says. "I try to create a safe space for them to say what's on their minds and to challenge each other to think more deeply about the attitudes they bring to their community practice. In a way, I can understand why they come in with these stereotypes, since we're working with kids who are functionally illiterate, kids who hate school, and even kids who are in the program because they beat up their teachers and were barred from their classroom. Yet all these young people have real potential as artists, as poets, as musicians, as readers and writers: our results show that again and again. So I work really hard instilling in my interns the idea that you should never define the person you're working with by their situation. We should all be defined by our potential, not by the fact that we're homeless or that we did something to get kicked out of school. No one wants to be defined by their worst moment or be pegged with a stereotype that other people have about their group. Most of the youth we work with are African American and poor, so even before they got expelled from school, there were all sorts of evaluative judgments made about their character and potential. So I tell the interns, let's look deeply at what we believe about these kids and at what we expect of them, and then look at them in terms of their strengths and possibilities. We need to ask ourselves, how can we work with young people that almost everyone has given up on in 'hope, humility and sympathy,' as Freire says? How can we recognize the barriers we have created to exclude them from the larger community?

"One way into this difficult topic is to talk about how we ourselves have been excluded," the instructor continues. "Many of the students who elect this class have been stigmatized at some point in their lives. There are always a good number of Jewish females, and that's a stereotype in itself. Some students are African American, and whether they're working class or upper class, most have felt the sting of racism. Then there are the Muslim folks who are not African American but have dark skin and have been snubbed or ostracized for that reason. Mainstream white females might think they have never been oppressed, but if they look closely, they can see the way sexism and internalized oppression have affected their lives. Even the white males may have been stigmatized for their religion, their sexual orientation, or just for being white. So this class is a place where we can talk about stereotyping and process it and be real with it, and not feel defensive or embarrassed or attacked.

"Another question that's really weighing on my student interns' minds is 'Who am I to teach?'" the instructor continues. "Nearly all of them *definitely* come with that. And the few that don't, I kind of worry about, because they come in with a banner flying that says: 'I'm going to go in and save these kids!' They come with that conceit, that belief in their own superiority, so we have to work on that so they know they're not coming in to save the day. But mostly, the interns are worried they're being presumptuous by entering into the community at all. They wonder, 'Who am I, a white girl from Bloomfield Hills, Michigan, (for example), saying I have something to teach you, a black kid from Detroit? I can't possibly know what it's like to be you. I will never know what it is to be black, much less black and poor. Who am I to teach you anything?' It's true that these questions represent some level of awareness, since at least they're recognizing the arrogance of thinking that mere exposure to their privileged world will change these kids' lives. But the question, 'Who am I to teach?'—a wonderful question, by the way—also reveals how alienated they feel from the youth they're working with. It's almost the flip side of thinking they're going to act like animals. They think they're just miles and miles apart.

"There's been so little contact between groups: the privileged and the poor, whites and people of color, and even groups of color from other groups of color, that students sometimes make enormous presumptions from the slightest bit of information," the instructor explains. "To give you just a couple of examples, if stories of abuse come out during our writing sessions with the kids—which can certainly happen when they want to say things that are deep and meaningful—the interns might assume that all the kids have violent parents, or that they have all experienced some kind of twisted relationship with someone in their extended family. Once when a group was working at a shelter that's a very safe space for LBGT kids, I even had an intern who said how surprised she was that so many African Americans are gay. She had so little knowledge of the African American community that she made this huge leap and presumed that all of them—well, there's an innocence about it," the instructor sighs. "It's not just these particular students, or even this generation that is so fragmented; it's our whole society. But if Millennial students want to be progressive, if they want to 'work for change,' they need to understand that divisions between people are real and meaningful, and at the same time, that they are not nearly as unbridgeable as they might think."

"It might sound a bit obvious to say this," remarks an instructor who introduces Spanish language students to issues of migrant labor, "but if they want to 'change the world,' Millennial students have to become aware that whole groups of people exist. For most people, the agricultural labor force is a completely invisible population—even in Michigan where we have as many as 45,000 workers in the fields every summer. Yet we are all directly and indirectly beneficiaries of their work. We are all a part of the agriculture system; we are all part of the economic system, we are all part of the global neighborhood. So first on my agenda for my students is knowledge: they need to know that migrant workers exist and that this has implications. It has implications for the agriculture system, for the consumer system, and for our society. And maybe most important for students to understand, if they *don't* know the field workers exist, that also has implications.

"I start by giving my students readings about who the migrants are, how the agricultural system works, who the growers are, what the agrobusinesses are all about, all these players," says the instructor. "And then we look at the larger context: the political interaction between the U.S. and Mexico, the trade agreements, the economic disparities between countries, the history of how the border was drawn. And then I ask them to discuss all this among themselves, and tell me what they see."

"But since migrant labor has been invisible to them, do they really see the system as a problem?" I ask. "Or do they see it as fine?"

"They never see it as fine."

"Why is that?"

"The migrant families, they earn on average $7,600 for a family of four, a year," says the instructor. "They all live below the poverty line. Their work is seasonal, remember. They work 40 to 80 hours a week picking crops, and for that, they make $300. So once the students consider this, it's a little hard for them to believe that the system works well for everyone. It's hard to figure out what to do about the system, but I've never had anybody say, 'Well, you know, that's life.' [11]

"I do bring up that the migrants earn here more than they do in Mexico," she continues. "I play the devil's advocate. Because students are very PC about things. They know that a good liberal is supposed to feel bad about inequality. So when they hear about the wages they'll say, 'Oh, that's awful.' And I'll counter, 'No, it's not awful, it's been going on forever.' And then they insist, 'No, that's really awful!' Okay, so they're feeling it, and that's good. But I want to get them to articulate *why* it's so awful. Because once you understand and can explain why, it's a lot easier to channel that energy into doing something useful about it.

"I don't just tell them what I think about it," the instructor continues. "Lecturing at them—no, it doesn't work. They have to actively figure out how to explain the system to each other. They have to make an argument out of it. I ask them to work together, to discuss, to analyze: 'What do you see as the central problem in this system?' Of course, the system is complex, so they could argue in a lot of different ways. So to help make their thinking more manageable, I give them an exercise where they have to draw a diagram that connects all the players in a way that shows how the system works. And they also have to indicate, based on their framework of how they perceive the problem, where is the weakest area, where would they attack it and how. Some students focus on consumers, who have the power of choice of what to buy. Some of them see the problem as the inequity between the U.S. and Mexico, so they would focus more on neoliberal economic practices and trade agreements. Others look at the agro-businesses as the central issue, so it would be a question of lobbying to change the rules about the extent of corporate power. When the issues are so intertwined, they can be perceived in a lot of different ways, but if you can't visualize and articulate your understanding of it, you can feel too overwhelmed to take effective action. So rather than just letting students say, 'Oh, it's too complicated' (which we always say), or 'It's always going to be that way because the big players are just too powerful,' they have to come up with ideas about how people like themselves can help make the system more fair. But then I tell them, 'I'm not going to do these things for you. You have to decide who you are, what your priorities are. I will give you the information and the arguments and the problems and help you sort it all out. Ultimately, you are responsible for what you do with this knowledge. You can act or not act. But you have no excuse for not knowing.'"

In *Pedagogy of the Oppressed,* Freire reminds us, "The oppressor is in solidarity with the oppressed only when he stops regarding the oppressed as an abstract category and sees them as persons who have been unjustly dealt with, deprived of their voice, cheated in the sale of their labor—when he stops making pious, sentimental, and individualistic gestures and risks an act of love."[12] Millennial students want to risk that act of love, an act that is almost unbearably meaningful to them in an age when so little else makes sense. But to do so, they must learn to see into people's lives and hearts, straight through the barriers and separations that keep us from recognizing each other.

Notes

1. Segregated housing and the unequal distribution of power and resources have long been features of U.S. cities. See Sugrue (1996) and Farley, Danziger, & Holzer (2000).
2. Dwyer, 2007. Nationally, the average square footage of new houses increased by almost 40 percent from the mid-1980s to 2000.
3. Interestingly, it is greater inequality, rather than a low income level per se that creates the persistent problems associated with poverty: violence, poor health, substance abuse, low educational performance, crime, and early death (Wilkinson & Pickett, 2009).
4. The disappearance of a sense of history is one of the defining features of our postmodern era (Irvine, 2004–2009). Yet this process seems to be even more pronounced among Millennials because of their fascination with the ever-increasing forms of electronic media. The routine practice of erasing electronically stored historical sources when Web sites are taken down also contributes to our historical amnesia (Brindley, 2009).
5. Nelson, 1991.
6. The Iran Contra scandal involved the secret sale of U.S. arms by the CIA to Iran during the Reagan administration, and the use of the profits to facilitate the overthrow of the Nicaraguan government, an action that had been made specifically illegal by Congress. A fascinating account of the Iran Contra hearings can be found in an eight-part video on YouTube (Iran Contra Coverup. n.d.), http://www.youtube.com/watch?v=35KcYgMPiIM.
7. Freire, 2007, 45.
8. An excellent visual history of racially offensive artifacts can be found at the Jim

Crow Museum of Racist Memorabilia at Ferris State University, http://www.ferris.edu/jimcrow/.
9. For example, see Lamont (2001); Reeves (2010).
10. For example, see *Huffington Post* (2009, April 16).
11. For an introduction to the living and working conditions of Michigan seasonal agricultural workers, see Michigan Civil Rights Commission (2010).
12. Freire, 1986, 34–35.

Chapter 4
_____

Connecting in a Digital Age

Regardless of Millennial students' disturbing separation from their local and global communities, they do maintain tight-knit social bonds with those who are closest to them. Since childhood, today's college students have been using electronic media to stay in touch, sometimes minute by minute, with friends and family. The rapid development of electronic and social media has produced profound changes in the ways this generation forms and maintains relationships. Cell phones arrived in elementary schools just after 9/11, when fearful parents insisted on immediate connection, and children found security in their parents' vigilance.[1] Instant messaging took off in the 1990s, and with the introduction of the "smart phone" with its keyboard features, low cost, and portability, Millennial children discovered they could keep in constant contact with each other through e-mail and text messaging. Social networking exploded in the early 2000s, providing endless opportunities for the exchange of gossip, photos, videos, news bits, and encouragement to chat, briefly and superficially at least, with friends, friends of friends, and entirely unknown friends across the world.

This constant connectivity has taken on the characteristics of an addiction, according to a University of Maryland study called "24 Hours: Unplugged." When researchers asked 200 college students to give up all their media for a day, students described their reactions as "frantically craving, very anxious, extremely antsy, miserable, jittery, and crazy," feelings most often associated with withdrawal from drugs or alcohol. Whether they are addicted to the technology itself or to the social connections it affords is a matter of scholarly debate, but most of the students attributed the intensity of their reactions to being abruptly cut off from their network of friends and family. "Texting and IM-ing my friends gives me a constant feeling of comfort," wrote one student. "When I did not have those two luxuries, I felt quite alone and secluded from my life. Although I go to a school with thousands of students, the fact that I was not able to communicate with anyone via technology was almost unbearable."[2]

We might think this craving for electronic connection is evidence that Millennial students are engaging in meaningful human relationships with more people than ever—even though the walls and barriers described in the previous chapter channel their connections to people like themselves. Yet research suggests that these constant, brief interactions add up to rather superficial relationships. A University of Michigan study found a decline in empathy among American college students since the 1980s, most notably since 2000. The reason, they speculate, is that the ability to interact on social networking sites takes time away from real-world relationships.[3] In a Ball State University study that surveyed nearly 5,000 college students about their mobile communication habits over five years, researchers found that text messaging had become the dominant form of communication for 59 percent of students, while only 17 percent were using their cell phones to actually talk to anyone.[4] With its instant connectivity, shorthand vocabulary, and "emoticons" that express simple, quick reactions (smile, hug, annoyance, sarcasm, tears, sexual arousal[5]), texting provides the feeling of connection with a circle of friends at any time or place. One can connect at any spare moment: standing in line, stopped a red light, at a boring moment in a lecture, or even between bites at lunch.[6] About 62 percent of students say they text during class, and some even text each other while sitting side by side on the couch in their dorm room. The average adolescent user sends and receives about 2,272 messages per month, or about 80 messages a day.[7]

"I think that we're losing that ability to hold a conversation face to face, or even over the phone anymore," Talia tells me. "My generation is too busy texting and sending instant messages to really have face-to-face contact with people. In fact, I think we feel even more comfortable texting than we do calling."

"Do you really?" I ask. I'm surprised Talia would go that far.

"Yeah. Because if you're texting somebody, you don't have to respond right away. So you can kind of hide, and take a second to yourself to process what the other person said and decide how to reply. When you're talking to someone, once you say something, you can't unsay it. But when you're texting, if you think what you're trying to say sounds stupid or isn't going to go over so well, you can just erase it and say something else."

"So does that mean that students are concealing their emotions more?" I ask Talia.

"Well, yes and no. I do feel like the whole texting and e-mailing thing is making people more guarded. But at the same time, people are texting long messages to each other that try to explain what they're feeling and why they're upset that their friend said whatever they said. They want to clear things up, but they also need that distance. But I think texting has definitely become a more accepted mode than face-to-face conversation. And that's unfortunate, because it makes everything seem more scripted. People get nervous. They don't always know what to say or how to say it."

These constant, superficial connections provide "the illusion of companionship without the demands of friendship," says MIT psychologist Sherry Turkle, who has been studying human relationships with technology since the 1970s. "The real demands of friendship, of intimacy, are complicated. They're hard. They involve a lot of negotiation. They are all the things that are difficult about adolescence. And adolescence is the time when people are using technology to skip and to cut corners and to not have to do some of these very hard things."[8]

Turkle points out that the stunting of emotional relationships is not just a characteristic of Millennial students—it's a natural outgrowth of the electronic networking capability that allows all of us to avoid awkward or complicated social interactions. "It's very hard to tell a colleague that they've disappointed you, that their work is a problem. It's extremely easy to send an e-mail that does that," Turkle reminds us. "There are all kinds of things that are really hard that virtuality smoothes over. But what technology makes easy is not always what nurtures the human spirit."[9]

Millennial students' difficulties with face-to-face interaction can be complicated by the ease of connecting with virtual friends they will never meet. "I do think this technology has created a new sort of emotional valve," says the Spanish teacher. "You can literally have invisible friends who live in god knows where who you tell all your secrets. And since you only have so much emotion that you can share, if you're sharing it with seven or eight people on the Internet, all that angst and happiness is not being productive in the here and now. It used to be that if you had an argument or you had a bad day, you either went to the gym and ran it out or you talked to somebody. Or you got into a fight. You didn't express your feelings to all the world with clever one-liners. You were forced to connect emotionally, with all the body language and unpredictable directions that kind of conversation can take. But now, students can talk about complicated human relationships in an abstract way in the classroom because it's not really about them anymore. Their persona is somewhere else. The technology gives them the option to evade being emotionally connected here."

These changes are not just about the ways people are using technology, says Turkle. "These are shifts in the inner life. . . . Do we want children to have social skills, to be able to just look at each other face to face and negotiate and have a conversation and be comfortable in groups? Is this a value that we have in our educational system?" she asks rhetorically. "Some people say, well, let's raise a generation that can do it all in their heads; I say, why would you want to deny the pleasures of the body? . . . We are evolutionarily designed to communicate at the highest level with the tiniest twitch of our voices, our faces. These are, in some ways, the highest expression of who we are as people."[10]

Even though electronic communication may inhibit the depth of their relationships, students do have a set of embodied friends on campus that they see and talk to every day. But the easy media connectivity with their known world can keep them from opening up to new people, thus missing an opportunity for critical intellectual and emotional growth. "Students in my classes are staying connected with people they're already connected with," says an instructor. "I watch them walking out the door—nobody's talking to people they just had class with. But—they're on the phone! You hear them: 'Where you gonna be?' 'I'll meet you on the Diag.' I tell them, if you don't pay attention to anybody else around you, how are you going to get to know anybody?"

"To be successful, you have to connect, whether in community work or in life," says the Spanish teacher. Certainly, for effective social justice work, the kinds of connections students need to make go far beyond the superficial. Developing an understanding of the people they want to help involves sustained interaction and dialogue across differences. It means developing a tolerance for awkwardness, for silences, for complicated emotions. Even in the classroom, Talia tells me, students need help making conversation. "If people get nervous and can't even talk to their friends about whatever is going on in their lives, then how can you expect them to say something they think might be stupid or wrong in front of a class of strangers?" she asks. "If you can't even express yourself to someone you're close to, how are you supposed to express yourself at all?"

Of course, Millennial students are far from antisocial. As numerous surveys have indicated, they are quite comfortable studying together, working on projects in groups, forming new campus organizations, and filling their lives with social and charitable activities. Because of the social discomfort Talia describes, these contacts may be quite shallow, skirting political discussion, depth of feeling, and complicated personal interaction. But Millennials who are care about social justice are not necessarily satisfied with superficial relationships; in fact, many are hungry for conversations that would edge them out of their comfort zone. I asked Chris Groscurth, an instructional consultant at the Center for Research on Learning and Teaching[11] and a Millennial himself, how he advises faculty to cultivate more authentic interactions in the classroom.

"For some students, their college experience is the first and maybe one of the last significant opportunities to interact across differences," says Chris. "So there's a curiosity, a desire to learn more, to test your assumptions about people you haven't ever had a chance to interact with. When I was in college, I wanted to understand my own biases, my own stereotypes, and as I continually encountered myself in these conversations and found a lot of my assumptions to be wrong, it kind of made me mad. And so that anger, and that feeling of being duped in some ways by my upbringing and education, motivated me to go deeper."

Growing up before electronic connectivity hit full force, Chris had spent a lot of time alone, fishing on a nearby lake, writing and playing his own music, engaging in reflective down time that later Millennials, especially those with access to a full range of technology, have rarely experienced. Now a U-M staff member with a passion for educating people about meaningful dialogue, Chris says, 'Because of the power I think language and conversation have, I'm not convinced that Millennial students don't have the ability to reflect just because the nature of their conversations is superficial. I feel like they're not reflecting with other people because they haven't been taught to ask the right questions. Once they learn this skill they can use the technology to have higher-quality conversations."

Chris mentions three questions progressive educators can use to set the tone for deeper interaction on the first day in the classroom: "Who are you?" "Where are you from?" and "Where are you going?" Perceptive students immediately see the philosophical and even spiritual nature of that third question. Although there are always some students who take the question literally, the incongruity of asking, "Where are you going?" at the beginning of a two-hour class prompts students to reconsider their straightforward responses to the first two questions. By the time several students have spoken reflectively, others will follow their lead. "And then you ask, 'Do you recognize those questions?'" Chris laughs. "'They're the three questions they ask you when you're crossing a border.' Now students are certain that this class is going to be different from what they're used to!

"I think my mode of constant questioning and reflective listening gives students a model for how to deepen their conversations in the classroom and with their friends as well," Chris continues. "Students don't need to be explicitly taught what questions to ask. Just hearing the kinds of questions I'm always asking gives them the idea. I ask a lot of 'What does that mean?' and 'What would that look like?' questions. 'Tell me about a time when . . . ' 'What could we accomplish if . . . ?' 'How does that work?' 'Where could we go from here?' Questions that start with who, what, where, when, why, and—my favorite—how—these simple words invite the participation of people interested in exploring opportunities and overcoming challenges. 'How should we proceed?' 'What would it look like if we did X?' And then, when we've exhausted all *those* questions, I challenge them by asking, 'Okay, based on where we've ended up in this conversation, what *new* questions did it raise for you?'"[12]

Chris is so used to asking these questions and so interested in where people take them that he's started an online conversation about effective communication in the workplace. I asked him what kinds of questions he asks the readers of his blog. "Well, I was interested in your idea that this interview should be a collaborative conversation," Chris replies. "So this morning I wrote, 'How collaborative are your conversations with students, with employees, with your co-workers? Do you listen and respond, or do you wait to insert your preformed, predetermined opinion? And what are the implications of *not* communicating collaboratively? What's being built as a result of that?' And the amazing thing is that in the last seven months I've tracked 1,000 unique visitors to my site. I have quite a few online readers in India, one in South Africa, several in Canada and Britain. For me, it's fascinating that I'm posing questions that people around the world are, at a minimum, being exposed to, and some are engaged by. Some leave comments. Some request more information and I'll send them a reading or something. Even though blogs can be used to just blurt out whatever and not really connect at all, they can also be a great tool for communicating about communication, about reflection, about depth and significance in our conversations."

"So you're saying that even though Millennials are using technology for superficial purposes, you can see its potential for something far richer?"

"That's right. Millennials have the tools! Right now, these tools may be a distraction from doing the kind of self-reflection that would lead to high-quality questions and interactions with others. But these tools could really leverage their social networks and amplify whatever insight or creative accomplishments they have so other people can organize around them or learn from them," says Chris with excitement. "At no other point in history has anyone been able to publish their thoughts or a video of themselves and have it disseminate as quickly and as widely as they can now! So if we can harness that with the ability and motivation to ask the right questions and engage in higher-quality conversations, that would be a pretty *amazing* contribution!"

True enough, I thought. But first things first. Students need to put aside their technology and take the risk of being real with each other in person before they spread their personal insights far and wide. Because without the skill to interact with each other in depth, what can they teach the world about social justice? Without the ability to fully connect, how can they know what it is to engage with people in radical ways, ways that relieve suffering, and speak truth to power, and move the world toward greater empathy, equality, and solidarity? And how will students even be sure of what it is they are working toward, if they haven't engaged in these conversations? Millennial students who want to "change the world" need to discover what political, social, and historical realities they want to challenge, and how they want to change them. These are not questions that can be answered by surfing the Web or catching a video online. These are weighty issues that people work out together over time. In a dialogue with Paulo Freire, Chilean popular educator Antonio Faundez affirms Hegel's contention that in the search for truth, "the true reality is becoming. Truth lies in the quest and not in the result . . . it is a process, knowledge is a process, and thus we should engage in it and achieve it through dialogue. . . . Perhaps I have part of the truth," Faundez says, "but I don't have the whole truth. You have part of the truth. Let's seek it together."[13]

The possibility of dialogue depends on self-understanding and self-acceptance as well as the ability to listen to others. Students' fears of "sounding stupid," as Talia says, are exacerbated by the intense competition and the "always on" culture that Millennials have lived since childhood. They need time to slow down, to think about their feelings and reactions, to accept the imperfections of being human. Getting away from their environment and into "the real world" may afford them that opportunity, as long as they are prepared for it. Yet our technologically connected students want their community experiences to be "awesome"—always amazing, always entertaining. An insight a minute, without the loneliness, confusion, disapproval, and doubt that community work inevitably brings. How do we help students break through the technology barrier and step into the world outside with openness and humility? I posed this question to a head of Global Intercultural Experiences for Undergraduates,[14] a successful U-M program that prepares first- and second-year students to connect with people on short service-learning trips to the Global South.

"Experiential education is not just a fad to these kids," the program director replies. "They are hungry for it. It's a response to having lived a virtual life. Students want to launch themselves into the real world because they've been online too long. But before we send them into communities abroad we need to teach some pretty elementary communication skills, where they have to interact with themselves and each other on a real-world, human level. We actually practice talking deeply. And before we begin," he says with a laugh, "I do this whole performance in front of them: 'Take out your cell phones,' (the program head makes a theatrical gesture of divesting himself of his electronics) and I take out mine, and turn it off, and tell them we'll put them all over here, in a box, so we can't even do a quick check when we see them light up. Because not only do we want students to pay close attention to their peers, they also need to get used to being without their electronic tethers when they get to their destination abroad. Because depending on where they're going, there might not be any connectivity at all. And even if there is, and even if their Millennial counterparts over there are texting and phoning just like they are—in Thailand or China for example—we don't want them phoning home every minute or posting photos and smart comments to their friends about every detail of their stay. We want them to immerse themselves in their surroundings and connect to their own experiences. We want them to recognize their reactions to the things that delight and trouble them. And we want them to be able to talk intimately about what they're seeing and feeling with the students who traveled with them."

"How do you get them ready for that?" I ask. "It seems like such a huge change. They're not only dealing with language barriers and cultural differences, but you're asking them to let go of their lifeline to their virtual community and begin to talk to people in ways that make them feel uncomfortable."

"So here's an example of one of the exercises we have them do before they leave town," replies the program head. "Students have to sit down together and write the answers to some elementary questions about themselves: their favorite food, their number of siblings, their favorite music, a slogan that is meaningful to them, a skill they want to improve and a talent they have, and so on. Then they share their responses with a partner, and let that lead to a conversation. The exercise actually sounds a lot easier than it is," adds the program director, responding to my quizzical look. "Try coming up with three words that best describe yourself and you'll see what I mean. And imagine sharing your response with a stranger and explaining why you picked those particular attributes."

"What words would I choose?" I wonder. "Writer? Yes, that makes sense. But writing about social justice? Would I want to share that with just anybody? Maybe not. It's always easier to tell new acquaintances that I'm a writing teacher. In a country where the mere mention of an interest in 'socialism' or 'peace' or even 'racism' can prompt derision, who knows what a stranger's reaction might be to 'social justice'?"

"Okay, I get it," I tell the program director. "This might be harder than I thought."

"Then we ask the students to interview each other," the program director continues, smiling. "And the questions we have them ask are sort of personal. Like, 'What did your family think about your decision to go to abroad?' Inevitably, there will be parents who are frightened of the part of the world their children are going to, or threaten us with consequences if their kid has problems over there. So students share these stories, and some might get into how they calmed their parents' fears about the risks and convinced them that the trip was worth it, which may have been a real moment of maturation for them. But despite the revealing nature of the conversation that these activities bring up, it's very common for our students to think they're only icebreakers—trivial, quick, get-to-know-you games that get people talking before the real work begins. Sometimes they even ask why we wasted time talking about these things in person when they could have answered the questions more efficiently online."

"So they don't understand that the conversation is the purpose of the questions?" I ask, incredulous. "Even if you tell them they're learning about communication?"

"Well, not all of them are quite so clueless," says the program director. "But we do have to explain, very deliberately, what skills they are learning and how they will be useful to them when they go abroad. I tell them, 'At your field site, when you're standing in line at the bank, or when you're on a bus, you have a choice: you can get out a magazine or text someone on your Blackberry, or you could *talk* to the person next to you. So what was that like for you, talking to a person you didn't know? And many of you, when you finished the exercise, you started thumbing through your folder of materials rather than continuing to talk with your partner. So this exercise is not only about connecting with others, it's about getting to know yourself. How comfortable are you with talking to a stranger? What do you get out of not tuning out? What is your *emotional* reaction to the experience of talking to someone you don't know?' We want them to go beyond the intellectual skills that they've learned so well in school and are so comfortable with. This is not about writing a paper where they sum up their analysis in a neat little answer. We put it right in their face: 'Conversation is a skill; this is something you might not be used to. There's a way to do it. How to make small talk. This is what we're doing!'" The program director is laughing, but his tone is insistent. In all his years in higher education, he never had to teach small talk until Millennials came along.

Once the students begin to share personal stories they begin to realize that they have not been placed together haphazardly. Although the GIEU program offers field sites in many different countries, students are not given a choice of where they go. Every faculty-led program is interesting: students have traveled to China to talk with their counterparts at Peking University about what it's like to be "children of empire." Others have gone to the Philippines to learn about global inequalities in health care. A group went to Brazil to study ecological practices of traditional ranchers, and another went to South Africa to help develop HIV education modules for people in far-flung villages.

"We intentionally construct our groups to mix students from various backgrounds, especially socioeconomic class," says the program head. "A student from a wealthy family who wants to do something positive in the world before heading off to law school might find herself on the plane to Vietnam with the daughter of a single-mother farm worker. Or a middle-class student might be confronted with the fact that his new friend from Singapore was able to get his father's corporation to donate $40,000 to the group's microfinance project in India—just like that! These are students who most likely would never have interacted on campus; in fact, their lives might never have crossed at all."

I wonder if this is awkward for the students, since most have so little experience in groups that cross class lines. "The privileged kids are taken aback by the working-class students initially," replies the program head, "but they quickly turn around. Most people—including the faculty program leaders, by the way—don't realize that many working-class kids are quite successful here at Michigan. They're never in somebody's office crying about all the stress; they just muscle through and get their degree. And they manage to come up with the money to go on these trips through a combination of grants and loans that have to be paid back the following semester. So when the 'ordinary' Michigan student of means sees these kids who are so bright, and gifted, and successful, doing this project altruistically even though they don't have resources, it raises their own sense of responsibility. They work all that much harder to make sure their trip is successful, and try to see to it that the people they meet abroad are getting something substantial out of the interaction as well.

"Originally the idea for this program was to get the working-class kids more involved on campus with stuff they might not have the time or resources to do," continues the program head. "Give them the full Michigan experience, get them up to speed. But then, the research started showing that our students were leading! A Marshall scholarship? A White House Fellow? The president of a new, highly visible campuswide organization? This isn't who these kids were when they came in to the program! We never thought of it as leadership training. So we started wondering, why are these students becoming leaders? And you know, it was really interesting. The reason they could make things happen on campus was that they had developed some unusual networks. Suppose they joined a student organization when they came back from their trip abroad, and someone suggested that the group coordinate an activity with Hillel, the Jewish Student Center. Well, then our student could say, 'Oh, I know someone in Hillel. I'll go talk to her.' Or 'I know someone in the Black Student Union—let's get them involved.' Or, 'I would feel fine about going to a meeting of the Cambodian Student Association even though I've never met a Cambodian in my life, because that's the kind of thing I did on my trip abroad.'"

I am just as enthused about the GIEU program as the director; many of my first-year students have gone on these short trips and some have come back significantly changed. One student in particular grew so rapidly through her experience working with impoverished women in India that her cynical, guarded, and somewhat impertinent attitude completely disappeared once she understood the nature of "real problems lived by real people," as she put it. GIEU training is not just taking students back to a time before electronic gadgetry and teaching them a few elementary social skills. Putting students together in an intense, reflective experience where they are intentionally confronted with their privilege, where they learn from the people as well as offer help, where they may contend with difficult physical conditions, and where they bond with their group over the trivial as well as the profound, this seems to be the beginning of a kind of connectivity that can "change the world" in significant ways.

The stakes are raised a bit higher for students when they find themselves in a significant position of authority for the first time. In a course that puts Spanish language learners into teaching roles in migrant labor camps, Millennial students are not only interacting with people they don't know, but are responsible for their achievement. "We take the students out to the fields in a van," says the instructor, "and on the first ride out there, you can see how momentous this is for the students, how scary it is to meet a population they've never spoken to in their lives, a population that they might not even have known existed until they saw the course description for my class. Their own education has been so incredibly goal oriented, so focused on 'success' in a very narrow way, that the fact that they're now in charge of someone else's learning seems like a huge task. So on that first ride over, there's silence. And then, a thousand questions: 'What if my lesson plan doesn't work?' 'What if they don't show up?' 'What if they don't understand me?' 'What if they don't like me?' And then, on the ride back, you feel that energy: 'Oh my god, they learned this, and they caught onto that, and I think I'm going to do this different next time!'"

"What if their class didn't go so well?" I ask, thinking back to my first teaching assignments. "Well, if the lesson didn't work, I ask them, 'Did you ask the workers if that's what they wanted to learn?' And they're like, 'Oh! You're right! I should ask them.' They never really thought of that before. And then, if only three out of their ten students show up, they're so discouraged. They just want to ditch the whole thing. And I say, 'Did you notice that it's been raining for three days and your students haven't been able to work? They might be a little bit frustrated because they're not getting any pay.' And if their class lacks energy or enthusiasm one evening, I need to remind them that this is a voluntary class. Migrants are not mandated to go. They don't even sign up for anything. So if the students talk with them after class—I require that they speak Spanish before and after class to shift the power dynamic a little bit—they might learn that they've been working for twelve hours before class started. I ask them, 'Would you go to a Spanish class after twelve hours of work?' And they're like, 'No.' So we start talking about what success means. Should you measure success by the number of students that show up?

"This generation has the energy and they have these great ideas," continues the instructor, "but they get much more frustrated than my students did in the past. To Millennial students, education is all about grades, goals, benchmarks, and tangible, measurable outcomes. Numbers of students means success. Remembering what you taught them last Thursday means success. Knowing ten colors rather than four colors equals success. So I ask them, 'How else can we think about determining success that is not tangible or visible to you? It could actually be something about you. Have *you* learned something? What did *you* learn today?' These are conversations we have to have, because they get very frustrated. Working in the community is frustrating; it's not as straightforward as studying for an exam and taking it."

"As student teachers, Millennial students have a lot of great qualities," the instructor says. "They can be very pragmatic, and very responsible and very respectful of their students. But their interactions have never carried much emotional weight. So when they do start feeling that emotional baggage as a teacher, they're caught off guard. Once they start caring, it no longer matters to them whether they're 'successful' or not. It's more what's happening on the inside. It's not just a social thing anymore; it's become personal."

"So would you say that, in the end, there are more gains for your students than for the migrants?" I ask. The Spanish teacher nods thoughtfully. "For the farm labor issue as a whole, teaching a little English doesn't do much," she agrees. "But for individual workers, the confidence they develop can be empowering. For the migrants, it's very important to be able to have biweekly contact with the white, English-speaking community when they're usually so isolated. It breaks down a lot of their personal insecurities, and that might allow them to be more willing to ask for something in a store, or approach someone on the street and ask for directions. The results are not huge. But for the individual, the experience can be very significant.

"But you're right," she continues. "It's the students who are really changed. Once they begin to connect with the workers—it's hard to describe. There's a giddiness about them, a charged atmosphere of excitement and potential. When we arrive at the camps, the children are always waiting for the van, cheering. And the men and women are standing there with their notebooks, ready to begin the class. And that's a very powerful image for a nineteen-year-old, to be expected and waited for. So overall, it's a very empowering experience. Teaching has become more than just an activity, or a task they have to do. It's like a sign of respect for somebody they care for. Their pride is no longer about getting a good grade. The pride is, 'I want them to learn. I want them to succeed because it will help them.' It's not just, 'I want to do a good job.' Earlier in the semester, there was all this focus on the lesson plan itself. It was almost as if the reason they needed the students was to teach the lesson plan! But later, you see a change. It's not about their own goals anymore; it's about their students. And I think that's the connection. The people have become part of them."

"That's really significant personal growth," I say, "and I think our students need that. But it seems like the experience is still so focused on *them*. Is this what we want to promote? Students who take courses like yours are so passionate about social change in the abstract, so distressed by the pictures they see on the news, so ready to jump in to action. Shouldn't we be teaching them how to be effective advocates for deeper social change?"

"I know what you're saying," the Spanish teacher says. "I do want them to advocate for migrant workers at the individual level, and at the local, or state, or national, or even international levels. But all that will come in due time. First they need to change themselves."

Notes

1. "[From 9/11] onward, having your child in constant connection became a parental virtue, and also something that children wanted." *PBS Frontline,* 2010 February 20.
2. Nauert, 2010, April 23.
3. University of Michigan, 2010, May 27. The author of the study suggests that students spend ten to fifteen minutes a day away from their personal technology in order to "try to remember what it's like to interact with people in the real world."
4. Cellular-News, 2009, April 7.
5. Wikipedia, n.d.
6. Lovetoknow, n.d.
7. Hafner, 2009, May 26.

8. *PBS Frontline*, February 20, 2010.
9. Ibid.
10. Ibid.
11. http://www.crlt.umich.edu/index.php.
12. For questions that can promote "transformative conversations" about teaching among faculty, see Palmer & Zajonc, 2010, 140.
13. Freire, 1989, 32.
14. http://www.gieu.umich.edu/

Chapter 5

Lighting the Fire

As instructors and progressive students have been telling us, social justice education for today's college students needs to begin with the development of their inner life. While social, emotional, and spiritual growth has always been part of the transition to adulthood, the Millennial Generation has new needs and new potential. Their unique place in history, their relationship with rapidly evolving technologies, the ways they have been educated and parented, and the effects of residential and economic segregation on their understanding of the people they want to help have shaped these students' abilities and willingness to connect with others from a deep place within themselves. They want to accomplish so much in a world that needs them so badly. But to begin to "change the world" more effectively, they need to develop their human qualities: slow their frenetic pace, learn to explore more reflective questions, and move from their anxious focus on right answers and instructor praise to a deeper understanding of what education might do for them as human beings. They need encouragement to connect more authentically with their peers, opportunities to get acquainted with people who have been made invisible to them, and the courage to look deeply into their unacknowledged assumptions and stereotypes that stand in the way of more egalitarian relationships. All this should be central to the college experience and available to every student, not just the ones who choose a social justice path.

But students cannot be forced to grow, or "to become more fully human," as Freire puts it. Personal and spiritual evolution cannot be made a graduation requirement. Students will come to maturity when they are ready, as long as their environment supports it. It seems to me that if more instructors would model the deep listening and caring we want our students to achieve, encourage their intellectual independence, and provide experiences that promote human connection, our students will find the space to grow. But what we can plan more deliberately, I think, are ways to draw students into a deeper awareness of injustice, its root causes, its present manifestations, and the need for reflective action.

Young people arrive in college with vastly different levels of knowledge about social justice and an array of attitudes about moving toward that goal. There are the uninformed or apparently uncaring students who might see themselves as good people and believe in equality in the abstract, but do not consider it worth their while to learn about the inequalities that so profoundly affect the lives of others. Then there are students who would care about injustice if they stopped to think for ten minutes, as Abby says, but are too preoccupied with academic achievement and their own personal problems to delve into issues that don't affect them directly. Other students are excited by a charity model of service that focuses on helping "worthy" individuals advance in life or adjust a bit better to a system that makes economic advancement exceedingly difficult, especially for the most excluded. The most committed and knowledgeable students are aware of global needs, and they are dedicated to working as partners with community organizations on specific projects: the engineering students who design sustainable technology to pump clean water to a village in Malawi; the linguistics majors who teach English in a Mayan community over their summer break; the students who create their own local nongovernmental organizations (NGOs) even before they have graduated. But even these students may not have asked why yet another neighborhood organization is necessary, or why traditional water sources have become so polluted, or why the Mayan people are losing their language and culture to an English-dominated world. How can progressive educators draw all these diverse groups of students into a heightened concern for social justice when they have such a variety of attitudes and feelings about the work we consider critical? How can we get them to the point where they are motivated, knowledgeable, and dedicated, with enough stamina and heart for the long haul?

The most difficult students for many of us to work with are the ones who seem to show no interest in the world around them. "What scares me most is young people who have been educated for indifference," a composition instructor tells me. "So many Millennial students who cross my path through writing classes or campus organizations are not only unaware of what's going on around them but they also seem content in their ignorance. 'We don't get cable at our house,' they tell me. 'We don't subscribe to any newspapers'; 'I just don't have time to watch the news.' Even when I show them it takes mere seconds to log on to free newspapers and progressive Internet sites, they can't be bothered.

"In my advanced writing class I will sometimes announce a 'news quiz' where students have to write about a national or international event they've heard about in the previous week," the instructor continues. "But many can't even identify a single story, especially once I rule out sports scores and celebrity gossip. This class includes senior education majors who are getting ready to start their student teaching in high schools and middle schools. So here's a new generation of teachers who will do nothing more than prepare students to pass standardized tests. What's going to happen when there is so much abject ignorance and indifference about the issues we are facing as global citizens? Who's going to be there to fight the violence and oppression and hate when so many people don't know that it's happening and don't care that they don't know?"

While intellectual conformity and apathy is hardly new—one could argue that schools have always kept students from becoming too intimately aware of people's struggles[1]—Millennial apathy can be particularly discouraging for progressive instructors, both because of students' "spoiled and bratty" attitudes and because of our sense of urgency for informed action. To reach the most indifferent students, I suggest an approach used by Myles Horton, radical educator and creator of the Highlander Center, who understood more clearly than most how to work lovingly and effectively with people who had been educated for indifference. Although Horton worked primarily with Appalachian people who had been silenced by stark poverty and the economic stranglehold of coal mine operators who controlled their conditions of work, he found he could apply his philosophy of education to all who came through the Center: community organizers, civil rights leaders, African American educators, idealistic college students, and ordinary people who had never completely believed in themselves.[2] Teachers of Millennial students who resist learning or caring about human struggles may be inspired by Horton's "two eye" method that he describes in his autobiography, *The Long Haul*:

> I like to think that I have two eyes that I don't have to use the same way. When I do educational work with a group of people, I try to see with one eye where those people are as they perceive themselves to be. I do this by looking at body language, by imagination, by talking to them, by visiting them, by learning what they enjoy and what troubles them. I try to find out where they are, and if I can get hold of that with one eye, that's where I start. You have to start with people where they are, because their growth is going to be from there, not from some abstraction or where you are or someone else is.
>
> Now my other eye is not such a problem, because I already have in mind a philosophy of where I'd like to see people moving. It's not a clear blueprint for the future but movement toward goals they don't conceive of at that time. I know they're capable of perceiving and moving toward those humane goals because I've seen other people like them starting where they are. [S]o I look at them with my other eye and say to myself, how do I start moving them from where they perceive themselves to be, to where I know they can be?[3]

Start with these students where they are, Horton tells us, even if that place is uninformed, self-involved, and resistant to anything but social acceptability, trivial gestures of charity, and personal advancement. Listen to them; show interest in their preoccupations, their joys and troubles. Don't give up on them. Keep reminding yourself that they're not yet all they can be. Lead them to consider issues that touch them the most deeply and personally, especially if they can be framed as controversial. This comes naturally in a writing class, where students need to learn how to construct an effective argument and will learn to do it better if they write on topics that move them. Let them write on questions that Freire would term "generative,"[4] issues that evoke the frustrations and preoccupations of their generation: the steep rise in college tuition,[5] the windfalls made by top executives while middle-class families lose their homes and livelihoods; the disappearance of the world's great beaches under rising sea levels; the effects of cyber-bullying; college students' addiction to texting; sexism and misogyny in video games.[6] Students with friends and relatives in the military can be drawn in by personal stories of deployment: a soldier's boredom and fear as he waits for action in a remote environment; his emotional distress at losing a friend in an unexpected attack; his suicidal thoughts, his longing for his children; his growing dismay and disgust with the war itself. [7]

Whenever students can identify with personal and ethical issues like these, they come alive. A psychologist who teaches a popular course called "Pills, Profits, Politics, and the Public Good" tells me that a particularly relevant issue for Millennial college students is the overprescription of drugs for corporate profit. "There's something about that course that shocks students, even the cynical and indifferent ones," the instructor says. "Among people their age, 30 to 40 percent are on some kind of medication. The overprescription of antidepressants is unbelievable to me. Half the students who visit counseling services end up on these drugs, although studies have demonstrated that, except in the case of severe depression, the new meds are no more effective than a placebo. Lots of my students are on these drugs, or their friends are, so there's a sense of reality and immediacy in this issue that's different from other moral problems like the Holocaust or even contemporary genocide, which is happening so far away. There's no escaping this!"

The psychologist has an ingenious take on how to move students from personal stories of what it's like to take these drugs to the interests of the drug companies that promote them. "Maybe it's a weird kind of luck that what the drug companies say about themselves is so much more revealing than what any outsider could say," the psychologist tells me. "So one of the ways I make it real for students is to show them some internal documents that I've persuaded someone in the industry to send me about how to get under the skin of the Millennial Generation and sell to them. If you're not used to reading this stuff it's a little chilling. You can see how the industry speaks in very stark terms about how to manipulate young people's insecurities and dependencies and stress in order to sell them a drug which promises to alleviate their suffering.

"One of my favorite readings is a kind of launch speech that a company spokesperson makes when a drug first comes on the market," he continues. "Every time there's a pharma litigation there's a leak of a number of court documents, so you can get hold of these texts. You have to imagine a thousand people assembled at Disney World being pumped up to get out there and sell. This particular example is from a company that was launching a hormone replacement product a few years ago for women going through menopause. They had turned menopause into a disease, and they claimed that the drug provided some benefits, which turned out to be quite the opposite. They had pushed the drug so hard that it was already being taken by lots of women. *Lots* of women. The company already had about 75 percent of the market share, but of course they wanted it all. The theme of the speech was 'No boundaries, no limits,' which the writer had turned into a call and response thing. 'No boundaries, no limits! Take it to a new level!' Every once in a while he would come back to it: 'No boundaries, no limits! Revolution! I want you to go out there—no boundaries, no limits! The power of a single fist!' It's dramatic, right? One can imagine a play based on some of these documents. The lights, the roaring crowd. It makes me think of Nuremberg, actually. Believe me, this kind of thing gets students' attention.

"As they read more about how the industry works I sometimes see students having what I call the 'octopus moment,' where they begin to see how this piece about some particular politicians fits with another piece about some aspect of history, and how all that fits with doctors and lawyers who have certain industry connections. And because I like to dig around in corporate communications, I've also found internal e-mails where some guy is literally writing to his pals: 'We buried studies X, Y, and Z and now we need to think about whether we're going to bury this one, and how we're going to spin it so that the good stuff shows up.'[8] There are other internal documents released after litigation that describe people in these companies celebrating that they 'created an illness.' Or the celebration might be about the enormous public preoccupation with potential risk—like all the worry about the H1N1 virus—which can mean billions of dollars in profits for whoever comes up with a preventative vaccine. So by seeing how all these pieces fit together, students develop a sense of how events in the industry are likely to work.[9] I'm not going to call this radicalizing for students, but I do think it's something prior to it, which is consciousness-changing. Even those students who come into the course with a certain distrust of the corporate world or, more specifically, of the pharmaceutical industry, even those students are thinking, 'Holy Cow! It's realer than I thought!'"

Students are attracted to this one-credit mini course for a number of reasons, not the least of which is that it can be added painlessly to a full schedule, or fill a gap in their general requirements for graduation. Students come into the course without any expectation that they will be looking at issues of social justice; they are not expected to take any action or adopt any particular point of view. They are only encouraged to listen carefully to the voices and arguments of the industry and the cultural norms and values in which the corporate world operates. Supplemented with speakers from the industry and the people who have been abused by it, as well as Supreme Court rulings against industry practices by its most conservative judges, the course can shake the world of apathetic students without pushing any particular agenda. Simply exposing students to information that is hidden from them is enough. "Whenever I can use information right from the horse's mouth, it's great," says the instructor.

Other students do not start out apathetic or uncaring; they might sign up for a social justice course if they heard about it, but after they've chosen a full schedule of other activities—marching band, a sorority or fraternity, glee club, peer tutoring, and the Lacrosse club, all in the same semester—they are too busy running from one thing to the next to deliberately look for a course that would take them into the community. Or, such students might become convinced—by parents, former teachers, or their peers—that the study of injustice is an unnecessary deviation from their route to a lucrative and prestigious profession. How do we light their fire?

"I think a huge part of drawing students into social justice work is the first-year experience," says Siobhan, a senior headed for law school. "There's a mob mentality in the freshman year, especially at a big school where there are so many things going on, so many opportunities and choices. So what do students end up doing? Well, they do the things that other people are doing. Why are there so many first-year students in Dance Marathon? Because it's really prominent on campus and they do a lot of hard recruiting, so new students get the impression that everybody's doing it. First-year students generally don't question whether the cause they support is a charity event or if it addresses any deeper issues. They don't even know the difference, most of them, in their first year. And they may never even hear about social justice courses, because they're not pushed that visibly on campus. There's no buzz around them. I don't want to say that social justice needs to be "marketed" to students, but for the average newbie who is so flooded with information about what clubs they can join and what classes to take, you have to make it obvious that social justice and peace and human rights are here on campus, that they are the coolest thing ever, and if they take these classes they're going to learn a ton about something they'll really come to care about.

"Right now, a lot of students never even come across these courses," Siobhan continues. "But if they do happen to luck into them, they really grow. My roommate is a good example of this. In high school she did a lot of work with kids with disabilities, and she felt really strongly about it. She did it because it's quote unquote 'good to do.' And it *is* good to do, it's awesome to do! But she somehow found a course in her first semester that taught her about institutionalized racism in the education system and how that affects kids with disabilities for the rest of their lives. And now, she's become interested in the issue in a completely different way. She's taking a lot of theory courses in sociology that are making her a much better advocate for these kids."

Siobhan also says that because first-year students often choose their courses on the basis of what their friends are taking, they "end up in really dehumanizing, giant lectures" and assume that's the best choice they could have made. She herself made the mistake of taking an introductory economics course in her junior year, though she dropped it rather quickly. "It was so hard for me to hear the professor telling all these first- and second-year students in this huge lecture hall how bad unions are, and how awesome free trade is," she sighs. "I do understand that professors have different opinions about what's good for the global economy, so I'm not against hearing a point of view I disagree with. But for all those young students, I feel it really shapes how they view the world ever after. Now if they were taking that econ class and, at the same time, they were in a community service-learning class, *that* might really stretch their thinking. I don't want to say that all large lectures are bad, because I've had some pretty awesome ones. But I think in the first year, experiential learning is so important—not only for the good of the world, but for the students, who can grow through learning more about the issues, working with their peers, and interacting with the community as well."

Indeed, community service learning or "real-world learning" has grown by leaps and bounds with the arrival of Millennial students on college campuses. Emerging as a trend in the mid-1980s, college-student volunteering rose sharply at the turn of the century, more than doubling the growth in the adult-volunteering rate.[10] Focused on tutoring and mentoring children and youth, homelessness and hunger, health care, the environment and senior services, students in Campus Compact's 1,190 member colleges and universities contributed 282 million hours of service to their communities in 2007–2008. Students in historically black colleges and universities and tribal colleges performed even more service—"well above the average amount of time per week."[11] According to the literature, students appear to reap many benefits from this work, including increased self-confidence, social responsibility, civic-mindedness, and personal efficacy, regardless of whether they volunteer as a purely extracurricular activity or as a component of a course that combines readings and classroom discussion with placements in schools and community organizations.[12] Their gains are higher when service is combined with activities that promote reflection on their experiences; in such courses students have been shown to gain significant "higher order" or critical thinking skills.[13] They also "experience new environments, learn to appreciate cultural differences, become more critically aware of social inequities and power relations, and envision a more democratic society."[14]

What all this service does for the intended beneficiaries is less clear. Certainly, there have been some gains: children have learned to read, teen drop-outs have been enticed back to school, and countless meals have been cheerfully dished out to hungry families. Volunteers have cleaned up streams, rescued pelicans and seagulls from floating sludge, repaired homes, planted gardens, and tenderly cared for hospital patients. These small gifts can mean the world to individuals and their communities. Yet, in my own community service–learning courses, I have seen more mixed results than these positive outcomes suggest. I have seen students who tutor impoverished children harden their hearts against parents who "don't care about their kids' education," despite extensive class discussion of all the reasons they might not be able to fill their homes with children's books or show up at parent-teacher conferences. Although I have seen some students awaken to their own race and class privilege as they notice inequality firsthand, others cannot seem to get over being called "white girl" by their junior high mentees. Students who ride the bus to their placement (which I require as part of the experience) might understand for the first time what it means to wait in the snow for erratic transportation. But others just see the requirement as a nuisance, or complain about the "racism" of the African American bus driver who scowled at them for not being quick enough with their change, yet allowed an elderly black woman to board the bus for free. While these uncharitable attitudes do not seem to affect students' willingness to work with young children (whom they see as innocent victims of their parents' irresponsibility) or even dampen their enthusiasm for providing services, companionship, and solace to adults, I wonder about the overall effect the conclusions they draw from these experiences have on their worldview and, as a result, on their readiness to support broader, political efforts at social change.

However, such concerns should not deter us from appreciating the positive effects the Millennial spirit has had on the nonprofit world as a whole. At an event that honored student interns' work with the incarcerated, a regional director of the national sponsoring agency told me how important some of my students had been to his ability to keep his program alive in hard economic times. "This generation saved us," the director said, clearly moved. "Their enthusiasm, their willingness to work, and their impressive numbers kept us afloat through the economic crisis when our fundraising efforts collapsed and we had no money for staff. We would have had to abandon so many of our programs if students had not filled the gaps."

I wondered how effective the students had been at working with prisoners whose lives were so vastly different from those of my privileged undergraduates. "It's true that today's students are a little naïve," the director admitted. "They need more of an understanding of the entrenched problems of the communities they serve, and more experience working in those communities before they can carry out all the dreams they are so passionate about. But that's what service-learning faculty are for, right?"

Right. But how far can service learning go to make students effective practitioners, allies, and advocates? The literature seems to agree that community service without a classroom component is distinctly inferior to what can be accomplished with instructor guidance. Classroom learning can involve background reading on the community's history and unique situation, explanations of institutionalized racism and classism, facts about urban development and inner-city politics, theories of community organizing, exercises that promote critical reflection, discussions of perplexing questions that arise in the field, and much more. All these approaches might help students move beyond explanations for poverty that center on the individual, and provide context that helps them understand the pain and devastation they see in our most impoverished communities. But so much depends on the goals of these courses, the political bent of the readings, the background of the instructor, and her ability to link students' experiences in the community with abstract ideas that students often find irrelevant to "the real world."

The spectrum of courses that are termed "service learning" can be quite varied in what they intend to accomplish. If we assumed, as some authors do, that all service learning is inherently oriented toward social justice,[15] we would miss important distinctions between curricular models.[16] Mitchell points out the differences between "traditional" and "critical" service learning. The "traditional" model emphasizes the service aspect, which focuses on ways to help people adapt to the system: teaching new immigrants to speak English more fluently; helping the unemployed gain access to food stamps; caring for children while their parents go for job training; or providing companionship to delinquent teens or elderly immigrants. While traditional service often stresses kindness and friendship between individuals and even across cultures, it does not specifically focus on making relationships between the helpers and the beneficiaries more egalitarian, or on changing the system that fosters advancement of the few at the expense of the majority. Classroom discussions in these "traditional" courses might touch on the nature of the social problems and some helpful ways to alleviate the pain they cause, but they do not delve too deeply into anything that might be construed as "political," that is, any suggestion that people have reason to be angry with the way the system treats them or that systems of inequality conspire to keep certain groups down.

Traditional service, if done with kindness, a good heart, and growing empathy through reflection and intimate connection, can provide students with an opportunity to grow personally and intellectually as they work with "the disadvantaged" in depressed communities. It instills them with a sense of community responsibility, and it can nurture a passion for leadership and a concern for what is often termed "the greater social good." But traditional service can also be condescending, and thus reinforce social inequality. Volunteers "provide" and the people "are helped" in their struggle for crumbs at the table, often with alarming racial overtones. In a church shelter in my own community, for example, volunteers set tables and serve breakfast to homeless families, but forbid them access to phones, make entry to the kitchen off limits while food is being prepared, and close up shop by 8:00 A.M., sending the families out into the Michigan winter to "look for work." Volunteers (inevitably white) congregate behind the kitchen counter, busying themselves with the simple tasks of food preparation while the residents (inevitably black) wait obediently at tables, or dress their babies (apologizing to the volunteers for their pretty new clothes), or try unsuccessfully to repair the sheet and blanket dividers that separate their makeshift "bedrooms." Volunteers are kind but distant; interactions with residents are mainly about protocol rather than anything meaningful or even superficially social. "False charity constrains the fearful and subdued, the 'rejects of life,' to extend their trembling hands," says Freire. "True generosity lies in striving so that these hands—whether of individuals or entire peoples—need to be extended less and less in supplication."[17] While such "service" may be necessary as long as extreme poverty is allowed to exist, traditional service learning can also reproduce and cement unequal relationships across race and class.

Most traditional service providers do not see their relationship with the poor as demeaning or insulting. Like the good people who staff the church shelter, they do not dwell on the inequality inherent in their charitable practices or notice the racial drama played out before them. In speaking about their work they might use terms like "the less fortunate" or "the needy" to describe the people they serve, suggesting that poverty is a matter of fate or bad luck, an inevitable part of the human condition. Freire called this worldview "magical consciousness," the belief that inequality is the misfortune of particular individuals, and that the poor should gratefully accept the authority—whether soft or harsh—of the "advantaged" or powerful elite. While Freire saw magical consciousness most clearly as internalized oppression in the poor themselves, his term could just as easily describe the good-hearted service provider (or policy maker or service-learning educator) who avoids overtly blaming the oppressed for their own condition yet ignores the ways that they are kept from realizing their true humanity. "As educators, we are artists and politicians, but never technicians," Freire reminds us. "Still, we must ask ourselves: to know in favor of what and therefore, against what to know; in whose favor to know, and against whom to know."[18]

The "critical" model of service learning, on the other hand, explicitly focuses on institutional structures that perpetuate inequality. In this model, "the goal, ultimately, is to deconstruct systems of power so the need for service and the inequalities that create and sustain them are dismantled."[19] Kindness and compassion, however deep and genuine,[20] are not enough. Relationships between volunteers and community members must be constructed as an equal partnership. "What we try to stress is the reciprocity of the relationship," the director of a service-learning office tells me, "whether it's between the university and the service agencies, or the student volunteers and the people they work with in communities, or the teacher and students in the classroom. The equal footing of power is what's important. It should be clear that everyone has something to contribute."

In the "critical" service-learning classroom, active learning, rather than "banking," is key. Readings and classroom discussions focus on the origins of inequality in its economic, social, or cultural guises. These frank discussions, which, as Siobhan says, "peel back layers" of the pretense that we live in a just society, may shock or depress students and dampen their feelings of efficacy, but in the long run, recognizing the extent of the injustice can motivate students to work on the issues in more meaningful ways. "I think more students need to question why their service is necessary in the first place," says Siobhan. "At Ronald McDonald House, why are we cooking dinner for people? At Food Gatherers, why do we need to pick up leftovers from restaurants to give to homeless shelters? And by the way, why does our wealthy society need homeless shelters at all? I think that if students knew more about the reasons for these things they wouldn't stop doing the work. They'd either get fired up about it or work really hard on the issue to make it come to an end."

As the critical model of service learning has gained more attention over the last decade, a consensus has developed in the literature that educators should help students move from charity to justice models of service. But "the irony of service"[21] is that most instructors find it difficult to provide opportunities for community involvement that actually challenge the structures of inequality. Readings and discussions can reveal the nature of institutionalized oppression, but the opportunities to address underlying problems with action are difficult to arrange, or even imagine. Our best students notice this and ask legitimate questions: "Why do you have us doing service which is at best only partially consistent with what you are teaching? Why do you teach change but have us help manage programs or do direct service?"[22] Students in a critical service-learning course might read about the racism that drives immigration politics, for example, but then volunteer in community programs that try to persuade undocumented teens to stay in school. They might discuss inequitable practices in the criminal justice system in class, but end up working with prisoners on creative writing projects. Their community service can be helpful and appreciated, and it deepens the students' understanding of the people they come to know, but it stops short of confronting oppressive structures and practices.

To add to the complexity of this dilemma, the assumption that "partnerships" with the community are truly egalitarian overlooks an obvious problem, that these relationships are most often made between academic institutions, programs, instructors, and/or students on the one hand, and service organizations staffed by professionals and community leaders on the other, an arrangement that ignores or at least sidelines the people themselves. "Critical" service-learning partnerships are created with school administrators and teachers rather than with parents and children; with homeless shelter staff rather than the homeless residents. This is not to say that educators and service providers do not have their clients' interests at heart, but the rhetoric of "equal partners" can obscure the reality: the oppressed are not "partners" at all.

On the occasions when partnership arrangements do include the people most directly concerned, students who try to advance a "critical" model may discover that the people are impatient with outsiders who want to "empower" them to demand fair treatment or dismantle the system. Often, impoverished people are just looking for ways to ease their burdens at work, master some skills, help their kids succeed in school, make the streets safer, and plant a few vegetables in a community garden. Seldom does anyone—students and "the people" alike—find the courage and will to radically transform themselves or their society: go off the grid, establish alternative institutions, break unjust laws, refuse to serve in the military, or shame their government into paying employees a living wage.[23] Perhaps the nature of the university, central as it is to systems that perpetuate class and race privilege, makes any form of service learning that would effectively dismantle structures of injustice and redistribute economic power and social capital an impossible endeavor. It might be that the best we can do is to educate students about the need for radical change and to show them that their egalitarian beliefs cannot be fully realized in a world where inequality is so firmly entrenched. Regardless, critical service learning continues to encourage students to think of themselves as change agents, to critique the status quo, challenge unjust structures and oppressive institutions, and reveal the systemic nature of inequality, injustice, and oppression that "lavishly reward the few at the expense of the many"[24] without trying to resolve the conflict between theory and practice.

Perhaps this compromise is realistic, given that Millennials tend to be team players who trust the core concepts of U.S. governance and the broader world system. Perhaps progressive educators, especially those of us who came of age in the 1960s and 1970s, should not assume that social change, for this generation, must directly oppose the system. The director of a community service learning–center on campus says that she has been struck by "the disconnect between the motivations of activists from the '60s," who were, in her words, "open to the conflict, open to the tension, expressive in their refusal to conform" and Millennials, who are much quieter and not motivated by agitation and change politics. Today's college students, she says, "are uneasy with the way politics is so polarized, and elected officials are at each other's throats. They would rather build community locally, one to one."

Be that as it may, I think that we need to pull our Millennial students in further toward a systemic analysis where they see that if they want significant change, they will need to oppose some very fundamental ways that the sociopolitical system functions, even if they don't decide to confront it directly. We need to make them more aware of the contradictions between the kinds of community work they are doing and the underlying, systemic problems they come to see through their analysis of injustice. But we should not assume that students will understand these issues quickly, within one course or in one semester. Nor should we expect that all our students will come to see the extent of the systemic problems, or accept the need to reconstruct or even simply reform our social and political institutions. Researchers have found that only "about one third of students involved in [service-learning] classes claim and appear to have undergone such a transformation."[25]

But perhaps we should not assume that students will learn to see the big picture through the "critical model" of service learning alone. Awareness of structural inequality may not need to come from explicit classroom discussion, or even from service learning per se. "Going abroad was really huge for me," says Siobhan, as she thought back over her most important college experiences. "I took a class where we went to Brazil to learn about environmental injustice, and along the way, we really had some interesting conversations, both with the people we met over there and among ourselves. One of the students on the trip was an economics major who had worked as a trader in the Chicago commodities market for a summer. I don't know why she had signed up for the class—maybe she just thought it would be fun to go to Brazil. Anyway, we were standing in this landfill, talking with a woman who makes her living gleaning through the trash, and she was telling us how the changing prices on the world market affect her life and the lives of her children.[26] And it was just a huge thing for my friend to hear that from this woman who was near tears, and to think about the job she had the summer before. We talked about this a lot, later, and I could see that she never realized that anything she did could have that kind of effect. Because when you're sitting in an office in Chicago it doesn't seem to matter what you're doing. The experience was just so shocking to her. And her reaction influenced all of us, I think. We had known, or at least some of us did, that the rich countries set the agenda for poor people all over the world, but the human connection made the reality of it so much more powerful."

A sociology instructor agrees that unexpected human connections can lead students to take action. In a course that takes students to the U.S.–Mexican border to study immigration issues, a powerful moment for students is meeting young people their own age who are preparing to cross the desert. "We ask the young migrants where they're trying to get to," the instructor says. "And they say things like, 'Oh, I have a brother in New York who has a job for me if I can make it.' Or they might even be trying to get to Michigan. And when we come back to campus, we focus on the situation of the Mexicans—of all ages—but predominantly young, who we met and who were getting ready to attempt to cross the border. We ask, 'Where do they end up in America? What kind of jobs do they get? What are their conditions in those jobs?'

"I had been giving my students a whole lot of background reading so they would understand what they saw when they got to Mexico," the instructor continues, "and my plan was that when we came back we would continue to read about Mexican labor and union issues. But what happened was that students started to say, 'Well, no! We want to know more about what we heard from those guys a few days ago. Let's read about that!' So then, I realized that yes, the remainder of the course should be about Mexicans in the United States.

"The most exciting thing is what has happened with the end-of-term projects," the instructor continues. "My students wanted to put their learning into concrete action, and do things that future students could plug into, not just something that would have to be created every semester from scratch. So a few years ago, a group of them founded a student organization called MIRA: Migrant and Immigrant Rights Awareness,[27] which continues to function today. Right now, they're working on immigration reform, and particularly the Dream Act, that would allow people who came to the U.S. as young children to attend public universities even though they're technically illegal immigrants.

"Then MIRA also got involved in putting together conferences that asked how do you improve the conditions of work for this migrant population, especially those who are undocumented? And one of the most important innovations that came out of these conferences was the idea of workers' centers. And out of that came the decision to start a workers' center here, in Washtenaw County. So out of that came Washtenaw Workers Center, which was created out of what we learned at the conferences, which in turn had been created by MIRA, which in turn was a student project. And all this came about because students made human connections with the people most directly concerned."

The sociology instructor allows that this approach isn't perfect, since he is convinced that structural inequality can only be effectively addressed by collective action. "Getting involved in movements that do organizing work is difficult for students, but it also is the most valuable. Because, really, social change comes from effective organizing. But we have very few courses about that and very few community opportunities to learn how to do it. When you think about it, what role can students realistically take when they have only a few hours a week to give? They can't be community organizers—that's a sixty- to eighty-hour-a-week job. They can't even apprentice; they don't have time for the amount of training they would need. They can be part of an organizing entity, but definitely not organizers. They can see what it's like, they can get a sense of contributing to it and supporting it in important ways, but not as organizers themselves."

I ask the instructor what he thinks we need to do to get around this problem. "Well, in the absence of internship possibilities in established organizing entities," he says, "we need to be creating pathways for students to become entrepreneurial and create their own organizations that do organizing work in areas and niches where they see the need. That means they would need certain skills, like how to run an effective meeting, and how to have one-on-one organizing conversations. But it's also about vision. It's about seeing what is possible once you move away from what you as an individual could do to what a collectivity could do. And that means students need to know how to identify common goals and common obstacles to those goals and a strategy for circumventing or overcoming such obstacles. And at the same time students are developing those skills, they need to be learning how to think in terms of collective action. It doesn't come naturally to us, at least not in this culture. We're used to thinking about individual solutions to what are often very big, social-structural problems. And this just doesn't work. So I think that getting out of the mind-set of, 'Well, individual effort is the best we can do. It's regrettable, it's certainly not adequate, but it's all we know how to do,' that is really a key thing."

Despite these obstacles, some students, on their own, are engaging in significant organizing work in campus and neighborhood organizations, learning effective skills from their more experienced peers. Building on the success of the United Farm Workers "critical decade of growth" from 1966 to 1976, tens of thousands of student volunteers and staffers of the Obama campaign went door to door to recruit significant numbers of new voters, which enabled his election.[28] United Students Against Sweatshops (USAS),[29] with chapters at more than 250 colleges and universities in the United States and Canada, pressures universities to sign on to a Designated Suppliers Program, which requires factories producing university apparel to pay a living wage and allow their employees to form unions. Students in USAS chapters work on a wide variety of issues from repression of worker rights at Wal-Mart and Nike factories, to the spiraling costs of college tuition, to the future of the union movement.[30] Students have organized to raise the wages of the lowest-paid workers on campus and have lent their support to Graduate Students' and Lecturers' Unions in their struggle for fair pay and sensible working conditions. Many of these progressive student organizations and campus chapters are created without faculty participation or support. Sometimes we only discover these efforts when our students come during office hours to ask us to sign on as their requisite faculty sponsor, or when they drop by just to share what excites them. It gives me confidence and strength to know that we don't have to do it all, that sometimes, our students are way ahead of us in discovering ways to work for significant social change.

Lighting the fire for justice, I have realized, is a messy process. It's disorganized. There are no mechanical or technical gimmicks, no straightforward, easily replicable methods, no neat lesson plans. Progressive faculty who are nudging Millennial students toward awareness and action do not work in concert, nor do they put students through a carefully crafted program that increases their knowledge, skills, and attitudes in measured steps, consciously providing support at one level while scaffolding the student up to the next challenge. Some of us are working on our students' personal growth, helping them connect with themselves and each other in meaningful ways. Others are breaking down barriers of class and race, making the invisible people come alive. Still other instructors are focused on language skills: building students' technical ability and confidence to converse, read, write, and study in another culture. Some are leading trips abroad or preparing students to work with progressive organizations in their own neighborhoods. Any of these faculty might be focusing on the big picture, the structures and institutions that hold back progress of oppressed groups. Some concentrate on the interpersonal; others, the historical. Some facilitate learning through intense reflection on community practice and what it means to be an ally.

Should our work be more organized, more coordinated, more carefully planned? Perhaps. But there's something appealing to me in the picture of faculty and program heads each doing what they do best despite the fact that their work may not assume the same idea of social change. Most of our students will be moved to care. Many will recognize that their country is not quite as free or as democratic or compassionate as it pretends to be. All of the students we touch will have had at least one college experience that questions and builds on their progressive ideals, their vision of how the world is supposed to be. We can take it further, and dream bigger. But for now, as long as we keep thinking, keep improving what we do, keep moving toward Freire's principled vision of praxis: "reflection and action upon the world in order to transform it,"[31] I think we will be doing okay.

Notes

1. See Zinn (2003); Loewen (2007); Illich (2000).
2. A compelling example of how rural Appalachian women grew from learned helplessness to confident environmental activists at the Highlander Center can be viewed in this dated, but surprisingly relevant, video, *You Got to Move* (Phenix, 1985).
3. Horton & Freire, 1990, 131–32.
4. Freire, 1981, 49–51.
5. Lewin, 2008, December 3.
6. *Guardian U.K.*, 2011, April 6.
7. For some compelling video testimony from three U.S. soldiers speaking out against the wars in Afghanistan and Iraq, see *Democracy Now* (2010), June 24.
8. For an example of a deliberate cover-up see Harris (2010, July 9).
9. Some of this instructor's favorite Internet sites that uncover connections between money, politics, corporations, and the media are Center for Media and Democracy, http://www.prwatch.org/, which reports on spin by corporations, government agencies, and the media; Open Secrets, http://www.opensecrets.org/, on the influence of money in U.S. elections and public policy; Source Watch, http://www.sourcewatch.org/index.php?title=SourceWatch:Purpose, which

"profiles the activities of front groups, PR spinners, industry-friendly experts, industry-funded organizations, and think tanks trying to manipulate public opinion on behalf of corporations or government"; and Pharmalot, http://www.pharmalot.com/, where "a certain number of industry people, under cover of anonymity, provide their perspective, as do whistleblowers, FDA people, and others."

10. National and Community Service, 2006, October 16.
11. http://www.compact.org/
12. Einfeld & Collins, 2008.
13. Fiddler & Marienau, 2008.
14. Hayes & Cuban, 1997.
15. Mitchell, 2008.
16. See especially Mitchell (2008).
17. Freire, 1986, 29.
18. Torres, 1998, 99.
19. Mitchell, 50.
20. See Morton (1995) for his interesting argument that both charity and social justice models can embody expressions of service that either have or lack depth and integrity, that is, "consistency between its ideals and its practice." Charity, in the original, religious meaning of the term, "begins with the radical act of recognizing the worth of every person," which an ostensibly more radical social justice approach might sideline. In the same way, direct service can be seen as redistribution, restitution, or giving back to the poor what was unjustly taken from them. A "social justice" approach, on the other hand, is based on anger at the way things are, which can lead to burnout, and ignore people's humanity.
21. Ibid.
22. Ibid., 29.
23. For an example of a community program that does directly challenge the status quo, see Detroit's James and Grace Lee Boggs Center, http://www.boggscenter.org/.
24. Marullo, 1999.
25. Strain, 2006, 2.
26. See Kaufman (2010, July) for an exposé of how bankers created an artificial shortage of wheat in the commodities market, driving up prices for bread and other basic foodstuffs, and adding 250 million people worldwide to the ranks of the food insecure. Also see an interview with Kaufman on *Democracy Now,* July 16, 2010.
27. http://sitemaker.umich.edu/mira/about_us.
28. Shaw, 2008, November 11.
29. United Students Against Sweatshops, n.d.
30. United Students Against Sweatshops, 2010, June 7.
31. Freire, 1986, 36.

Chapter 6

Radical Equality

Progressive faculty who teach courses on race and racism face a particular challenge with this generation. On the surface, Millennial students' "colorblind" attitudes seem promising. "Students today have a different attitude toward race than they did when I was in college," an African American psychologist remarks. "Watching TV with my kids over the years, I've been struck by the way some programs have tried to normalize relations between the races. Even though Millennial students don't live in very diverse communities, the idea of diversity is there, in their consciousness: 'Well, this can be the norm. It's not a big deal.' And that's the way a lot of young people look at it now: Race is not a big deal. For good and for bad, you know what I mean? In some ways, it's a good thing. In other ways, it's probably sweeping under the rug problems that we all know still exist. But these TV shows seem to have opened white students up to the idea that blacks can be in the world with other people, that they don't have to fear them, and that in some ways, they're just like everyone else: they want to date, they want to get married, they want to have children, they want to live in a house, the house should be nice. I grew up in a largely segregated African American community. My race mattered and was always in my consciousness as an important part of my identity. Even now, race is salient to me. But many young people in this generation have grown up very differently. It's not that race is totally negated, because students of color do encounter racism and discrimination. But the fraternizing across racial boundaries is more fluid now."

A white psychologist agrees. "I wouldn't go so far as to say we live in a post-racial era. But there's less race consciousness, less sensitivity. Millennial students have grown up in an age when they can take diversity for granted in ways that we just didn't in my generation. It used to be that if there was a black person in the room we'd trip all over ourselves trying to make it not make any difference. I don't sense that discomfort now in the same way. Of course students have issues. Race is part of our consciousness quite deeply in this country. You can't escape it. But regardless of that, the students in my classes, at least, are much more comfortable being together in a multi-racial environment."

Studies of the Millennial experience support these instructors' observations, at least up to a point. Without question the United States is becoming more multiracial. Twenty percent of all Millennials are children of immigrants, and the majority of these immigrants are people of color. By 1990, fully half of the new immigrants were coming from Latin America, a quarter from Asia, and only 15 percent from Europe,[1] reversing the "nearly white" or "white on arrival"[2] immigration of generations past. This surge in immigration has made this generation the most ethnically diverse in our country's history.[3]

But Millennial students, so diverse in the aggregate, seem to have less opportunity to get to know each other across racial lines than many of their parents did. Growing income inequality over the last twenty years has isolated whites and wealthy immigrants from both historically underrepresented U.S. groups and poorer immigrants and refugees, leading to a "resegregation" of the nation's public schools. When some liberal school districts tried voluntarily to reintegrate their classrooms, the Supreme Court declared their methods unconstitutional. "Under the new decision," says a report by the UCLA-based Civil Rights Project, "local and state educators have far less freedom to foster integration than they have had for the last four decades."[4]

It's true that suburban schools do sometimes achieve a rainbow effect by the inclusion of upper-middle and upper-class second generation Millennials like Sanjeet, whose parents came from India as graduate students, as well as other students of color whose families have done well professionally. And it's true that these students seem more comfortable with each other than did those of past generations. White students no longer shift uncomfortably in their seats when a black student walks into a classroom. College and high school students pal around in ethnically mixed groups more than they did in years past. Cross-racial roommate assignments have increased the likelihood that white college students will make friends across the racial divide,[5] while greater diversity of the campus community has promoted more interracial friendships among students of color.[6] Interracial dating and marriage are more common than they were a decade ago and are seen increasingly as normal. According to a Pew Center research study, "almost all Millennials accept interracial dating and marriage,"[7] at least in theory,[8] in marked contrast to their elders.

But the apparent camaraderie between the races evaporates quickly when "race breaks out"[9] in the classroom. White students sit in shocked silence when someone mentions how painful it is to hear naïve remarks that insult or patronize people of color, or if a student asks why there are no perspectives of blacks or browns in the syllabus. A white student is called out by her peers after she makes a particularly ignorant remark, and she leaves the room in tears. A student who speaks knowledgably about everyday racism against blacks, Asians, and Latinos suddenly blurts out an ugly stereotype of Arab Americans. Everyone shuts down when the instructor blanches at the mention of a racially charged subject. On Internet blogs, where anonymity encourages blunt reactions, comments on sites that appeal to Millennials can be unabashedly racist. And in a study that allowed college students to respond to researchers' questions "as if they were writing on a friend's Facebook or Myspace page," students with a "color blind racial ideology"[10] were more likely to express racist views when shown graphic photos from "racial theme parties" (such as a "gangsta party" celebrating Martin Luther King Day) than did students who acknowledge the salience of race.[11] Under the illusion of getting along just fine lies a chasm of ignorance, fear, anger, and misunderstanding.[12]

What accounts for these contradictions in Millennial college students' attitudes toward race? Abby's experience in an unusually progressive private high school may shed some light on this paradox. Abby's high school, she tells me, is well known for its strong social justice curriculum and its devotion to multiculturalism. Unlike many other schools in suburban Michigan, a diverse student body is a "huge priority" and is achieved in part by offering generous financial aid to help with the $21,000 yearly price tag. "We celebrated diversity as an idea," Abby says, "so we could all exist together in this small school where everyone got along and we just didn't talk about race."

I raise an eyebrow. "*That's* a good way to get along!"

Abby laughs a little in embarrassment. "My family and a lot of my teachers were *so, so* politically correct that we wouldn't even mention someone's race," she admits. "Like if you're trying to describe a black person, you'd sort of say, 'brown eyes . . . um, you know,'" she laughs a little at the absurdity of it. "I always sort of felt like I was instructed to know that racism exists, yet do everything in my power to make it seem like I wasn't a part of it at all."

An astute observation, I thought. I ask her if she sees herself as part of it now.

"Well, I can kind of see that I was part of it even then. You know, I grew up in a mostly white suburb, and we'd go to Detroit to—I mean, we'd almost *never* go," Abby laughs nervously. "And if we did, it was like a *big deal*." Abby stage whispers "big deal" like whites in my parents' generation did when they talked about black people in public. "And being in the city was made to feel like a scary experience! Like, 'Don't look at those people!' 'Make sure you lock the car!' And that made me unsettled. It seemed strange that the way we acted was so different from how we talked about things."

"Looking back at it, do those warnings seem kind of racist to you?" I ask.

"Well, yes and no," says Abby, hesitantly. "I think it's more like a class thing."

"A class thing? I don't understand."

"Like, 'Don't look at those poor people.'"

I must have looked unconvinced. "Abby, if you were never allowed to talk about race and you were never really encouraged to explore what racism is . . ."

Abby interrupts me with another observation: "I think what shocked me the most about coming to college was that, here, people sit like in *racial boundaries*. I was so surprised by that and it's changed my beliefs about what should and should not be talked about. I mean, before coming here I just thought we could politely operate in an accepting community because that's what we were taught and that's how we acted in my high school. But now . . ." Abby trails off, unsure of herself again.

"What's different in the way you're thinking about race now?"

"Racism still exists, and I don't think I really knew that before I came here," Abby laughs. Like Sanjeet, who said he had never really known of the existence of poor people in this country until the day he took the bus to Ypsilanti—despite the fact that he knew quite well that inner-city blacks were poor—Abby hasn't thought through her racial attitudes clearly enough to notice she is contradicting herself. And like Sanjeet, Abby is a top-notch thinker who will graduate with one of the highest grade point averages a student can achieve at Michigan.

While Abby's experience in a determinedly "colorblind" elite high school may be unusual, her confusion is classic for high-achieving Millennial students. Few white college students, even those who are the most energized and determined to "change the world," are aware of the extent of personal and institutional racism in this country. Nor have they engaged in sustained, challenging conversations about race. Even if they have studied some of the histories of people of color, have a passing acquaintance with the concept of white privilege, and are proud of their friendships with students of different ethnicities, they fall silent in the classroom when they are expected to discuss the significance of race.

Abby relates her experience in the small art history seminar Expressive Cultures of the Black Atlantic.

"In a lot of ways, that class was a great experience," says Abby. "We did a lot of theoretical, anthropological reading. The material was fascinating. But the room was *so quiet,* I couldn't believe it. It was unreal."

"Why do you think nobody would talk?"

"Because it was about race?" Abby laughs, as if stating the obvious. "And the class was three hours long. It was *painful* to sit there with no one saying anything."

"Do mostly white kids take that class?" I ask.

"Yeah. Well, it was a small class. Fourteen students. Two blacks."

"The instructor was African American?" I don't know why I thought so. Maybe it could help account for the silence. White students so often admit they don't want to offend anyone by saying something that could be construed as insensitive, certainly not to the person who is evaluating them.

"No, the professor was white," Abby replies. "But he really wanted us to talk about our own relationship with the topic—with race, I mean. So the first assignment we got was to write a three-page essay called 'My Black Friend.' We didn't get any other instructions for it. And everyone *freaked out.* So I thought to myself, 'What could this really mean? 'Cause I bet I'm not supposed to find one of my three black friends and write an essay about them.' So I wrote this story about my futon that's black? It was like making fun of things that white people say about black people, pretending that the futon was a person. I guess the professor must have liked my approach, because after that, during the break, he used to come up to me and say, 'Abby, why isn't anyone saying anything? What's going on? What can I do?'"

"Was he really that clueless?" I ask.

"I think he knew why the class was so quiet," Abby says. "But he didn't know what to do about it. It was too bad, because all the reading was so good and interesting. But no one wanted to have to mention race."[13]

Like so many elite Millennials that I've taught, Abby is dissatisfied with the silence around race, yet uncomfortable and self-conscious about delving into it too deeply. Abby, you may remember, is the one who dragged her friend to hear the rapper M1 denounce global imperialism, and who was so gratified when her friend broke down in tears afterward because it showed her that people could care. Despite the fact that M1 is a former Black Panther whose message, Abby tells me, is about "people of color resisting imperialism in all its forms," what attracted her to his talk was not his views on the racial world order but his opposition to capitalism. While she knows that M1 and his group Dead Prez are carrying on the legacy of the Black Panthers—"he was wearing a Free Huey t-shirt,"[14] Abby laughs—in her way of thinking, Pan-Africanism and resistance to white police brutality are not really the issue. In high school, she had learned the importance of speaking out against abuses of human rights. So when M1 asserts that the United States is playing the role of global bully, charging into impoverished countries that can't defend themselves, and forcing them to accept economic agreements that benefit U.S. multinationals, Abby applauds.[15]

Ignoring race is one way to make it seem like "no big deal." But the pretense of colorblindness requires a fair amount of evasion and subterfuge to pull off. Silence does not effectively mask the tension, embarrassment, or resistance that most white Millennial students feel when race is mentioned, or when the nature of the readings requires a response that shows some degree of sophistication about racial dynamics. But their silence isn't necessarily a sign of moral indifference. In fact, the opposite may be true. "Silence suggests shame," says social critic Arundhati Roy," and shame suggests conscience."[16] Millennial students may know very well that something is wrong, even within the ranks of their own upbeat generation, and that they are somehow implicated.

It is this vague sense of shame, I believe, this uneasy relationship with race that drives so many Millennial students—even those who are most excited by social justice work—to focus their energy on human rights abuses in the Global South rather than in their own country. And they *are* energized! "The persistence of world poverty has a special meaning for this generation," says Ananya Roy, director of the Blum Center for Developing Economies at Berkeley. The students who crowd into her class on the challenges of development in the new Millennium have an "intimate relationship with global poverty." It is "their issue; it define[s] their place in the world."[17] Indeed, Millennial students' intense interest in "making poverty history" is shared by their parents' generation as well. "The turn of the century has been marked by the emergence of a remarkable global conscience," says Roy. "The stark fact that of a world population of 6.7 billion people, 1.4 billion live under the unimaginable conditions of earning less than $1.25 a day is now common sense.[18] . . . In short, a new global order, what I call 'millennial development' is taking shape."[19]

All this interest in making life more livable for "the bottom billion"[20] is a wonderful thing. But over the seventeen years I have taught my own course on grassroots development in the Global South, I have been struck by the growing numbers of elite students who have studied, interned, or volunteered in "third world" countries and the delight they take in their travels, compared to the aversion so many of them feel at the prospect of spending time (or even passing through) impoverished communities of color at home. I don't think they make this distinction consciously. Media images of beautiful people in remote places have awakened their sense of adventure, and stories of starvation and disaster in the world's "failed states" have evoked their pity and indignation. They have not heard the blatantly racist admonition, "Don't *look at* those people," in reference to the inhabitants of the shantytowns of Thailand, or Morocco, or Brazil, or even South Africa. While parents do admonish their children to be cautious when they travel abroad, they also encourage them to follow their dreams to other continents. "Go ahead," they say, "I trust you. Go forth, conquer, experiment, explore! Find your way! Find your path!"

And so, these young, confident Millennials do go forth, not only to look at people in the world's most impoverished countries but also to photograph, videotape, interview, research, and reside among them. They blog to the world about their new friends; they raise money for them, stay in their homes, share meals with them, learn their cultural ways, exchange gifts with them, and come home stimulated to learn more about them and to help them better their condition. They do not, for the most part, see "those people" as thugs, con artists, carjackers, addicts, or lazy good-for-nothings who don't care about their children's education. Instead, they are more likely to experience oppressed people in the Global South as fun, interesting, warm, hospitable, wise, artistic, happy despite their poverty (a common observation), unjustly afflicted, and full of potential. Both caricatures are false, of course. Oppression wreaks havoc everywhere, yet people have always resisted and adapted to their condition in remarkable ways. But Millennial travelers rarely meet the fun, interesting, warm, hospitable, gracious, wise, artistic, impoverished people of color in their own country, at least not those living in neighborhoods they have learned to avoid.

I remember a student, a leading-edge Millennial, who had traveled to the highlands of Bolivia to learn the ways of the people who send their children to beg on the highway to supplement the few potatoes they coax from the rocky soil in that remote, wretched environment. My student had gone out to beg with the children every day of his two-week stay, scrambling down an embankment with them at the approach of a car, extending his hands in supplication alongside theirs. Over the course of his visit he had taken some remarkable photographs of the families he stayed with that revealed their luminous spirit as well as the tragedy of their dehumanization. At the opening of his exhibition on campus, surrounded by friends and family, my student was quiet and withdrawn, trying—and failing—to enjoy the lavish celebration of his talent. Watching him, I could see that he had been shaken to the core by his experience and would not easily readjust to the life of wealth and opportunity that was unfolding before him. I was concerned about his state of mind, yet, like Abby, I was also buoyed by his sadness, as it reminded me that people can care—no, not just that we can care—that we can be touched so deeply by the humanity that binds us as one people. Yet how many elite students have had such a marvelous, terrifying revelation in their own country? It is true that people here are not so poor that they are reduced to eating leftovers flung from car windows. Yet if one looks closely, one can see the same abyss of deprivation in the eyes of North Americans: the Vietnam veteran who has spent every day and night of the last thirty years in a filthy sleeping bag on the streets of our nation's capital, the child sent with a rotting milk carton to procure a bit of soup from a mobile food pantry, a rail-thin man on a bicycle—a man with a *briefcase* on a bicycle, trembling as he notices the food truck and stops for his first meal of the day. Where are their photographs? Where is the sadness? The outrage? [21]

In a strange way, this contradiction between the compassion that many elite Millennial students feel for the most impoverished people in the Global South and their fearful avoidance of their counterparts in their own country has to do with their confusion and denial of their race and class privilege. It's not that elite Millennials are averse to people of color per se—this is clear from their enthusiasm for the people they befriend abroad. And it's not that they are disdainful of poor people for the same reason. But if they focus on problems in the Global South, Millennials can live out their egalitarian beliefs, their urge to help, and even their uneasy conviction that color doesn't matter without ever being confronted by the word "race." International development discourse does not, for the most part, use terms like "whites" or "blacks and browns," or point out disparities using racial data, or mention, as do so many people in the "developing" world, that it is "the whites" who manipulate their lives.[22] Changing the world is framed as championing programs for basic education and the prevention of communicable disease; it means securing small-business loans for entrepreneurial women, providing access to technology; it means clean water, sturdy shelter, and food security. Even when one looks into the deeper causes of underdevelopment, the conversation is about institutions and international agreements: fair trade, debt relief, equal rights for women. Democracy. Peace. The rule of law.

All of these goals are laudable, of course. But they do not require our elite students to think about the racialized systems that created such vast inequalities and how these systems still operate today. Raceless discourse about human rights and development is a far cry from M1's "people of color throughout the world opposing imperialism in all its forms"—a refrain that, for obvious reasons, does not make its way into mainstream, that is, economically powerful—conversations about global improvement. And so, Millennial students who make world poverty "their issue" do not need to ask why it is the blacks and browns (not to mention "yellows" and "reds") of the world who must be organized, demilitarized, democratized, treated, trained, fed, educated, and exhorted to excel, and why it is the whites, in overwhelming numbers, who intern among them, research them, measure and count them, test them, videotape them, and make grand plans for their improvement.[23] When the indignity of the racial divide is ignored, Millennial students—as well as their parents and grandparents—can save the world guilt free.

Why should race matter, we might ask? If elite Millennials are doing good work without having to dwell on their race and class privilege, why should they have to confront it? If we can be friends across the world, global citizens all, why not just leave the bogus idea of race behind? Racial categories were an eighteenth-century idea anyway, a relic of the fledgling scientific establishment that justified exploitation; a fiction of slave traders and colonizers, missionaries and corrupt royalty, like King Leopold II of Belgium, who in the guise of bringing civilization to the Congo, worked millions of black Africans to death in forced labor gangs in order to amass a personal fortune in rubber and ivory.[24] Those days are gone . . . aren't they?

Even if we put aside for a moment the disturbing modern parallels to Leopold's exploits: the fabulous wealth extracted from the diamond mines of Zimbabwe by black workers in ragged undershirts; the grueling, punishing sweatshops of Bangladesh; the echoes of scientific racism in educational testing and welfare policy in our own country,[25] even if we ignore all that, race and race privilege remain entwined with this generation's ideas about how to uplift the so-called developing world. In my classes, the word "dependency" inevitably surfaces in students' initial conversations with each other about what "good development" might look like: The poor must avoid being dependent on the benevolence of the rich countries that fund their development, students say. We must create projects and institutions that are "sustainable"—that is, self-generating, self-funding—so that the wealthy countries, the lending institutions, and caring individuals are not constantly funding projects for the poorest of the poor. I sometimes point out that dependency isn't necessarily a bad thing: as adult students many of them are still dependent on the benevolence of their parents and will continue to be until they find their foothold in the world. This comment usually elicits a perplexed, "Huh? That isn't what we . . ." and then an embarrassed, amused "Ohhh, okay," as they suddenly see that "dependency" might be understood as an ordinary human need for help and indulgence that people like themselves enjoy. Even further, the idea that the rich countries might owe the poor something for the theft of their resources and human capital doesn't immediately occur to these students, or, if it does, it is quickly dismissed as an unfortunate chapter in the distant past. To this generation, social justice is not about dredging up old wrongs; it's about what's happening now, what's practical, what's workable, what they can contribute to, and what doesn't need to remind them of the old master-slave, civilized-savage, parent-child, teacher-student, human-provisionally human relationships between whites and people of color that still echo today.

Of course, the Millennial approach to development might seem quite positive: "Wipe the slate clean!" "Start anew with a better attitude!" But ignoring oppression built up over centuries of exploitation and racial distain does not help Millennials understand the resistance they will inevitably encounter. When the Global South doesn't respond as it should to the generosity, good ideas, superior institutions, and organizational excellence of the fortunate people in the fortunate countries who want to help, Millennials become confused and disheartened. A third-year student writes from India where she is interning with a local NGO that provides microloans to impoverished women: "I feel more and more discouraged each day, less optimistic about the people's will to change or look at things from a different perspective," writes Sarah. "I also can't help but think that all the NGOs in the world could come to India and work, but until there is a way to make people demand accountability from their government, the same problems will be perpetuated and the inequality will grow."

"Make people demand accountability." The gentle arrogance of this generation of world shapers, their idea that they know (or should know) what is good for oppressed people around the world is at its core, an elitist, even racist idea. Of course this attitude is not unique to Millennials. My own Boomer generation, myself included, carried this same kindly, arrogant, colorblind, ahistorical attitude into our service both at home and abroad. Fortunately, there has been much more criticism of this position from scholars and practitioners since the 1960s, and some of that critique has filtered into the consciousness of the Millennial generation. At least they're *thinking* about partnerships, about "Who am I to teach these people?" about which development alternatives might appeal to different communities, and about why their own country should live up to its human rights rhetoric.[26] Yet their plans and projects belie these stirrings of radical equality.

An international program director affirms my notion about this generation with his own observations of students who take it upon themselves to design projects for communities in the Global South. "Millennial students have much more interest in being engaged in the world than students in the past," he says, "but their activism also has an element of 'on my terms.' Sometimes they'll come to us with a proposal—well, it's not even a proposal. They don't *propose*—they *tell* us: 'Hey, we've got this student group and we're going to do such and such project in Country X.' So then it's my job to say, and I say it all the time," the program director laughs, "'Wait, we don't just give you money to do things!' And if they listen to our advice: if they go out and do some serious research about the issues: find a faculty member to head their project, line up their resources, figure out a way to evaluate what they've done, stuff like that, they can be really interesting and fun to work with. But the students who just go ahead and do these projects on their own haven't thought any of those things through. They'll dream up a project in education or health in the belief that these services have never been provided or even considered in the country in question. Plenty of countries are like—'Project? The Ministry of Education or the Ministry of Health has to approve it!' The students haven't even considered that, actually, health care is supplied by experienced providers who are authorized by a government agency. And teachers have to be licensed, you know? But these students haven't considered that, and actually, they find it more or less irrelevant. The ones who insist on carrying out projects on their own tend to be well-resourced kids who have accumulated a good deal of social capital in their own communities. They have leadership experience from high school that sort of jumps out at you. And they've got an idea to help end poverty that they believe is—*just amazing!*"

"So do you feel they're over-confident, or naïve, or . . ."

"Well, it's a dual naivety," the program director replies. "There's a naivety about certain procedures that need to be followed. You need a visa, for example. You need to coordinate your plans with the officials in that country. And have you thought of consulting the people about your great idea to improve their lives? There's also a naivety about the value of their ideas. Students are thinking, 'This will be a great experience and I'll be so helpful,' and I'm saying, 'Well, what exactly will you be doing? You want to build a school? Have you ever built a school before? How are you going to do this?'"

I'm laughing at the director's characterization of so many of my students in recent years, but I recognize the frustration in his voice. I've heard the same critique from program officers in Senegal, Togo, Côte d'Ivoire, the Solomon Islands, India, almost everywhere I've spent time in the Global South, and it embarrasses me. "Who are these young kids?" they wonder. "What qualifications do they have? A degree in *what*? And they want to do—*what?*" Well, these reactions are seldom expressed so directly with quite that tone of outrage, yet the sentiment is often right there, beneath the polite veneer.

"So we have to kind of walk these students through their proposal," continues the U-M program director. "'Okay, so you don't know how to build anything. Well, what *can* you do?' And then if they stick with you, you help them make a plan. But if they go off on their own they can get stopped in their tracks pretty quickly. They might get the idea that they can raise money to give to the community for a project—send a child to school, donate a bunch of medical equipment, that sort of thing. And then they'll get all disillusioned because they raise all this money and then they don't even know what happened to it. So there's a lot of wasted effort. They did their project in good faith but they never realized there has to be follow-through, accountability, and sustainability built in. That takes planning and experience, connections, and knowledge which they in their youthful enthusiasm don't yet have."

More important even than proper planning, I think, is a previous step, that is, asking themselves why they think they have a solution to complex problems they have never had to think about before, much less live with intimately. Nor have they asked for the people's ideas and the people's indulgence to work together. Paulo Freire remarks that one of the questions he has to ask himself again and again is, "In company with whom do I translate my vision into reality? . . . If I work *on* and not *with* the people, I contradict my revolutionary words about the creation of a just society."[27] Privileged people who want to help, yet feel guilty about their advantages, tend to deal with their own guilty feelings by treating the oppressed as children, says Freire. Yet "rationalizing [their] guilt through paternalistic treatment of the oppressed, all the while holding them fast in a position of dependence, will not do. Solidarity requires that one enter into the situation of those with whom one is solidary."[28]

Committed Millennial students are certainly open to learning how to enter into solidarity with the people. But it's hard for them to slow down. The ninety-six-year-old Detroit activist Grace Lee Boggs tells of the young people who attended the fiftieth reunion of the Student Nonviolent Coordinating Committee (SNCC) that she and so many others had joined during the civil rights movement. "Some were the children of SNCC veterans," she writes, "but most were a new generation of activists who, having been energized by the 'Yes We Can' Obama campaign, wanted to learn from SNCC veterans what it takes to build a movement." They were looking for history, yes, but also for courage. "'Don't just regale us with stories,' the young people insisted. 'Tell us what it was like to risk death!'" The SNCC veterans were happy to share their memories with this new generation. But their message was not about the moments of high drama; it was about listening to ordinary people. When they were young, they had come to the movement with their own ideas, "their own stuff," but what they discovered was that the people knew their own situation best. When you truly listen, they counseled, you'll be as amazed as we were at how much you have to learn from the grassroots.[29] The young activists who came to the event were mainly students of color and a few radical whites, and their focus was on community development in their own country. But their reaction to their elders' advice was similar to that of Millennials who want to solve problems of poverty overseas: "Yes, all that sounds reasonable and right. But I want to do something amazing *right now!*"

Listening to the people takes time. And helping oppressed people achieve their hopes and dreams can be confusing. What do you do when people say they don't want change, despite their dire circumstances? Or that "it is written"—or that God has willed—that they should live in destitution? Or what if they are only willing to work on small improvements that help them adapt to their oppression? Freire would describe these reactions as "fear of freedom" or "magical consciousness." This is what Sarah was up against in her short summer internship in India. She believed that the impoverished women needed to demand accountability from their government, but she despaired of them ever taking the initiative to do so. The politics were complicated, she told me, as were the religious tensions in the community. She had only a few words of the local language, and no background in Indian history or culture other than the few books I recommended that she take along to read on the plane. After several weeks of frustration, Sarah retreated to a Buddhist monastery, where the harmony and structure of daily life helped her deal with the stress of getting nowhere.

And what if the people are in a state of "naïve consciousness" about the local and global systems that ensnare them? Even Freire found this stage challenging. "Almost always, during the initial stage of the struggle, the oppressed, instead of striving for liberation, tend themselves to become oppressors, or 'sub-oppressors.' . . . Their ideal is to be men; but for them, to be men is to be oppressors. This is their model of humanity."[30] People in a state of "naïve consciousness" do not yet see themselves as oppressed persons or as members of an oppressed class. Their idea of development is to become bosses, or overseers, or landowners, tyrants, even, over their former friends and neighbors. They fear freedom, Freire says, yet they are the ones who need to lead the struggle for liberation. What is the role of the eager Millennial in this case—probably the most common situation that good-hearted students will encounter? What if they are asked to help prepare teenagers to pass national exams that have been explicitly constructed to weed out the vast majority of their impoverished peers? What if they are called upon to help traditional birth attendants upgrade their skills so they might find work in a hospital that excludes the poor, or to train teachers to give lessons on safe sex to people with HIV who have no access to antiretroviral therapy at a price they can afford? Will our Millennial students even recognize the irony of these "internship opportunities"? And if they do, how will they decide what to do with that knowledge?

Freire addressed the people's fatalism and fear of change with "education for critical consciousness,"[31] a participatory style of learning that builds on what people know and persuades even the most oppressed and impoverished people that they are skilled "makers of culture" who are worthy of human dignity. But this approach has obvious pitfalls when the would-be facilitator is a young U.S. Millennial, whose ignorance of the language and culture and whose racial, class, and "passport privilege"[32] separate her from the people she wants so much to help.

Youth are by nature naïve; that is why they need teachers. But what worries me is that this Millennial Generation is not only naïve. They are *passionate.* They feel competent. They are incredibly hard workers. They're super-organized. They've succeeded at everything they've done in the past. And they believe that if they get right to work with their good ideas and good heart, poverty will be history. But development is never that simple.

What kind of guidance do these Millennials need in order to be of real service internationally? They need to hear people from unfamiliar cultures talk about what makes life worth living, and how those values might challenge common assumptions about economic and social development. They need to hear people express themselves in culturally unfamiliar ways, and to understand their apathy and resistance in terms of power dynamics and historical context. They need to learn about the activists and organizations and social movements in the Global South that are already "doing development" in ways they might learn from before they offer their handy inventions and ideas for improvement. They need to learn to put aside their intense, youthful desire to be themselves in cultures that may not recognize their choices as respectful or proper. They need far less encouragement to parachute into another culture for a few weeks or months, far fewer opportunities to carry out their own research studies on captive populations in the Global South. They need a more detailed understanding of the global economic and political order, its racial origins and implications, and their place in it.

But even before all that, they need to confront the ways that race and racism operate in their own country. They need facts. They need progressive history. They need to see how race privilege operates in their intimate environment: their school, their social scene, their media, the world of their professional prospects. They need courage to confront the widespread denial about racism, and to speak frankly and from the heart about the social and economic disparities that are staring them in the face. As Freire says, "the people have the right to know better what they already know."[33] Millennial students already know much about race-based inequality. What they need is to know it better: to understand it from the point of view of those who are most painfully affected, and to confront it without illusions. Once they do that, they will be able to see more clearly what Freire means by "solidarity": working with people to support—rather than orchestrate—their struggles for liberation.

Notes

1. Howe & Strauss, 2000, 83.
2. Despite the racially charged atmosphere in the early twentieth century that did not fully accept Southern and Eastern European immigrants as "white," these and other European immigrant groups were accorded "white" legal status (Brodkin, 1998; Guglielmo, 2003) and generous social welfare assistance compared to blacks and Mexicans (C. Fox, forthcoming).
3. Howe & Strauss, 85.
4. Orfield & Lee, 2007.
5. Stearns, Buchmann, & Bonneau, 2009.
6. Fischer, 2008; *ScienceDaily*, 2008, September 2.
7. Pew Research Center, 2010b, February, http://pewresearch.org/pubs/1480/millennials-accept-iinterracial-dating-marriage-friends-different-race-generations.
8. "Accepting" interracial relationships does not necessarily mean engaging in them: "The Pew Research Center's recent report on racial attitudes in the U.S. finds that an overwhelming majority of Millennials, regardless of race, say they would be fine with a family member's marriage to someone of a different racial or ethnic group" (Pew Research Center, 2010b, February).
9. Fox, 2009. The title of my book, *When Race Breaks Out*, comes from a quote from the African American social critic Michael Eric Dyson: "Like a camel on the loose, [race] has the capacity to do greater injury when we attempt to coop it up as opposed to when we let it run free. A classroom is an artificial cage for the animal of race, and race breaks out everywhere" (quoted in Dobrin, 1997, 170–71).

10. A "color blind racial attitude," common among white liberals, is the idea that noticing a person's race is inherently wrong.
11. University of Illinois, 2010, April 21.
12. Other studies have confirmed that college students' negative racial attitudes lie just beneath the surface of their apparent comfort and tolerance of diversity. See, for example, York University (2009, January 9); Kansas State University (2010, January 13); Tufts University (2009, December 18).
13. See Fox (2009) for a discussion of racial dynamics in the classroom and how instructors can promote deeper, more informed discussions of race.
14. Huey Newton was arrested for the murder of a white police officer in 1967, and was thrust into the role of revolutionary hero to publicize the Black Panther Party's determination to end police brutality, http://xroads.virginia.edu/~UG01/barillari/pantherchap2.html.
15. Thetalkingdrum, n.d.
16. Roy (2009) made that remark during a speech in Istanbul on the first anniversary of the assassination of the Armenian journalist Hrant Dink, in reference to the silence in Turkey about the Armenian genocide (pp. 143–44).
17. Roy, 2010, preface, x.
18. Ibid., 6.
19. Ibid., 7.
20. Collier, 2007.
21. Not since Walker Evans photographed Alabama tenant families for James Agee's "Let Us Now Praise Famous Men," http://xroads.virginia.edu/~ug97/fsa/gallery.html; and Dorothea Lange chronicled the faces of dustbowl migrants for the Farm Security Administration, http://www.historyplace.com/unitedstates/lange/index.html, have we seen such dignified portraits of the U.S. poor. Through these photos, the face of white poverty during the Great Depression touched the white middle class deeply. Blacks, of course, had been living this way for generations.
22. For a notable exception, see Easterly, 2006.
23. See, for example, Winant, 2001.
24. Hochschild, 1999.
25. See Dennis (1995) for the history of scientific racism and its modern equivalents.
26. Mokhtari (2009) points out that even critiques by the U.S. political left that exhort the United States to practice what it preaches to other countries are rooted in the notion of self-congratulatory American essentialism, the notion that Americans are "natural" human rights leaders.
27. Freire, 1989, 55.
28. Freire, 1986, 34.
29. Boggs, 2010, May 9–15.
30. Freire, 1986, 29–30.
31. Freire, 1981.

32. Passport privilege, like race privilege, refers to the metaphorical backpack of unearned advantages, both formal and informal, enjoyed by people from powerful countries. While its power is not absolute, passport privilege does confer special status and can call upon economic, social, and diplomatic resources when the traveler is in danger. For example, international accompaniers are able to protect human rights workers in Colombia by their presence, their country of origin, and their skin color as they travel through contested areas. Likewise, U.S. "prisoners of conscience" who have been jailed for crossing the line onto the military base at the School of the Americas generally serve short sentences, and then are recognized as "heroes" or even "saints" for their activism on behalf of victimized people of color in Latin America. See Koopman (2008) for an explanation of how playing the role of "good helper" in such situations "can fall into colonial patterns, even as it works against empire."

33. Freire & Macedo, 1987, 83.

Chapter 7

Millennial Leadership

"I get a little frustrated in class sometimes," Carrie tells me—a bit hesitantly, since it's my grassroots development course we're talking about. "Sometimes it's just not *real* enough to have all these classroom discussions. There's so much information, so much context to consider, so many different opinions among students; it's all so rapid fire. There's no time to just look each other in the eye and develop real relationships. That's the most important thing, whether you're sitting in a classroom, or working as an organizer, or travelling in impoverished communities abroad: to know that authentic relationships between human beings are not only important, but that they're *possible*."

Carrie had been particularly taken with the idea of authentic relationships when she read *Pedagogy of the Oppressed*, which, she says, has become a kind of life manual for her. "The biggest thing I got out of reading Freire is that we're all incomplete," she tells me. "And that means 'the oppressor' needs to be in the kind of dialogue with 'the oppressed' where they both come out 'more fully human.'" She puts in the quotation marks with her fingers, laughing a little, as if she isn't entirely comfortable with Freire's language. One of Carrie's most memorable attempts at getting into an authentic relationship was at a conference of Latina domestic workers in California where she went almost on a whim. She had learned the basics of organizing by volunteering at a workers' center near the university, and had become fascinated with the idea that immigrants who do informal, unregulated household labor could be organized and empowered through interaction with college students like herself. So when the California conference came along, and with it the opportunity to use her fledgling Spanish, she hopped on a plane and arrived at the organizing conference, ready to offer her support.

"I kept telling the domestic workers I was there to help them," Carrie reflected. "And I was forgetting everything Freire says about where that impulse should come from. The women accosted me so many times for that! They were like, 'How dare you? Why would you think we need your help? Get over yourself!'"

"And how did you feel about that?" I ask her.

"Like, oh shit!" Carrie says, laughing. "I thought that just by going to that conference, showing my interest, using my privilege to help empower the workers was what Freirian dialogue was all about! But of course that's not at all what Freire had in mind. My attempts at conversation were so patronizing. It was—just all wrong! And then I started thinking, 'What am I doing here?' And when I couldn't come up with a good answer to that, I thought maybe I should just sit back and listen to what the women are saying. And while I was taking it all in, I started thinking, 'Wow, this is the first time I've been the only white person in the room.' I just reflected on that for a while. So then I tried to backtrack, and during the break, I went up to the women who'd yelled at me, and I tried to apologize: 'Thank you for challenging me—um, not to belittle you by thanking you for that.' I was trying so hard not to step on toes! Of course, they were still dubious. But I just kept on talking, saying the first thing that came into my mind: 'I know this is wrong. I don't need to keep making these mistakes. Just tell me what I need to say instead.'"

"So did they help you out?"

"They did! I think they could see that I got why they were so annoyed. Here I am this white girl from a little, all-white town in

Michigan. I'm not a domestic worker. I'm not Latina. Why would I show up at their conference when I knew so little about how I might actually be useful? But they ended up helping *me* out, and I made some great relationships in the process. That's so important, I think, so critical to the kind of social justice leadership I'm trying to figure out. I mean, as much as these barriers are real, and as much as race and class privilege need to be acknowledged, I think we can end up paying so much attention to our differences that we no longer see the other person as just another human being. That's what I'm always scared of. I'm scared I'll forget that we are all just people."

Carrie has good reason to dwell on these relationships. Growing up on a cozy apple farm in rural Michigan, she and her favorite doll, Allison, each in their matching red aprons, would help her grandma sell fresh cider and sugar doughnuts to passersby, or roam the orchard with the "pickers"—seasonal workers from Haiti and Jamaica who lived in dilapidated shacks out behind the barn. Carrie had become special friends with Slim and George, the loyal workers her parents often referred to as "part of the family." The time she spent with these men defined her childhood, Carrie tells me. They were her protectors, her role models, and along with Allison, her best friends. They would stand with her at the school bus stop, keeping her safe from traffic in the early morning dusk. They would join the family for Thanksgiving dinner and breakfast on Christmas morning. And when George surprised her by showing up at her ten-year-old birthday party with a small gift, Carrie threw her arms around him and burst into tears. "It was an affirmation of our friendship," Carrie says. "Or so it seemed at the time."

One day just before she left for college, Carrie was sitting on the porch with her dad, reading the paper, when she came upon a piece about the Coalition of Immokalee Workers in Florida, who were organizing a strike against tomato growers for better wages and working conditions. "I was reading this news article and then I was like, 'Wait! Dad! There's something wrong here!'" Carrie laughs, thinking back to her sudden revelation. "'This article I'm reading right now about the Immokalee workers, this is what *we're* doing! We live in a seven bedroom house, but the pickers' quarters are horrible—the roofs are leaking, the floors are sinking in, there's broken glass everywhere. We're white and everyone that works for us is black! Dad—this is problematic! What's going on?'"

Carrie's dad took her accusations calmly and with a touch of good humor, for his daughter's liberalism had always been a gentle joke. "I was the token 'you should recycle that,' and 'let's not refer to people in that way' person at my high school," she told me. "So my family sort of expected me to take that role at home." Carrie's dad explained that he could not really see himself as the "exploiter" and the workers as the "exploited," since those terms did not acknowledge the complexity of human relationships, especially when your workers are "part of the family." The housing he provided was the best in the state, according to the local newspaper. And without the migrant workers, he reminded her, the farm wouldn't have survived as long as it had.

Carrie had written about all this in her first college paper for my seminar on human rights. And even before that, when she was on the farm drafting her admissions essays, she had begun reflecting on what those relationships meant, despite her father's attempts to smooth things over. "I know now," she wrote, "even though admitting it tears open my heart, these men were not 'playmates, protectors, role-models, and family,' but workers, probably illegal workers. I would like to believe that the jobs our family gave them were better than any other they might find, but I think that our orchard serves as an example of the capitalist system that exploits human beings in order to make a profit."

Every semester Carrie comes back to this essay and "finds new layers in it." She writes endlessly in her journal, reflecting on the child she was when those relationships were fresh, and the young adult she is now. She remembers how as a teenager, after the farm had failed and the migrants had found work elsewhere, she ran into one of her old "best friends" at the bank. "It was such a strange interaction," she tells me a bit wistfully. "I was so excited to see him. But he just sort of looked away as if he didn't recognize me. And I was just like—'Ohhh.'"

"What were you thinking at that moment?" I ask.

"That maybe we weren't quite the friends I had always thought. That there was a lot of hierarchy in the situation that I wasn't aware of, and that we both had internalized certain expectations about how we had to act with each other—he the Jamaican picker, me the boss's little girl. I don't know. It was not good. It made me very sad."

"Sad how?"

"Just sad that we were unable to interact comfortably, normally, as human beings. I see it now as very much the result of a situation in which we came to know each other, which was racialized and . . ." Carrie's voice fades into indecisiveness and embarrassment. She is not sure what to think now. There had seemed to be no distance between her and her childhood friends and now that she understood the relationship more fully a barrier had become visible. Had she constructed it herself by dwelling too much on the imbalance of power? Had there actually been an "authentic relationship" between friends, despite the exploitation? Or had she been lulled into believing that her father was a "good master" as in the days of old?

Carrie's willingness to reflect so intensely has been fruitful for her. At least she is asking the right questions. But endlessly interrogating one's relationships across class and race can be debilitating, especially when it is laced with shame and guilt. Carrie tells me about the summer she spent in Argentina, where the poverty so shocked her she felt "paralyzed by difference." She had been trying to help out at an orphanage—unsuccessfully, she confesses, since "teaching children is really difficult, especially in Spanish"—so instead, she would spend long afternoons in a nearby barrio, getting to know an indigenous family who let her hang out with them, help with the laundry, eat and talk, "stuff I would do with my friends at home." Carrie had been so appalled by the family's condition—the dirt floors, the crowded spaces, the racism and exclusion they suffered—that at first, she could not even greet them with a smile and a few words of small talk. Perhaps, in her awkward silence, she heard echoes of her family's relationship with their loyal pickers; perhaps she was just disoriented by culture shock. But the old questions kept nagging her: How was she going to build the authentic relationships she so desired? How could people who were so different come to appreciate each other across the barrier of privilege, "the huge, huge privilege" that she now understood that she brought to the relationship?

How could she reconcile such vast inequalities with her strong need, an almost spiritual need, I thought, to see the core of the human being through the barriers that keep us apart?

"I think recognizing one's own part in an oppressive social system is a necessary stage," says Dana, a senior whose sense of her own race and class privilege had been impressed on her by her family for as long as she can remember. "But guilty reflection can take you only so far. I've seen people like my parents doing social justice work for decades out of guilt. And when I look at my white, middle-class peers, I see a lot of struggle reconciling personal privilege and suffering, and this creates a very unhealthy situation. It can be hard to even validate your own existence, given that you embody the oppressor. The problem is there's no positive model out there for antiracist, anti-oppressive activism—for whites at least. So there's a tendency to shrink into the background and be kind of invisible while you're doing social justice work in poor communities. You can't allow yourself to be proud of your contribution—in fact, it can even feel kind of shameful. Anti-oppressive, antiracist leadership requires self-creation, not self-annihilation."

Dana's insight is profound, I think, and speaks to Carrie's dilemma: How can we develop authentic human relationships within the oppressive social systems in which we are all entwined? How can elite Millennial students create a new leadership style that fully acknowledges the oppression of the social system, yet offers their skills with pride and confidence? Dana doesn't think faculty can help much in this endeavor. "I don't mean to sound pessimistic," she says, "but I think that what the university at its most progressive does best is to provide the theories and the classroom-based discussion and maybe some opportunities to get involved in the real world. I don't think there's any way for students to develop a visceral awareness of oppression and privilege, and out of that, create a positive, anti-oppressive identity except by following their own process. It's something that students need to work out for themselves."

So should we just let our best, most reflective students find their own way as they become the leaders of their generation? Critical self-creation, as Dana terms it, is such a central aspect of a progressive personal development, it seems unlikely that young people will find their way on their own. So many things are still confusing to Carrie. Her loyalty to her family, her strong bonds to her decent, hardworking parents and grandparents, her need for authentic connection, her difficulty—despite her devotion to Freire—in saying the words "oppressor" and "oppressed" without scare quotes and a little laugh, all suggest that she has a lot to work through as she tries "to figure out what social justice leadership is all about."

But as I talked to students like Carrie and Dana, I began to realize they are already constructing a model of progressive Millennial leadership without the benefit of faculty supervision. Within the university, yet existing alongside it like a parallel universe, is an entirely separate system of education, one without exams or grades or carefully managed opportunities for intellectual growth. In this universe, nearly all the faculty-directed experiences that the university provides—the classes, the research assistantships, the work-study jobs, the study abroad programs, the service opportunities, the counseling and career planning—all these fade into the background. Within their social justice organizations and in their dorm rooms and co-op kitchens, our most progressive Millennials are teaching each other how to be social justice leaders, learning from their more experienced peers, and opening up space for newcomers to join in. And they are learning with a level of excitement and energy that would astonish most faculty.

Carrie ventured into social justice leadership when, as a requirement of my first-year seminar to join a human rights organization, she got herself appointed to the Michigan Student Assembly's Peace and Social Justice Commission. There, she became acquainted with "older activists"—third- and fourth-year students—who saw her as a willing worker who was eager to learn how to get things done. As Carrie was ending her term on the Commission, a new student initiative, Stop the Hike, was organizing a campaign to convince the University Regents to freeze Michigan's tuition, which in 2008 had topped $11,000 for in-state and $33,000 for out-of-state undergraduates. One of the organizers suggested that Carrie come along.

As she plunged into the organizing work, Carrie found no carefully constructed syllabi, no lectures or required reading to orient her to the issues or lay out the skills she would need to learn. "In fact, I had no idea what I was doing," she says. "I was the only freshman working with a whole bunch of second-semester juniors and seniors who were incredibly knowledgeable and effective." The ground work for Stop the Hike had been laid by an experienced student activist who was alarmed about the proposed tuition increase and who happened to know an engineering student with the same concerns. The two of them, the activist and the engineer, had become very excited about a cause that could involve all students, not just the social justice types, but economics students and science and math majors who typically had their own, separate organizations, or kept to themselves and concentrated on their schoolwork. Their strategy had started with coalition building among student organizations. They began contacting students who had influence on campus: the president of the Interfraternity Council, students from the business and engineering schools, people from all the student assemblies across the huge campus, and a lot of leaders from student of color organizations.

"That campaign was *such* a big deal!" Carrie recalls. "There was so much energy that whole year. We used to meet on Wednesday nights—late. We'd start around ten, and we'd be there until midnight or one. And at first I would just look at all those people and ask myself, 'What is it about them that I admire so much? How can I get myself to be like them?' Just being in the room with them, I could feel the dedication, the passion, the hard work, the energy, the people skills! You felt that the administration would *have* to take us seriously, and that felt incredible. Especially because the things we were studying in our classes seemed so far away. This was really hands-on!

"I think I really value energy," Carrie continues. "When people are 'somewhere to be there,' you know? And when you hear the passion in their voices. I would get so excited when someone would say, 'Okay, we need to e-mail this key person,' and then someone else would take out their computer and e-mail them, right on the spot. Or a bunch of people would stay for half an hour after a meeting just to follow up on the things they said they would do. It was the dedication, the commitment that got me. Because sometimes in work like this, it's hard to keep that hope and that belief so solid all the time. These issues are complicated, and you sometimes question, 'What am I really doing?' But when everyone is so passionate and so effective in putting an action together, you don't have those doubts. What we were doing, it wasn't just academic. It wasn't just lip service. It was something we really, really believed in.

"Coming back to the dorm I'd be all fired up, and I'd talk with my roommate about it for hours," Carrie continues. "To work with the president of the Greek system was such a big deal, because fraternities and sororities are generally so disconnected from the progressive peace and justice network. They have their own charitable events, but they don't generally consider themselves politically progressive or even political at all. But this was a cause that could unite all students. And we weren't just doing it because we didn't want to pay more tuition. It wasn't a self-serving thing; it was an issue of social justice."

In their strategy sessions, the students discussed the arguments they could use to convince the administration that holding down tuition costs could be cost-effective as well as ethical. Hard data were critical to their argument. "We decided to research the percentage of students who were dropping out because they couldn't pay," Carrie says. "So we conducted a thousand surveys, did the analysis, and used the results to have conversations with key people in the administration. Then we did an in-depth study of the university budget, and someone found a group of math majors who agreed to analyze it and help the rest of the coalition understand it. We set up meetings with the University Regents—some of them one-on-one—where we explained our reasoning to anyone who was the least bit sympathetic. Then we'd go to the Regents' meetings and we'd take every single slot at public comments time and explain our position formally, with the news media present and a protest outside that we'd organized beforehand."

"So what was the outcome of all this?" I ask.

"Well, the administration raised tuition by 6 percent—which was a lot," says Carrie matter-of-factly. Remarkably, she is not demoralized by their failure. "The longer-lasting outcome was that a lot of relationships were built between groups that had never interacted before, as well as between the university administration and specific students. We saw it as an example of what could be accomplished by building student power across campus. "

"So the process is everything."

"That's right! Of course, the goals are important too, but for me, in my freshman year, that campaign was a moment when the students said, 'We matter. And the administration is going to listen to us, no matter what!'"

"And you felt they listened?"

"I think they listened to the students more during those two months than I've seen them listen since. And that was a really, really big thing."

So during her freshman year, besides carrying a full course load and working to support her financial aid package, Carrie had put herself through an intensive, extracurricular tutorial in the basics of organizing: how to communicate with strangers and fire them up about a cause; how to conduct research and make a convincing case to potential supporters; how to speak at a packed assembly of powerful people who might judge or patronize young students; how to contact the media, put out a press release, and organize a group action that could make a significant impact. For a sheltered first-year student who was just beginning to understand the dynamics of power and privilege, the work was both exciting and intimidating. Carrie would sit in organizing meetings packed with confident, knowledgeable student leaders from all across campus and try to get up her nerve to speak. Even forming her own opinions could be difficult because of the gender dynamics at play; the "big men on campus"—alpha males from fraternities and student government—dominated the conversation with their confident, booming voices, their habit of interrupting each other, their high energy laughter. Watching the more experienced female activists not only hold their own in these meetings but also come up with some of the best ideas, Carrie began to force herself to speak up "after gathering so much courage and trying really hard not to cry" from all that effort and emotion. And when the whole room listened to her respectfully, she says, she learned a lot about herself and what she might be able to accomplish. All through the process, Carrie was making the lasting human relationships she so valued with people she never thought would notice her, much less work with her on an equal basis.

Of course, Carrie's parallel education did little to prepare her for her visit to the domestic workers' organizing conference in California, where she never did have a chance to use the leadership skills she had developed during her first year. Like many progressive white students, Carrie needed more knowledge about why class and race do not just fade into insignificance when people unite around an issue of social justice. In fact, learning to organize around a tuition increase that affected so many students regardless of their race, ethnicity, educational interests, or even class, may have reinforced her tendency to ignore or minimize these differences. But for other students, peer-to-peer learning that focuses their attention intently on a progressive cause can expose and complicate identity issues as well.

Students might start their informal education with a version of the "bull sessions" that previous generations of activists might recall from their own student days. Gathering late at night in someone's dorm room or co-op kitchen, progressive Millennial students are talking about political change, labor organizing, global inequalities, environmental activism, food security, immigration, race, and class. Of course, some of these sessions, then and now, are more political posturing than serious inquiry. But the topics get to the heart of the issues students find most intriguing, and the conversations, unlike most of their experience in classes, can take on the toughest questions.

Such conversations might start out simply, with two students chatting as they study. Maybe one of them has taken a course that touched on the subject of race privilege. She interrupts her roommate to share an exchange that happened in class, a disturbing video clip that has been circulating on the Internet, or an insight she had come up with while writing a paper. As the friends discuss these ideas together, they may be drawn into an extended conversation that continues for the rest of the semester. Lauren, a second-year student, who, like Carrie, was drawn into activism through her friendships with older students, tells me how she started learning about oppressive relationships with a friend who was training to be a facilitator in a class on social identities.

"We spent a lot of time talking about my friend's experiences with other students in her class," Lauren recalls. "And for me, that was really enlightening. It's the first time I've really been challenged to step back and realize there are certain things about you that affect other people, whether you're conscious of it or not." She took these new insights to Guatemala where she and another friend traveled over spring break. Lauren wouldn't have noticed this before, but now she was conscious of how she was treated differently "as an American—or maybe as a white person," she says. "Even doing local things, like riding the rickety buses that most people take, I felt we were given more attention by the bus drivers, or maybe treated with more courtesy and respect. At first I thought, 'Well, that's just a cultural thing, they are hospitable people.' I was enjoying it, actually. But then I started wondering . . ."

"How are you thinking about that now?" I ask.

"I don't know. I don't think I've thought enough about it yet," Lauren answers thoughtfully. "It probably has something to do with the tremendous influence for good or bad of the United States on Latin America and how entrenched we are in the fate of other nations, in their economic or political policy. Somehow those power relationships must filter down to the local level. I don't know how. But I definitely want to understand it. Trying to think these things through is a really uncomfortable process for me. But I'm glad it's happening. It's certainly been a major influence on my personal growth this year."

As students reflect on these kinds of experiences and explore ideas together, some are gaining hands-on leadership skills by joining a student group or club focused on social justice issues. This might just happen by chance, or at the invitation of a friend, or, less frequently, through a class or internship. Like Carrie, students generally just watch and listen at first, then find the courage to contribute as they begin to understand the issues and develop the ability to act on them. Their willingness to volunteer for mundane tasks and put in long hours gets the attention of the more senior student activists, who take them on as protégés. These relationships, and the new tasks and challenges that grow out of them, change them profoundly.

"Before I came to college I really didn't have a social consciousness," Lauren tells me frankly. "I went to a private high school with a homogenous population that was superfocused on academics and not at all on social justice issues. Nobody would have started a chapter of Amnesty International at *my* school! The administration would never have supported that move. It was just academics, academics, academics. So when I came to college, I never thought anything politically progressive was going to happen to me. I started out as a creative writing major because I had always loved stories and literature. I thought I'd want to study abroad for a while, maybe in Latin America, just to get out. But then I got involved with SOLE and it just took off from there."

In her first semester, as a requirement of my class to join any organization on campus with a concern for human rights, Lauren had joined Students Organizing for Labor and Economic Equality (SOLE), a campus group that was trying to convince the university administration to sign on to the Designated Supplier Program, a nationwide effort to have university apparel made by factories that pay living wages, offer worker protections, and allow collective association. Lauren chose that group "because of all the organizations on campus, SOLE had the reputation of being the rabble rousers." The most radical thing that SOLE had actually done was to organize a brief sit-in in the president's office to underscore the need for students to be heard. But in an era where most students are team players who, at best, are content with "tweaking the system"—like holding tuition costs to $33,000 a year—a peaceful campus sit-in can seem truly risky. Lauren was tired of her quiet life and "wanted to join a group that was actually doing something, not just talking about it."

"In SOLE, we had some very dynamic seniors who were willing to work with first-year students," says Lauren. "They were really into teaching us skills related to organizing, strategizing, and action, as well as educating us on global labor issues that were totally new to us. I really like the structure of the organization. We don't have a hierarchy. It's very open. You can bring your own projects to it, and we do things by consensus, so there's a strong community feeling."

As Lauren developed more of a sense of race and class inequalities though her discussions with peers, she brought these issues into the organization. "Something we've begun to talk about among ourselves is the composition of our group," she told me. "Like, we're all white. And I don't think any of us comes from a working-class background, yet we're all organized around the issue of labor. That's kind of weird if you think about it. Why would we of all people want to do this work? We don't really know. But even more important, how can we broaden our membership? We can't just assume it will happen of its own accord. So we're asking ourselves, is it the way we portray ourselves to outsiders that's the problem? Or is it our group dynamics that's made us so homogeneous? So we're thinking about these things very hard, very intentionally. But it's hard to see if we're making progress. I think it takes a long time and definitely a strong interest in race and class issues in order to understand what's really going on."

Lauren's parents are not pleased with the direction she has chosen. "Every time I go home, all we do is fight, fight, fight," she tells me. "My dad keeps saying, 'I can't believe this is what you're doing with your life!' I've tried to foster an understanding with them. I've explained why I might want to do something where I'm not going to be making a ton of money, something more service oriented, not supercapitalist. But that's been a difficult process for my parents. They're very apolitical. They still have this delusion that I'm going to come to my senses and transfer to the business school. But I've always been pretty independent, and I think I've made my peace with our disagreements."

Developing a vision of Millennial social justice leadership can be easier, in a sense, for students of color, immigrants, or impoverished students whose life experiences have made the social and economic inequalities crystal clear. Justin, an immigrant from China who arrived in this country with his dad when he was fifteen, went to work in a restaurant owned by a relative to help with the family's meager resources. Right away he began to experience the barriers of ethnicity, privilege, and power that Carrie and Lauren are still struggling to comprehend.

"I'm always aware of global inequalities because of my background," says Justin. "Even at my young age, I could see how the restaurant employees struggled and toiled doing that tedious, repetitive work. Of course, I had to do it too. It was one of those all-you-can-eat buffets, and I was the one who had to bring out the huge dishes to fill the hot and cold bars. And I had to constantly communicate with the kitchen staff, telling them what we were running low on and what we were out of, and of course the cooks were struggling to get all the stuff ready and they weren't exactly in a good mood. It was a miserable job, just bad in every way. All I could think was, 'This sucks. I hate it.' I was so young, and I was studying so hard because English is my third language, that I didn't get much further in my thinking.

"But once I got to college, I started to reflect," Justin continues. Something that really struck me was the hierarchy of employees: the owner and his family lived on the first floor of his house, the Chinese employees all lived on the second floor, and the Mexican workers were stuck in the basement. And this system was repeated in the restaurant: the owner's close relatives worked the easiest, most visible jobs—cashier, for example—while the other Chinese immigrants worked in the kitchen cooking the food, and the Mexicans were washing dishes and taking out the garbage. So I started to wonder, 'What does this mean? Why this hierarchy? And why do I have to work at this restaurant? Why does my dad have to work here? We came all the way to the U.S. for this? We are working for so many hours and never see the sunlight, while other people enjoy life!'"

Justin's experiences and his observations of other immigrant workers led him to dream of a world without borders, "a world where you don't need a passport." This thought came to him when he learned in my grassroots development class that one of the internationally recognized human rights was freedom of movement. "If we have the right to move freely within our own country, and the ability to leave and return to any country, including our own as it says in the Universal Declaration of Human Rights, why shouldn't we extend this freedom to the whole world?" he wondered. "Why shouldn't anyone be allowed to cross international borders at will? Monitoring and regulating people's movements just increases the opportunities for exploitation."

Justin had learned to reflect on his experiences through his first-year writing course, which had focused on personal narrative. But aside from a few small classes like that one, Justin was enrolled in large lecture classes—stats, psych, English lit—"like everyone else." He might have continued on this conventional path had he not stumbled on a course that offered something called Asian American Community Service.

"I had *no* concept of what that class was," Justin told me. "In China—and even in my high school here in the States—you don't take classes about your heritage, and you don't get credit for community service. I didn't even intend to take the class when I showed up on the first day. But the idea of it intrigued me so I stayed." For the service requirement in that course, Justin got involved with the Asian American Heritage Month Planning Committee. And that innocuous organization became Justin's introduction to hands-on social justice leadership and eventually helped him achieve the status of skilled campus organizer, and from there, to a job with Teach for America in one of the most challenging communities in the country.

Like Carrie, Justin was awed and a little intimidated at first by the "big people" in the student organizations, the juniors and seniors who knew the ropes. "I would just sit there quietly in the Multicultural Student Affairs office, taking notes for the Planning Committee, watching what the others were doing, because I had no idea how organizations are run," says Justin. "But that was the gateway that really got me started. In the summer, I actually got a job in that office. I was just a student clerk, answering the phone and filing stuff, but by talking to the staff members and student leaders who came in, I learned about all the events and issues that involved the Asian community on campus.

"So now I knew a lot of the student leaders because of my job," Justin continues. "And in my sophomore year, I took the same job again, but now, I was involved in organizing and logistical support of Generation APA, the pan-Asian cultural show, the biggest event of the year! Since it was summer, most of the student leaders were at home, or away doing internships. But I was on campus taking classes and working, so I could see that a lot of things needed to be done, and I just sort of jumped in. I reached out and had conversations with the service-learning people about what kinds of projects we could undertake the next year. I reached out to the Student Affairs Office and talked with people there about how to work with other student of color groups. And I took on what turned into a huge project of publishing a little magazine to send to all the entering Asian American freshmen. For that project, I had to be in touch with various organizations about funding. Then I had to communicate with the graphic designer, and the writers, and with the printing company about prices and deadlines, as well as report back to the board and the co-chairs about all I had done that week and try to get their ideas about it. And if they wanted the printing or the design to be done a certain way, I had to communicate that through different channels and sources. So I was kind of like the middle person doing all the communication from multiple sides."

"So you were learning by doing?"

"Exactly. There was no communication coach! You just had to learn from your mistakes. And I made them, for sure. The worst one, I was so worried about deadlines, I became really harsh with the printing company," Justin laughs sheepishly. "And that really backfired. I kind of threatened them: Do this or else! Of course my supervisors and mentors jumped all over me for that, and I realized right away how wrong I was. That was a real learning experience for me."

By this time, Justin had declared English as his major, "which was an outrageous idea at the time," he says laughing. "It was pretty naive for an international student who can't really speak English right, and who can't read well or comprehend a lot of the texts. But it was pretty progressive idea, I guess!" Despite the difficulty, or maybe because of it, Justin loved the focus on reading and writing, especially after he got into U-M's New England Literature Program, where students live cooperatively in unheated cabins in the Maine woods in early spring, studying regional authors, writing intensely, discussing everything. "NELP had an educational philosophy that really caused you to reflect on your life," Justin says. No distractions were allowed: no cell phones, laptops, iPods, no electronics at all. "The meaning of life, the meaning of your choices, that's what we were constantly writing and talking about. They taught me to be really conscious about why I was making certain decisions.

"What is the purpose of life?" Justin asks rhetorically. "Most students don't think about that when they come to college. They have a certain professional destination: medical school or law school, something really conventional, really safe, something their parents approve of and that will make them a lot of money. They know that if they apply themselves, they're going to succeed. They know exactly how it's going to turn out. But they don't think about what they really want to do with their life.

"But the staff at NELP really gets you thinking about these unreflective choices," Justin continues. "They encourage you to try new things, take risks. They force you to write in different styles. If you are always using the same voice they want you to try something new. If you're stuck in a formal, academic style of writing they want you to branch out. Or if you always write about your personal experience, they want you to change that, too. And not only in writing—I think there was one week where they forced us to do something we'd never done before. And they encouraged us to challenge them, even though they are the teachers. They said we can all learn from dialogue and open discussion, from everyone sharing their personal stories and points of view. This was a new idea for me. In China, teachers are at the top of the hierarchy. Even if they're wrong you have to be respectful of their authority."

When Justin came back to campus for his junior year, he brought all these new skills and experiences with him. "One day in class I found myself challenging an instructor's idea about the texts she'd chosen for discussion," he told me. "'Why is minority writing always about victimhood?' I asked. 'Why is African American and Latino writing always about gang violence and social inequality? Why is Native American writing always about alcoholism and suffering? Doesn't that just reinforce stereotypes?' And the instructor was saying, 'Oh, let's not talk about it.' Maybe she didn't want to confront the topic. But I was like, 'Wow, I'm like a totally new and different person!'"

With his growing confidence to ask tough questions about educational norms, Justin started looking critically at the social segregation on campus, especially in the student of color organizations. "Can you believe, there's an African American Medical School organization, there's the Asian Medical School students, and then they break that down into

Asian American and International Asian, and then into Chinese and Taiwanese. And then there's a Taiwan Student Association and a Taiwanese *American* Student Association, which don't really work with each other because one group speaks English and the other speaks Chinese, or as they would say, 'Taiwanese,' so they break it down even further! And there's an even greater divide between East Asians and South Asians. There's absolutely no solidarity! I thought, 'There's something wrong with that. No one's working with each other, despite the fact that we all went through the same struggles as immigrants.' And as you know, Asian students score a lot of academic achievements but we have very little political power in this country. So there's a need for us to work together and to reach out to other groups of color. Once I understood that, I decided to join the NAACP."

"Really!" I exclaim.

"Yeah," laughs Justin. "I remember the first meeting I went to—I walked in and everybody was like, 'Can I help you?' 'Are you in the wrong room?' I'm pretty open-minded and outgoing, and by then I had a lot of experience working with different people, so right at that first meeting I managed to join into the conversation. And by actively volunteering to do a variety of tasks and by adding my own perspective as an immigrant and a first-generation college student, I think I contributed something. Of course I learned a lot, too, since I had no clue about African American issues before I came to this country."

During his junior year, "a frantic time," Justin admits, he was a resident advisor in a dormitory responsible for communicating with forty students, their parents, the director of the residence hall, and the other resident advisors. He had become the community chair for the umbrella organization for all the Asian American student organizations on campus. He was the convener of the Asian American Heritage Committee (where as a freshman, he reminded me, he was the one meekly taking notes), "responsible for recruiting people to join, convincing them to join, and convincing them to convince other people to join." And then, just because he "wanted to do something different," Justin looked online to find an organization that worked with immigrants and "just showed up" at one of their meetings. Migrant and Immigrant Rights Awareness

(MIRA) was a small organization, he told me, "so they welcomed me with open arms." Soon he was working directly with Mexican immigrants, fighting for change in immigration law. He met restaurant workers in church basements and worked with student groups to provide volunteers for the cause. Many nights, after an evening packed with organizing activities, he would be up until dawn writing e-mail, making sure groups were getting funding, reaching out to other student organizations, recruiting more students to join in. "I was really, really involved," says Justin, "and everyone in the community knew me. I reached out to a lot of university departments and offices, so I was really connected and engaged. It was hard! It was a *lot* of work. A crazy year. But I loved it."

Finally, Justin, by his account, had done everything in terms of student organizations on campus and had become "a kind of advisor for other students, a role model. You have to be sure the next generation has a smooth transition into leadership positions because you're not going to be there forever," he says. "You're not going to be able to do everything. You have to delegate. And there are students—like me when I was younger—who are very excited to take those responsibilities from you. And there are others who are kind of shy, but you see their potential. So you have to train them. And since you're the one with all the connections, you have to make sure you take them around to various offices and establish those connections for them. You have to put them into a position to succeed. And that's so rewarding! You pass on to the younger students what older ones did for you."

I ask Justin what were the most significant things he learned in college.

"I took a lot of good classes," he replies diplomatically. "Small classes, like yours, where you really have the freedom to think and discuss. But the real learning came from organizing with other students on campus. I think a lot of my peers have had the same experience. The biggest lesson I learned is not to get deterred. Leadership is learning by doing. And by struggling. My thing is that you have to struggle to make progress. I definitely went through that struggling phase. And year by year, I improved myself. So, as I told all my mentees, explore the possibilities and jump into them with open arms. Take risks. If there's any opportunity, you should reach out for it, even though it might not appear compelling or attractive at the time. That's really why I'm where I am right now. Because the sense of possibility took me really far. Because I just showed up. Not many people do that! Most people tend to take the safe, conventional, and prestigious opportunities. But I just jump onboard. If you show up at an NAACP meeting, people look at you like you're crazy. But it takes these struggles for you to make progress."

Beyond these personal challenges, Justin, like Carrie, sees authentic relationships as central to social justice leadership, though he's less obsessed and more pragmatic about approaching them. "I think leadership starts with little things," he tells me. "Things I learned at Michigan, mostly just through observation. Like, I hold the door for everybody." Justin smiles at everyone, too, and his smile is so genuine that everyone gravitates to him. "I think you can't accomplish large-scale social change if you can't do little things to reach out to other people," Justin says. "If you have stereotypes about other people—and who doesn't?—if you don't actively approach them with a smile and understanding, you're not going to be successful. You can have the best social vision in the world, but without a genuine human connection, it's not going to happen."

As this generation leaves college, they expect to become leaders. But college doesn't explicitly teach leadership, and even if it did, it is questionable whether traditional leadership models would be adequate for this generation and the world they inherit. What Justin, Carrie, Lauren, Dana, and other Millennial student leaders are trying to work out with such intense intellectual and emotional energy is a model of leadership that goes far beyond what progressive education can offer them. The components of the model are critical self-reflection, real-world argumentation, concentrated attention to detail, and research and study that is motivated not by grades and authorities but by the needs and expectations of the group and the issue itself. It involves a highly efficient group process, productive mentoring relationships, and intense, multifaceted communication across boundaries of race, class, age, gender, and authority that have been cemented in place by previous generations. For many elite Millennials, this new, progressive leadership also requires what Dana called "critical self-creation": recognizing one's part in an oppressive social system, coming to terms with one's privilege, understanding the historical reasons that barriers between groups were constructed and how they are kept in place, and developing the skill to reach across these barriers with humility, tact, and persistence. For the students who come to college with a "visceral understanding of oppression," critical self-creation means developing the ability to reflect deeply on one's own life, finding the courage and knowledge to speak one's mind, and reaching out to other groups of color and trusted white allies. Above all, Millennial leadership, as these students describe it, means searching for connection, peering through artificial barriers into the heart and spirit of the other, trusting, as Carrie says, that authentic relationships between all human beings are not only important, but that they're *possible*.

As progressive instructors know all too well, elite Millennial students arrive in college with lofty personal goals and the self-confidence—sometimes nascent, sometimes overweaning—in their ability to change the world. Many do not rise above their hubris, and they allow their energy to be frittered away in superficial activities, anxious conformity, obsessive attention to Facebook, and plodding from one huge lecture class to another with the goal of a prestigious career. But the best, or the luckiest, find a way to develop as Millennial leaders and, in the process, as human beings.

Chapter 8

Teaching Peace

Millennial students' gentle vision of a better world is one where systems are fair, where no one goes hungry or suffers from curable disease, where human rights are respected, and where everyone has ample opportunity to reach their potential and contribute to the greater good.[1] While Millennials need to radicalize their notions of equality if they are to work effectively in the service of this vision, just as urgent, I believe, is their need to think deeply about how that kinder, more peaceful world is to be achieved without resorting to the brutality and wreckage of war.

My own conviction about the futility of violent solutions to human conflict was shaped by a brief but startling trip I had taken just before the September 11th attacks on the World Trade Center and the Pentagon. In Cambodia for a conference on language and development, I stumbled upon an opportunity to talk with high school English teachers who had survived the genocide of the 1970s, when in a pathetic attempt to uplift the exploited rural population, Cambodia's Communist Party had abolished formal education, burned libraries, put an end to money, shot the intelligentsia, and sent two and a half million people, including children, the elderly, and invalids roused from their hospital beds on a forced march into the countryside to work as laborers for the new regime.[2] Hundreds of thousands of teachers, doctors, artists, engineers, technicians, and students were starved, tortured, and executed by the Khmer Rouge as enemies of the people.[3] I visited a former high school, the infamous S–21, where 17,000 men, women, and children had been chained on the cement floors with their fingers smashed and genitals electroshocked, starving, for months, before they died. In the countryside, children were often recruited to do the killing. Ten-year-olds learned to slice people's throats, or drown them in rice paddies by wrapping their heads in plastic bags and shoving them under water.

As I talked with ordinary Cambodians, I asked them what they remembered about that brutal period. A beautiful young woman, a teacher-trainer, told me in a whisper how she lost her father to the killing fields and two older sisters to starvation. A translator had seen the Khmer Rouge execute an old man in his village for stealing a potato he had grown himself. A high school teacher told me about the fourteen-hour days he had endured in the rice fields and the single meal of gruel—a bit of rice boiled in water—that was allotted to him at the end of each day. We sat at the conference lunch table talking, and three times he went back to the buffet to heap his plate with pats of butter, which he ate straight—without bread—still remembering, perhaps, the feeling of near starvation after twenty-five years.

Who were these monsters that inflicted such suffering, I wondered. They were not an external enemy, nor were they a group that distinguished itself from others by ethnicity, or race, or religion. They were Cambodians who had turned against their neighbors, their teachers, their colleagues, even their own families in their zeal to create a revolutionary society. This is what still haunts Cambodians today, that they did all this to themselves, that they committed such atrocities out of fear, revenge, and cold-blooded self-righteousness. Looking around as I walked through the streets of Phnom Penh and the villages and towns I visited, I realized that many of the people I saw had been adults during those terrible years and had either been very, very lucky, or had participated in some way in this perverted system.

But strangely enough, I did not see a nation of people degraded by evil. In fact, I found Cambodians to be some of the most gentle, hospitable, and delightfully sunny people I have ever met. As a nation of Buddhists (which they have been since at least the fifth century), they revere all forms of life and deplore inflicting pain on others. To get angry in public over a cab fare or some other petty complaint is considered childish and embarrassing. Even raising one's voice is culturally inappropriate. This is not something that arose recently, after the experience of such opposite sentiments. These values have been present throughout Cambodian history. I was also struck by the connectedness people seemed to feel in traffic jams. Trucks, cars, and motor scooters were all over the road, going any direction, the roads deeply potholed, the potential for accidents extreme, yet everyone seemed to watch out for each other, passing within centimeters without incident, without fear, without a hint of road rage. Were these the same people who gave rise to the demented fanatics of the Khmer Rouge regime only a generation ago, I wondered? Or was the concept of "demented fanatic" somehow wrong?

The conclusion I came to was this: Most people who commit unspeakable crimes and who aid and abet such crimes, whether technological, or suicidal, or up close and personal, are not "inhuman." They are not monsters. They are very ordinary people who have become overcome by an idea—whether that idea is a militant political philosophy, a twisted interpretation of a religious creed, or a government's call to the defense of the nation. Most important, they happen to live in a time and place where conditions are right for that destructive idea to take hold and feed upon itself, blooming and mushrooming until it explodes in violence. And as that violence begets an ever more violent response, the idea grows even stronger, and those who hold that idea, who are in a sense the victims of that idea, believe more and more firmly that they must carry out these crimes and that their society, their values, their dignity, their way of life, all depend on it.

As I reflected on my Cambodian trip in the light of the newly declared War on Terror, other examples of the mutability of good and evil came to mind. The Japanese, so incorrigible as to merit a nuclear holocaust at the end of World War II, quickly became our trading partners and esteemed colleagues. Vietnam, once a rogue state whose people were considered so brutish and worthless that they could be maimed, burned, and genetically deformed with impunity is now a traveler's destination of choice. ("Beautiful!" say the American tourists. "Especially the North. And the people are so hospitable. You must go.")

Surely, it's illogical to say, as all governments do when they prepare the nation to commit unspeakable crimes of violence, that there are the bad people and the good people, the immoral countries and the responsible countries, and that if we annihilate or violently reform the "bad guys," we—the good and responsible people—will be safe and evil will be defeated forever, or at least kept under control. But it is not people, or even governments, that cause these problems, I mused; it is the idea of war itself. Not only are most human beings mutable—complicit in horrible crimes one minute and gentle and loving the next—we are also all emotionally gullible: easily swept away by notions of patriotism, honor, revenge, fear, blind obedience, and self-righteousness. Our attachment to war leaves us bereft of ideas for addressing human conflict more intelligently.

Convinced that the wars in Afghanistan and Iraq were pointless and futile and that "war is not worthy of human beings" (as I was beginning to repeat with annoying frequency to friends and family), I created an upper-level seminar that addressed the complex causes of war and violence and the kinds of nonviolent responses that have successfully mediated intractable conflict. Later, in 2005, I began a research study to better understand how Millennial students were thinking about these issues and what more they might need to understand. For this project I employed three undergraduate research assistants to help draft a questionnaire and conduct many of the interviews, as my experience told me that students would be more voluble and honest talking with their peers than with a faculty member. The interviewers found volunteers for the study through their personal networks of acquaintances and classmates, and students in my nonviolence seminar used the same protocol to interview themselves and their friends. Our final sample contained an approximate balance of males and females, students of color and white students, and students pursuing a variety of academic majors.

My young research assistants suggested, rightly, that a discussion of the heavy topics of war and peace should begin with the personal, so we asked how respondents had been affected as children by the events of

9/11, their feelings about the Iraq war, the images that came to mind when they thought about war in general, whether they had ever been approached by a military recruiter and how they had responded, and what they would do in the event of a military draft if one were to be reinstated—which, though unlikely, had been discussed in the media.

We then asked respondents to think about broader questions of war and peace: "Why do you think terrorists want to attack the United States?" "In your opinion, what is the best response to terrorism or terrorist threats?" "Do you see war as a reasonable way for nations to settle their differences, a necessary evil, an unacceptable way to conduct foreign relations, or something else entirely?" "Do you think war could become universally rejected or condemned at some point in the future, like cannibalism, human sacrifice, and slavery?" "What do you think humans would have to learn in order to solve global conflicts more peacefully?" The purpose of these kinds of questions was twofold: we wanted to know what respondents thought and felt and what information they lacked, and we wanted to give them a brief opportunity to reflect on common assumptions about war that too often remain unquestioned, which we thought would be a valuable end in itself.

The interview questions were intentionally open-ended in order to elicit as much information as possible from respondents. Interviewers asked encouraging follow-up questions ("Why do you feel that way?" "Can you say more about that?"), occasionally posed questions of their own that deviated from the interview protocol, and allowed answers to take their own paths even if they veered somewhat off topic. While this conversational approach made the interview data hard to quantify, we felt it gave us a more complete picture of what these respondents thought, and, from the perspective of peace education, what questions should be addressed in classes like mine. In this way, we completed in-depth interviews of eighty University of Michigan undergraduates, about a quarter of whom had taken my nonviolence seminar. These interviews, in addition to student essays from my nonviolence classes and my reflections on teaching nearly eighty additional students over a period of five years, provide the data, the reflection, and the recommendations in this chapter.

Strikingly, the students we interviewed made no attempt to avoid taking a position, or carefully sidestep political questions, or meekly confirm the attitudes of their elders, as their Millennial profile suggests they might. Most said bluntly that the Iraq war was "pointless," "ignorant," or "unnecessary." Some of our respondents were angry about the war; others, deeply cynical. A first-year student said, "I totally did not approve of this war. It sounded really stupid from the beginning. I've heard it mentioned that this will become another Vietnam, and that's what it seems it's going to be, a long, drawn-out war where in the end there is no benefit, there is no end result. Just nothing. Just a lot of people coming home angry and depressed. Nothing really to show for it."

Another expressed her disdain for the individual who had led the country into war: "I'm looking down at President Bush because I'm like, 'Why are you putting us through this? What are we getting out of this?' I think a lot of us are looking at Bush like, 'What the hell are you thinking? What is *wrong* with you?'"

Unless they had family members in the military, many of our respondents said they were emotionally disengaged from the war itself. Some didn't even follow it on the news, either because they couldn't make sense of why the United States was in Iraq, or because they believed that the media or the administration were deliberately downplaying the war or had lied about it. A first-year French major who said he had been horrified to discover that there were no weapons of mass destruction in Iraq, responded emotionally when the interviewer began, "Do you feel the news media plays the role of a mediator and deliverer of information, or as an instigator that—"

"Instigator! Instigator!" interrupted the student, almost shouting. "And they try to scare you with a lot of things that aren't true! We've got all these TV channels competing with each other. So they all try to come up with things that make their stories more spicy and sizzling so more people will listen to what they have to say. We used to get good information when we had about four news channels. Now that we have twenty-four-hour news channels, most of it is like, lies, or false situations!"

If a military draft were to be reinstated to supply personnel for the Iraq war, the majority of respondents said—rather rashly, I thought—

they would flee the country, go to prison, or somehow make themselves unqualified for military service. Many said that their families would support their decision to avoid the draft—or even lead the way in an escape to a neutral country. When asked, "If there were a draft and you were drafted, what would you do?" a second-year female student replied, "I'm not going! I'm not going if they try to draft me!"

"What would you do if you were drafted?"

"Get pregnant. Get very pregnant!"

"How do you think your friends and family would respond to your decision?"

"They'd say, 'Good job!' They all know *they* ain't goin.' And *I'm* not goin' either! They wouldn't *let* me go!"

A fourth-year male student told us, "I would have great trouble killing someone, or working for someone that I knew was supporting killing people. So I would try and dodge it as best I could. I've heard that new agreements with Canada don't allow draft dodgers there, and the college exemption no longer works. So I don't know what I would do. Maybe I could become blind spontaneously?"

A majority of our respondents believed that the United States had brought the September 11th attacks on itself because of its tendency to bully other countries or treat them as inconsequential. In reply to the question, "Why do you think terrorists want to attack the United States?" a second-year student said hotly, "Every country wants to attack America! Because America has been holding its thumb down on every other country for the past 100 or so years, with all its weapons. Oh my God, did you know there's over 200 nuclear facilities in our country alone? And we get pissed off at North Korea or Iran if we find *one!* And we bomb it all of a sudden. No wonder people want to fight back; we're like an oppressor, we're like the biggest superpower with the biggest military and the biggest weapons, it's like, you know, who wouldn't want to come in and bomb [the United States] and destroy it?"

A third-year student responded even more graphically: "Why do terrorists want to attack the United States? Because the United States thinks they're the high shit and they can do whatever the hell they want to other countries, and then they think everybody's supposed to be okay with it. But the terrorists are fed up, they're like, they want to be heard, and they don't *like* the United States. Like a lot of countries don't like the United States! Which people in the United States don't realize. People say oh, we're such a great country, we do a lot of great things—well, we do a lot of horrible things, too."

Almost all students said that the U.S. response to the September 11th attacks did not make them feel safer and that war is not an effective, fair, or rational way to deal with terrorist threats or attacks. Many suggested that only the individuals behind the attacks, rather than entire countries, should be brought to justice. Some pointed out the uselessness of trying to annihilate terrorism as an idea or tactic. One student suggested that the potential for terrorism is in all of us, even those our government is trying to protect. She related the story of how her friends and neighbors had turned violently on the only Arab American family in her small community after the September 11th attacks, attempting to torch their business and effectively running them out of town. "I don't think that a war on terror is the best answer," she told me, "because that [incident] just shows you that anyone could be a terrorist. What happened in my town was an act of terrorism. And the majority of the citizens were involved in it!"

While some students upheld the need for war in limited circumstances after careful and repeated attempts at diplomatic solutions, many said that any war is pointless, self-defeating, or hypocritical. As a fourth-year student explained, "War is a paradox, because it can be justified by anything. Anybody can find their own reasons to start a war. At the same time, somebody else can feel that your reason for war is totally unjustified. So there's really no good reason for war. It's just ridiculous. It's not even a paradox, because a paradox makes sense. It's an inherent contradiction. It's a self-defeating philosophy!" A first-year student added categorically, "I don't think anybody has the right to kill anyone regardless of anything. So, just the simple fact that we're sort of saying, 'Hey, it's your time to die now—boom!'—I'm not ready for that. So that's how the Iraq war affects me. I'm not down with the killing."

Yet despite their abhorrence of war and violence, the overwhelming majority of our respondents said that wars will continue eternally and that the dream of a nonviolent future is unrealistic. The students gave a variety of reasons for their pessimistic view. Some confidently asserted that humans are inherently violent, self-centered, or irrational.

"Is the thought or dream of a nonviolent society realistic?" asks my research assistant.

"No!" responds a third-year political science major. "It's just not realistic. Because human beings are—we're not reasonable. We don't think about what's in everybody's best interest. We just think about our own. We're selfish, we're jealous, there's a whole list of all the negative things that human beings are."

A computer science student explained that humans just aren't logical.

"So what would you suggest as an alternative to war?" the interviewer asks.

"You know, people always say, 'Talk it out,'" he replies. "So that's what I want to say. That's the right thing to do. But we don't just live in a perfect society where you can just like, talk out problems, so everyone can go their separate ways, 'cause human beings aren't rational people. We don't think logically. People don't think about the other side. They don't ask if they have a valid point. They only think about themselves. We're selfish people, I guess."

A third-year student who believed that President Bush's response to the 9/11 attacks "unveiled our government's true nature," suggested that humans are unable to give up the will to power: "I can't imagine a world without war. That's unfortunate, but it's reality. As long as there's a world, there will be wars. Because humanity will have its people who want more power, they'll want more control over others, they'll want to continue to rule the world. And as long as there's a mentality that 'I need to rule,' that 'I need to control,' that 'I need money,' that 'I need material things,' that 'I need to satisfy myself at the expense of others,' and as long as there's fear, there will always be war."

Some students even suggested that human nature is so problematic that almost any dispute must be resolved violently. A third-year student remarked, "War and violence are just part of who we are. It's pretty difficult to solve problems with just peace. Such as who owns land, who controls resources . . . these are issues you can't solve peacefully because of the way people are. Or because of the difference in cultures. Or something as simple as a language barrier or whatnot. So I guess it's whoever can take it, it's theirs. I mean, that's just something that's part of being human."

Students who didn't go as far as attributing war to inherent human flaws sometimes pointed out that violence is by far the easiest way to settle differences. A first-year student told us he "totally did a 180"—conservative Republican to liberal Democrat—when he discovered that the Bush administration had lied about the reasons we had gone to war in Iraq. Yet he does not feel optimistic that anyone, Democrat or Republican, will put in the effort to address differences rationally.

"Why are people so ready to use violence and war to solve problems?" asks the interviewer.

"Because you can get it over with, you can just kill someone. You don't have to sit down and actually make a compromise. Because in war, whoever is the most powerful will like, come out on top, but when you have to actually sit down, go over your flaws, fix the things that are going wrong, listen to another party's views, to actually sit down and try to come up with a plan, people don't want to do that."

Other students suggested that weapons technology promotes war or that powerful people gain from violence and chaos. A third-year psychology major noted with a touch of sarcasm, "Will war ever become obsolete? I don't think so. Not in this day and age, because we're getting more technologically advanced, developing more strategies and weapons and all that stuff. So you know, you gotta use 'em, so why try anything else? Why try to listen when we have weapons? Ha, ha, we've got the big gun!"

A first-year chemical engineering student pointed out the economic gains from war: "I don't know about other countries, but America has this big industry manufacturing guns and weapons. And the only way we can justify how much money we're putting into building all these weapons of mass destruction is using them every so often. And then people will profit from that, and then the companies will make even more money. So then we have to go and use them and sell them to other countries."

Some students see cultural norms as getting in the way of the elimination of war. A second-year student who had three family members stationed in Iraq said reflectively, "I think war is just a very traditional idea. A lot of people think it's just what they're called to do: the men have to defend their country, the women go over there as nurses to take care of the men that are getting hurt. It's something that's socially built in to our culture. Like a chip in your brain, where guys are like, 'Okay, I'll go.' You don't have to think about it very much."

Some students saw mere differences in personality or lifestyle as barriers to getting along without war and violence. When asked, "Is the thought or dream of a nonviolent society realistic?" a first-year student who shared with us that he lost two extended family members in the 9/11 attacks responded almost gaily: "Nope. It's impossible."

"Why do you think that?" asked the interviewer, a bit taken aback.

"Everyone's too different," replied the student, serious again. "I mean, there are those of us who are really aggressive and those of us who are not. There will always be that imbalance. And because of that there will always be fighting, always some kind of conflict."

And a third-year student contended that people are so ornery that they would find a way around any attempt to solve problems peacefully: "The only way to get rid of war and violence would be to establish rules, and of course by establishing rules, people would just break them anyway. And this would just lead to anarchy. People are gonna—it's just the way people are."

"How do you think we'll get to a nonviolent society, then, if ever?" asked the interviewer.

"I guess the only way I see it happening is by finding some way to enforce the rules around the clock. But basically you'd have to remove a lot of people's freedoms."

I found these responses somewhat puzzling, because so many of them seem to ignore the ways disputes between people and groups are solved nonviolently every day, through the judicial system, through laws that promote fairness, through civil and religious education, and through peace-enhancing values and practices that can be found the world over. We found it fascinating that students tended to think of large-scale national or international violence in the same terms as interpersonal disagreement. People will always get angry at each other, they said, or use violent language to put each other down, or even just assert their will, and that means that in order to avoid violence, we would have to agree about everything, and that would mean we would need some kind of thought police to avoid divisions between people. Humans would have to be perfect to outgrow the need for war, they said, and that will never come to pass.

A first-year student put this quite clearly: "No matter what, there's always going to be violence, there's always going to be that one guy on the block who abuses his wife, there's always going to be that one woman on the block who abuses her children, there's always going to be that one country around the corner that disagrees with our policy, there's always going to be that one president who's *out of his mind* that would bring us back to war."

These reasons for the inevitability of war were almost always given in a tone of cynicism and even despair. Yet when asked how humans could learn to avoid war, almost all students gave answers that reflected their optimism about human nature or human capabilities, saying that tolerance, respect, and communication are key, or that we just need to sit down with the other side and work on problem solving together, or that more cultural understanding will help, as will alleviating global poverty.

A second-year student who described the reasons the United States went to war in Iraq as "immature" suggested, "In regards to warfare, just negotiate instead of jumping the gun and starting a war. Just negotiate with the other heads of countries. And I'm sure people could be civil and figure things out. If the U.S. poses ideas to the other country and tries to handle the situation in a calm, rational kind of way, then it could work towards, first of all, making countries hate us less, and second of all, making *us* less violent, then the violence against us would decrease too."

Another student told us that she reacted to the 9/11 terrorist attacks by intentionally traveling to as many countries as possible "because I feel that's the best way I can show what a real American is like." "How to solve global conflicts peacefully?" she mused. "This is really cliché, but we need to remember that everyone's just a human trying to live their life, have their family, everyone's got things in common. So there's no reason to blow each other up! To oversimplify. But it's like Palestinian and Jewish families, they have the same Semitic values, the same structure. If you have a room full of Palestinians and Jews together, they look the same, basically. It's like if people would just realize how much they were alike and came together, it'd be better."

And a first-year student told us that watching graphic war movies made her give up the idea that war is a reasonable last resort, and that even some TV shows are more forward looking than governments: "On *Star Trek* they have gone beyond war now, and I think that's kinda cool. If we decided we're really going to get rid of this war, I think it'd be about a year before we could get it done. Same thing as if we decided to give electricity to all countries—six months. If we decided to make a way where everyone could have fresh water to drink—nine months. If we decided to put our energy, time, and effort from fighting each other into uniting as one to make the world even better? Hot damn, we couldn't be stopped!" Trite as these responses might sound, they were offered to the interviewers seriously, even passionately, as if these alternatives to violence had never really been considered before.

Many students also claimed that wars of liberation or armed humanitarian intervention in cases of extreme oppression or genocide are quite different from the greed- or fear-inspired wars like Iraq or Vietnam that they so deplore. These students see World War II as a "good war," claiming (erroneously) that the United States entered into it to liberate the Jews from Nazi oppression. Some also cited the U.S. Civil War as morally necessary, saying (again erroneously) that it was fought primarily to free the slaves.[4] This strong impulse to justify armed intervention to protect the weak and vulnerable was echoed by the majority of students who have enrolled in my nonviolence class. "Just war," to these students, is not about their own national or even personal security. It's about stopping rape and pillage in Darfur; it's about caring enough to send in armed peacekeepers to end the Rwandan genocide; it's about supporting an armed revolutionary struggle in Chiapas that fights for an impoverished indigenous population considered so inconsequential that, as one student wrote, "nobody cared whether they protested nonviolently."

If Millennial students like these are to move us toward a world where global conflicts are worked out fairly and without bloodshed, what do they need to know? First, I found it striking that when students were asked to name strategies other than war that had been used to solve disputes in the past, they give very vague, general answers: "Diplomacy, I guess. Negotiation." While several mentioned the most famous exemplars of nonviolent resistance—Gandhi, Martin Luther King—virtually no one mentioned any other nonviolent leader or movement (there have been hundreds[5]), nor did they bring up any specifics of regional or international conflict resolution or any other nonviolent methods,[6] such as those that have long been used in the labor movement, the peace movement, or the worldwide protests against neoliberalism, such as in Seattle in 1999.[7] These omissions shouldn't surprise us, given that nonviolent tactics are rarely celebrated in history textbooks and are often downplayed, even ridiculed, in the mainstream media. Likewise, negative judgments of human nature abound in our culture, leaving the distinct impression that despite countless everyday examples to the contrary, humans are incapable of controlling themselves or their institutions. And while many of our respondents were convinced of the horrors of war—the vast toll in human lives, the physical and mental cost to survivors, the deceit, the profiteering, the tolerance of racism and sexual violence, the acceptance of torture, the deliberate[8] or, as Howard Zinn argues, "inevitable" targeting of civilians,[9] and the suspension of civil liberties—students mentioned these negative outcomes only in regard to wars they disapprove of; few pointed out that they pervade "good wars" as well. Indeed, progressive educators, curriculum designers, textbook writers, and program developers have much work to do.

Peace education is not entirely absent, of course; worldwide, there are more than 450 undergraduate, master's, and doctoral programs and concentrations in more than forty countries and thirty-eight U.S. states.[10] Wonderful models and lesson plans exist for all age levels,[11] and knowledgeable teachers add information on nonviolence to the standard curriculum when they can. But clearly, basic knowledge of the power and efficacy of nonviolent direct action is not reaching enough students, even those (or maybe especially those) who attend elite universities like Michigan. In both high school and college, standard history and political science classes teach "realist" models of world politics, which assume that nations are motivated by irrational or base notions of fear, honor, and profit; that human nature is intrinsically violent, sinful, or "fallen" in the Christian sense; and that national and personal security can be gained only through a struggle for power.[12] Each year, armed with their knowledge of the irrelevance of human generosity, compassion, cooperation, and morality, thousands of high-achieving Millennials pack up for law school and then go on to influential positions in think tanks, lobbying organizations, political offices, and the nation's diplomatic corps.

My own course, which I have been teaching since 2003, is one of the few seminars on nonviolence available to Michigan's undergraduates. I deliberately keep my class small—fewer than thirty students—out of my conviction that students learn by wrestling with complex issues in small discussion groups and through writing successive drafts of their arguments, insights, and ever-expanding questions. I never lecture; students are expected to come to class prepared with questions for discussion and debate. I tell them I don't expect them to adopt my blatantly pacifist stance, since I know that opposition to all war on principle is a rather extreme position in our culture, but that they do need to listen to the arguments that support it, and I welcome their challenges and questions.

Some students enroll in the course because they are looking for ways to convince their friends, or their parents, or indeed, themselves, that their impulse toward nonviolence is valid. Others take the course simply to satisfy the university's advanced writing requirement, so they come with an interesting variety of viewpoints. One of my best students did most of her previous schooling in India where she had become frustrated by the prevailing "Mahatma craze," as she put it, the glorification of "Gandhi's bloodless war" that defeated British control. She had come to the University of Michigan to study war, actually, since she had wondered all her life if the terrible violence between Muslims and Hindus at the partition of India and Pakistan could have been avoided by armed intervention. She was taking my course "to get the other point of view." Some students arrive in my class full of masculine bravado, believing, as one put it, "that pacifists are worthless cowards, and that walking away from a fight is cowardly as well." I recently had an ex-Marine who had served two tours in Iraq, an angry-looking young man who had joined up when he was seventeen and was still trying to process his experiences seven years later. He had come to the conclusion that the war was a playground for politicians and CEOs and a disaster for everyone else, but he was proud of his unit and, like most of the other students, he was vague about alternatives to violence.

The most common view of entering students is that nonviolence is irrelevant. "When I came into this course," one student wrote at the end of the semester, "I had a rather odd misconception that being non-violent meant having a lot of crappy bumper stickers on your car. Not much to it besides participating in a few peace marches that are largely ignored."

I start the course by asking students to define "violence" and "nonviolence." My students inevitably want to define violence extremely broadly, including emotional and spiritual violence and even the violence of ideas: "It seemed that by the time we finished our list even breathing could be considered a violent act," one student recalled. Nevertheless, allowing students to define their terms, even if they have to reconsider them later, seems to set the tone for the intellectual and personal engagement I expect of them throughout the semester. We look at what anthropologists say about aggression and cooperation in human nature, especially the work of Douglas Fry, who provides fascinating ethnographic, cross-cultural, and archeological evidence to support his view that humans, though capable of a great deal of individual violence, are not warlike by nature.[13] We look at the psychology of war, particularly the claim made by former army ranger and paratrooper Dave Grossman that humans are innately loath to killing their own kind, an instinct that accounts for the difficulties many soldiers have in firing during wartime,[14] even to save their own lives or the lives of their friends. We look at the roles of shame and humiliation in the decision to become a suicide bomber,[15] and question the common assumption that religiously motivated violence is unique to Islam. Students analyze and attempt to diagram in some way the dozens of causes of war that we've studied.[16] I remind them that they're not looking for the usual reasons for war that are given in history or political science texts: struggles over resources; differences in ideology; political and social repression; self-defense; and so on. Such "reasons for war" assume that, at least in some instances, war is necessary and right, whereas I want them to question why we resort to organized killing to solve those conflicts at all.

We look at some of the personal effects of current wars: the shocking suicide rate among military personnel, the physical maiming of combatants and civilians on both sides that is so carefully kept from the public eye, the trillion dollars that could have been put to better use,[17] the psychological numbing we experience toward violence we neither see nor fear. Leaked videos of recent military strikes, complete with video game–type commentary—the laughing and joking about driving over bodies, the "wasting" of people running for cover,[18] bring the reality of modern warfare into the classroom.

Once students have an understanding of how violence can be defined, understood, regulated, promoted, and justified, we turn our attention to alternatives. We explore how addressing spiritual and other "core values" of groups engaged in peace negotiations can help break an impasse.[19] We look at teachings of nonviolence in various religions—not just Christianity, although that tradition has the most extensive and striking literature, but also Judaism, Islam, Hinduism, Jainism, Buddhism, Confucianism, and some Native American spiritual practices. Discovering commonalities and differences among faiths can get students talking in ways they rarely do in other classes. One semester I had two fundamentalist Christians, one Sufi Muslim convert, five Jews ranging from Orthodox to Reform to Secular, and one Russian Orthodox, with the remaining students defining themselves by their politics and personal ethics rather than any particular faith. Since I want students to speak from their own experience and knowledge as well as from their understanding of the texts I assign, it was not unusual for one of the Christian fundamentalists to whip out his pocket Bible to explain why the world would be more harmonious if we all accepted Christ as our personal savior, or for a conservative Jewish student to invoke Zionist principles to justify Israeli settlements in Palestine, or a Muslim student to argue that men and women are considered equals in Islam. Although these discussions can be charged and difficult at times, I encourage them, first because they expose students to points of view they may never have considered before, and second, because there are so few venues on campus where such opinions can be aired without disintegrating into loud, angry denunciations of the opposition.

Having a relatively safe space to listen and be heard can give students the courage to confront their own unacknowledged tendencies to dismiss, devalue, or fear other people. A reflective Jewish student writes at the end of the semester that she was barely aware of how her "us and them" thinking began:

> Perhaps it was my education in Hebrew school, learning that Israel was surrounded by Arab neighbors who disliked Israel's existence. Maybe it was the fear in my parents' voices when they discussed the suicide bombings by Islamic extremists in Israel and their concern for our family living there. Perhaps this image was perpetuated by the events of 9–11 and the anti-Arab sentiment of the U.S. When our class began discussing religion, I didn't know anything about Islam. I didn't care to understand a religion that preached that becoming a suicide bomber would guarantee you a spot in heaven surrounded by virgins. I was shocked to discover that *jihad* is not a reference to holy war; rather, it means struggle or effort. *Jihad*, I learned, is divided into two struggles, the Greater Struggle to improve yourself and the Lesser Struggle to improve the world around you. What I knew of Islam was just a small extremist faction that has received much media attention. Ironically, the moment I came to understand the meaning of *jihad*, I was partaking in the Greater Struggle. I was actively breaking down perceived lines of separation, developing my internal nonviolence. This was the first time my beliefs were shaken and I was forced to question the values that I grew up with.

To help students talk openly about such emotional topics I introduce a model of dialogue called the LARA Method, which was originally developed in the U.S. civil rights movement and adapted for community discussions of LGBT issues by Bonnie Tinker of Love Makes a Family. The technique involves a series of steps: Listen, Affirm, Respond, and Add, that both students and instructor can use when discussions become contentious. Tinker explains the method:

> **Listen** behind the words until you can hear how a person of principle could possibly hold the view being expressed. Listen until your heart understands how what they are saying connects to something you believe to be true. Don't

say anything until you have heard this. **Affirm**, with the first words out of your mouth, that you share some principle or value with this person. Don't talk about the shared belief, but demonstrate it by using an "I" statement. **Respond** with a direct answer to the concern expressed. By not dodging the question or issue, you show that you respect the other person, and you show that you are not afraid of their opinion. **Add** some fact, or better yet, something from your personal experience, that gives some new information, or a different point of view. Repeat this process for as long as you are willing and able to engage with an open heart and clear mind.[20]

After students practice the LARA Method in class (generally using topics unrelated to the course) they can be reminded to use it later if their discussions begin to escalate. As Tinker says, "I can't claim that I use this method every time I am hurt, or angry about injustice, but I can say that I have seen amazing changes using this kind of dialog with a great variety of situations and issues. Using the LARA method is not so much an accomplishment as it is a practice."[21]

Although the LARA method is more difficult to practice than it might sound, the mere fact of having tried it seems to make productive discussion more likely. A student who had been skeptical of pacifism and critical of what she saw as easy, liberal solutions to complex problems writes at the end of the course:

> What made the class for me was my fellow classmates. We had such a dynamic group of people who learned to listen, to trust, and to cross barriers in order to communicate with one another on a deeper level of understanding and discussion. Hearing the comments of a variety of people coming from different backgrounds and experiences was incredibly refreshing and challenging. I was interested to hear people talk so passionately about philosophies I completely disagreed with.

At this point—about a third of the way through the semester—students are getting the idea that a peaceful, secure, and fair world cannot be achieved through the habitual use of violence. Yet nonviolence is still very abstract to them. Like the interview respondents, my students are quick to point out the obvious, that skill in dialogue, problem solving, intercultural understanding, and a just distribution of the earth's resources could lay the foundation for a nonviolent future. But these are long-term goals, they say, and violence is happening now. They envision a crisis: machete-wielding mobs attacking their neighbors; marauders on horseback raping defenseless villagers; or their own country's military gearing up for an "antiterrorism" campaign in yet another country that will inevitably destroy thousands of lives. What can possibly deter these madmen from violence but more violence, they wonder? Even when they see the circular nature of that position, it is not enough for them to hear that the world should simply quell the violence by creative, nonviolent means, since they don't yet know what those means might be. Their education, both formal and informal, has so neglected the range of diplomatic and political tactics that have been or could be employed to deter violence that they see no clear path to follow.

This deficit cannot be fully addressed in a single semester. But providing them with some examples of successful nonviolent movements and an opportunity to analyze their methods and tactics gives them a start on what they're looking for. For this section of the course I rely on a video series, *A Force More Powerful*,[22] which depicts, through news footage, interviews, and commentary, nonviolent movements in Poland, Chile, South Africa, India, and the Philippines, among many others. I also use videos from the series, *Eyes on the Prize*,[23] with its thrilling historical footage of nonviolent tactics from the U.S. civil rights era, and from *Chicano!*[24] a series that documents Mexican American activism in the 1960s and 1970s, particularly Cesar Chavez's boycott of grape growers in California. I also sometimes use chapters from Mary Elizabeth King's book, *A Quiet Revolution*,[25] with its story, always surprising to some, of the nonviolent philosophy and methods used by Palestinians in the First Intifada. Students meet in small groups for the three or four weeks that we devote to these case studies and look carefully at the goals, leadership, tactics, and cultural and historical context of each example, reporting on what they found and comparing them to other nonviolent movements they have studied. They read Gene Sharp's pragmatic analysis of the theory, politics, and tactics of nonviolent struggle,[26] as well as excerpts from Gandhi, Martin Luther King, and Cesar Chavez, all of whom emphasized the spiritual nature of nonviolent resistance and the ways it can transform both oppressors and the oppressed during the struggle.

Next, I introduce students to a few of the personalities of the peace and justice community both past and present, including Leo Tolstoy, Dorothy Day, Jane Addams, A. J. Muste, and Thich Nhat Hanh. We might read Art Gish's moving testimony of his experiences confronting the Israel Defense Force in his *Hebron Journal*,[27] and the frank confessions of Israeli soldiers and conscientious objectors in Ronit Chacham's *Breaking Ranks*.[28] We might look at stories from the international accompaniment movement in Latin America[29] and read blog posts from a former student who works with the Fellowship of Reconciliation protecting human rights workers in Colombia. We might hear from students or local activists who attend the yearly protest against the School of the Americas (now renamed the Western Hemisphere Institute for Security Cooperation) in Fort Benning, Georgia, whose graduates have participated in acts of extreme violence and repression in Latin America.[30] And if we're lucky, a former student might come back to talk to us about what it's like to work with an international peace team in Iraq, Sri Lanka, or Palestine.

In some versions of the course, students apply their knowledge of nonviolent theory to a current movement such as La Onf[31] in Iraq, or the more recent "Facebook Revolution" in Egypt, analyzing the tactics and philosophy, the leadership, the actions they have taken, and the apparent effects of those actions, and then evaluating the movement (respectfully, I always caution) from their new understanding of how nonviolent techniques have worked in other contexts. This challenging exercise, which is always preceded by group discussion and planning, sharing of Web resources, and peer feedback on drafts of their papers, helps students draw connections between theory and contemporary events.

In other versions of the course I have included a community action component, another way of addressing the gap between classroom learning and real-life experience. A few weeks into the course, students form small groups to plan projects that can be carried out on or off campus. Some of the most successful of these have included teaching some of the themes of our course to students in a local secondary school; arranging a peace art show on campus that included paintings, sculpture, visual media, and spoken-word performance; recording reminiscences of Holocaust survivors in an elder-care facility and presenting them to the campus community; and interviewing local peace activists, posting the transcribed texts on a Web site of the students' own design.

By the end of the course, most students feel confident and ready to put their new learning into practice. They are energized by video footage of successful nonviolent action; they are moved by testimonies of peacekeepers without arms; they ask themselves under what conditions they too would be brave enough to enter into a violent situation without the means to defend themselves. They completely give up their view of nonviolence as passive or weak. And students who had trouble defending their idealism from the condescending remarks of their friends find that their deepest beliefs and hopes for a nonviolent world have been given substance and dignity. A future teacher writes:

> I have always been a nonviolent person; I am highly sensitive and have a deep sense of compassion towards others. I had no idea there was a way to embody my values on a worldwide scale. . . . I had always been taught to believe that man was violent by nature, and therefore the idea that violence could be eradicated was preposterous. This course has taught me otherwise.

I have no doubt that humans are intelligent and courageous enough to address our differences without resorting to war. But to get there, we must convince young Millennials that peace is possible. High schools and even elementary schools need required courses in peace education that would teach nonviolent solutions to both interpersonal and international conflicts. Standard political science courses in universities should explain the major underlying causes of violent conflict: global inequalities, militarism, religious extremism, and disputes over dwindling energy resources, with special attention given to points of view of countries and individuals most directly affected by these problems. Courses in history and international relations should give central consideration to the extensive record of successful nonviolent activism, and these courses should challenge students to come up with their own ideas about how specific international conflicts could have been addressed without violence.

All these courses must be grounded in the personal: the stories, testimony, and deeply introspective accounts of the people we call friends and enemies. This is what touches students and gives them pause. At the end of my course, many of my students report that their new understanding of nonviolence has come to them as a meaningful, personal revelation. As one student wrote in her final reflection:

> I do not identify as a pacifist. But I do identify as part of the human race. And as such, I feel obligated to protect the rights of other humans. I am striving to see every person as human. I am striving to attain nonviolence within myself, for then I will be able to separate people from their actions and love my enemy. I have come to understand that nonviolence is not the absence of violence or even the opposition to violence, but something much deeper. It is actively refraining from violence; it is a way to bring about change; it is a conscious decision about my own actions; it is an attitude toward other human beings; it is an internal commitment to better myself. In my pursuit of knowledge, I can begin to think nonviolently. Because I believe that once peace is achieved internally, outwardly acting towards peace is inevitable.

Notes

1. A version of this chapter first appeared in Brecher (2010). Reprinted with permission from the publisher.
2. Peace Pledge Union, n.d.
3. See Ponchaud (1978); Chandler (1983). More than two million Cambodians were killed during the period of Khmer Rouge control (1975–1979), both by execution and by starvation and disease (B. Sharp, n.d.).
4. See, for example, Kurlansky (2008).
5. For summaries of many nonviolent campaigns see http://www.nonviolent-conflict.org/index.php/movements-and-campaigns/movements-and-campaigns-summaries.
6. See Sharp, 1973, for a catalog of hundreds of nonviolent methods that have been used in conflicts around the world.
7. See Tormey, 2004.
8. See Tanaka & Young, 2009.
9. Zinn, 2006, September 2.
10. Peace and Justice Studies Association, 2006.
11. See, for example, Workable Peace (n.d.), an innovative high school curriculum developed by the Consensus Building Institute and the Program on Negotiation at Harvard Law School.
12. See Freyberg-Inan (2003) for a discussion of the dominance of the "realist" school of international relations.

13. Fry, 2006. "The evidentiary base supporting the dark-sided, demonic view of humanity is in fact very limited," writes Fry (p. 5). Nomadic, egalitarian, hunter-gatherer societies, in which humans have lived for 99 percent of their history, do not seem to have engaged in organized warfare, that is, "relatively impersonal aggression between communities" (p. 91). This practice, Fry argues, began with the rise of complex, sedentary hunter-gatherer societies that created hierarchies based on wealth or heredity (p. 103).
14. Grossman (2009) presents evidence that "only 15–20% of American riflemen in combat during World War II would fire at the enemy" (pp. 3–4).
15. See Jones, 2006.
16. See, for example, Addams, 2002; Andreas, 2002; Chappell, 2009, 2010; Grossman, 2009; Hedges, 2002; Power, 2002; Reardon, 1996; Stramer, 2010; Thomas, 2006; Weiss, 2007; Wolff, 2006.
17. If I had a trillion dollars, http://www.youtube.com/user/IHTDVideos.
18. See, for example, McCord's Eyewitness Story, http://www.mediasanctuary.org/movie/1810.
19. Atran, 2007, August 24.
20. Tinker, 2006, April.
21. Ibid.
22. York, 1999.
23. Hampton, 2006.
24. Galen Productions, 1996.
25. King, 2007.
26. Sharp, 1973.
27. Gish, 2001.
28. Chacham, 2003.
29. Mahoney & Eguren, 1997.
30. Books and videos on these protests can be found at https://salsa.democracyinaction.org/o/727/t/10867/shop/shop.jsp?storefront_KEY=777.
31. La Onf, or "No Violence" in English, began as a peace movement in Iraq in 2005 when a group of local activists posed the question, "Can nonviolence be a tool for change in the midst of occupation, violence, and suffering?" http://www.warresisters.org/node/508.

Chapter 9

Visions of the Future

"I ask you, as people in power, to follow our lead. You don't need to lead, just follow us. There are plenty of us that will stand in front of you."[1] This is the voice of the Millennial Generation: brash, confident, optimistic, and outspoken in its idealism. Where are they taking us, we might wonder? How do Millennials, especially the most progressive among them, envision the future—both the future of progressive activism and a future society that embodies their notions of social justice? I talked to Mark and Soufiane, two student leaders whose visions of where we should be headed seem to resonate with so many of the Millennials I have taught in the last ten years.

Mark arrived in college with the first wave of the Millennial Generation, and developed his vision gradually, learning from his progressive peers, his adventures abroad, and his evolving relationship with activism. Always a philosophical thinker, yet craving human connection and deeply committed to an egalitarian global order, Mark envisions "an intimate kind of activism," rooted in local communities and connected across borders through the new technology and social media. When I talked with him he was about to leave for South India where he will spend a year doing research for a dual Ph.D. in anthropology and social work. He is interested in how activists in the Global South make ethical and practical decisions about strategy as they work to counter the negative effects of corporate globalization on their societies and cultures. He is intrigued by the camaraderie and alliances that South Indian activists have made with each other, and how they build their network of connections through list servers, social media, and international conferences. Whether they are fighting multinational demands for cheap labor, or teaching each other how to use open-source software, or trying to stop the World Tourist Organization from recognizing their region as its "destination of the year," with the environmental destruction and child prostitution that seem to inevitably follow it its wake, these activists are taking advantage of the speed and global reach of the new technology and the kinds of discussion forums they can provide.

"The new media are really changing the face of activism," Mark tells me. He is amazed and energized at the thought that there is a whole network of activists and researchers who are talking to each other all over the world, strategizing, coordinating, getting ideas from one another, developing relationships and friendships through their work. At a recent activist anthropology conference in Texas, Mark met a South Indian activist who turned out to be good friends with someone he had been chatting with extensively online but had never met in person. "The crazy thing is, the two of them go way back to high school," said Mark. "They both work in the state of Kerala in different locations and on different social justice issues. But they're talking with each other all the time. And they don't confine their activism to South India—the guy I met is also studying social movements in Bolivia!" Mark is eager to exchange ideas through these networks, both to learn from other activists and to contribute to the development of better strategy. "I'm not only interested in studying activists, but collaborating as an activist with the people I'm studying," he says. In his first year of graduate school he cofounded the group Ethnography as Activism in order to exchange ideas with people worldwide about how academic and activist work can be combined. "When I made the decision to go to grad school I realized

I only wanted to go the academic route if it was going make me a better activist," he says. "So I made a commitment that I would always use my academic knowledge to be a better ally, and to integrate activism into all my academic work."

Mark's interest in India began when he signed up for a study abroad program as a first-year undergraduate. "That trip didn't focus on social justice at all," he says, "even though it was led by former Peace Corps volunteers. But just by looking around, I was struck by the huge gap between people's life chances in that country and our own. I mean, yes, India is one of the economic powerhouses these days, but the level of poverty, especially among the poorest people, is astonishing to me. Families living in rags and filth, people with horrible deformities, lots of kids working—little kids! Teens who end up selling stuff on the street when they should be in school. So that started me thinking. I had come into college as a marketing major with the idea that international business would be the way I could do some good in the world. But once I saw the poverty over there, I started thinking that working in development could be more useful."

When Mark returned to campus, he joined an Indian American student organization that sponsored a variety of development projects run by Indian NGOs. The students were very critical of the politics of development assistance and the powerful global interests that set its priorities, says Mark. "And just by talking with them I had my preconceptions about how the world works challenged at every turn. I was pretty open-minded and quick on the uptake at that point, since I was so concerned about the inequality I had just witnessed. I could see how the World Bank, even though it has this big development face, can end up disempowering people, and how the international corporations that I thought would be so helpful in the Global South are actually responsible for some of its worst abuses."

The next summer, Mark volunteered to go back to India to do a promotional video to raise money for the projects sponsored by the campus group. "I learned a hell of a lot on that trip," Mark says. "I was riding the train all over the country carrying all this video equipment, and at each place I stopped I would visit two or three NGOs and find out about the work they were doing, and get them to talk about their programs on camera. And then they would invite me to stay with them, so I would hear all the scuttlebutt about development at the local level, which wasn't all that pretty either. Some of the NGOs were doing really good work, but I could see how difficult it was to make any lasting improvement in people's lives, given the corruption and in-fighting at the grassroots, and the power politics and financial interests of the big players who never even meet the local people, or who have never been to India at all! The NGO staff were really knowledgeable about all these complications, and they would give me books they thought I should read, and I would immerse myself in them on the train until I got to the next place I was supposed to film, so that whole summer was like an incredible crash course on third world social justice issues."

Mark's travels led him to the Narmada valley[2] where thousands of Indian farmers have been conducting Gandhi-inspired protests since the mid-1980s against a complex of megadams that are destroying their lands and livelihoods.[3] At the protest site one evening, Mark had a memorable conversation with Indian novelist Arundati Roy, a high-profile activist whose participation has brought the struggle worldwide attention.[4] Smoking a cigarette with her around a campfire in a rare moment of relaxation, Mark told her how inspired he was by the people's movements for a just society and how he was thinking of trying combine his interest in creative writing with some form of activism on Indian development issues. Roy bluntly told him to go home. "She thought I had too much of a salvation ethic," Mark told me. "She said, don't work here, basically. 'Work in your own culture, be an activist in your own culture. Indians need to work in India.'"

Looking back on that unnerving conversation, Mark thinks that Roy was right—up to a point. "It's true that I could do a lot of good work if I just restricted my activism to the U.S. and that it is ethical to think about activism in those terms," he says. "But the people of the world can no longer be so neatly divided into national or cultural categories as Roy was suggesting. What I've come to understand is that the problems in India have very much to do with policies of countries that make the decisions about how the global economy is run. Since the centers of power are in the rich countries, people in the less-powerful countries need to gain access to those power centers. So if activists on both sides can collaborate, the privilege and social capital that we have here in the Global North can be spread further."

But Roy's frank remarks started Mark thinking more deeply about issues of equality. "I had been thinking of social justice as something that only needs to happen in India," he says, "but that conversation really got me interested in what I didn't know, in any detail at least, about my own country." So when it came time to do his senior project for his social science concentration, Mark and a friend showed up in my office with the idea of making a documentary about homelessness in Ann Arbor. Despite the fact that they knew very little about the problem of homelessness in general or what local agencies were trying to do about it, they had been talking to the homeless men who hung around the student dormitories, warming themselves on the grates over the steam vents that emanate from central heating. And from these men they had learned that passersby would give them spare change at times, or buy them coffee or even an occasional hamburger, but few would look them in the eye, or ask their names, or inquire how they were doing. Fewer still asked their opinion about their predicament or listened to their stories without judging them. Mark decided that being despised and ignored might be even more of a problem than their lack of resources; it was an issue of human dignity. The documentary would be called *Listen,* he told me, and the only people in it would be the homeless and formerly homeless they had met around town.

"Making that film was a profoundly transformative experience for me," says Mark. "It got me thinking about the importance of community and the importance of human relationships. We were going around to all these sites where homeless people might be: the breakfast program, the soup kitchen, the woods behind the parking lot of one of the big box stores, the camps down by the river. And we were meeting all these different homeless people who had contacted us about being in the documentary and developing pretty close relationships with some of them. It was an intensely local thing."

Determined to make the film a collaborative effort, Mark decided there would be no voice-over, no explicit analysis or point of view offered by the filmmakers other than the choice of stories and their placement within the film—kind of unusual for a social science project, we decided, but interesting. As Mark and his collaborator began deepening their interactions with the people they hoped to film, they opened their house to them, sharing their food and, at times, the use of their couch. They spent weeks just getting to know people, fostering their trust and willingness to speak openly on camera. And indeed, they got some remarkable footage.

The film opens with Shawn, a disabled young man who has been sleeping under a bridge near the campus medical complex. A flashlight illuminates Shawn's face as he speaks frankly about what it's like to live amid broken glass, garbage, and human waste. "When you're homeless, it's like you're suddenly *silenced*," he tells the camera. "You're *invisible*. You *don't exist*." As he struggles up the steep hill from his den by the river to the road that winds around the U-M Medical Campus, the viewer is struck by the contrast between the massive buildings where he had been outfitted with devices to help him manage his disability and the only "home" he had to retreat to upon discharge. In other memorable scenes, men and women offer a wide range of stories and opinions about how they became homeless, what they think about other homeless people, and how they have been treated by the system that has been set up to help them—or make their lives more difficult, depending on their point of view. The film was a hit when Mark showed it in restaurants and cafes around town, drawing scores of community people, students, and even local government officials and professionals who work on issues of housing, addiction, and disability. After each screening, Shawn and other members of the cast would help Mark lead a discussion, answer questions, and talk about what should be done.

Soon after Mark graduated he went to work in Washington, D.C., with a documentary company that makes videos for the Bill Moyers show, quite an unusual opportunity for a young person right out of college. He was in the midst of making a video about the feminization of poverty worldwide, when a friend from back home sent shocking news: Shawn had died, probably by suicide. Mark was devastated. "For a long while I felt really guilty about just picking up and leaving town after creating such a ruckus about the homeless issue, and building relationships with all these people, and then—skat! I was gone!" says Mark. "It's true that the issue of global poverty had become very important to me. But our work was not the intimate kind of activism we had been doing in Ann Arbor." Shawn's death made him rethink his idea of the kind of community that activists should be creating and the importance of deep and lasting human connection with the people he was advocating for. "What made it really hard was that I had developed such a friendship with Shawn, yet I wasn't there for him when he died. I shouldn't have been just kind of zipping around doing this and that! I should be really valuing people."

Now, five years later, Mark's vision of Millennial activism has evolved from his early, naïve belief in the efficacy of any sort of "development" to a more mature understanding of the intricacy of such an endeavor: the power of global institutions and their distance from ordinary people's lives, the complexities of culture, the different ideas of "development" from the point of view of various individuals and communities, and the shortcomings of well-meaning programs, even those run by allies of the people at the grassroots. He is more likely now to see the local as a piece of the global, with actions of people and institutions all over the world shaped by the reach of powerful institutions, yet with the potential of intimate human connection. Though he has always believed that people should be responsible for one another, his vision of how those relationships should be forged and maintained is informed by work that at its best is "intensely local," as he puts it. Inspired by some Catholic Worker houses they visited, Mark and his wife have bought a house in a Detroit neighborhood that they hope one day to open up to like-minded friends and the residents of the surrounding community. He's thinking he might like to join the faculty of a local college or university and combine classroom teaching with "some new, more radical variety of service learning" that gets students organizing local people for economic justice. And he would like to see his students move beyond their discomfort with controversy and get them to listen more closely to arguments from all sides of the political spectrum.

"Undergrads tend to feel that 'what's true for you is true for you, and what's true for me is true for me,'" Mark says. "That way, everyone can just be satisfied with their own truth and not argue about it. That's what they think tolerance is: not being too loud with your ideas, not trying to persuade other people to look at things your way because everyone has a right to their own opinions. But I'd rather say that we *should* try to persuade others, especially when we think they're wrong. Tolerance should be more than live and let live. Tolerance should be about respect, and caring, and a willingness to listen, and a willingness—even an obligation—to try to influence other people. If we have an ethic of persuasion in the classroom, we can all hear a lot more good ideas, which can help inform our own choices."

Teachers should engage in persuasion too, especially on issues as critical as social justice. Neutrality in the classroom, though comfortable for Millennial students, is not enough. "I like to think that people need someone to challenge them," says Mark. "Someone to tell them, 'Hey, this is a problem and you need to be doing something about it.' Something to get them started thinking about why they should take it personally that the world is the way it is. And further, people need to know what I learned the hard way—that you have to change yourself and the way you see the world if you're going to be effective. If you want change, you need to live that change. You can't just do a project and then pick up and leave. You can't be satisfied with charitable works or with the feeling that you're on some high moral plane because of the way you're living your life. You need someone or something to make you feel that you're not so awesome for helping out."

* * * *

Soufiane's vision is more concrete than Mark's, though he shares his Millennial emphasis on the local and the search for authentic connection. He, too, is focused on building community: connecting with neighbors, promoting native ecosystems, and working for policies that support the health and welfare of the immediate environment. His ideas do not seem nearly as radical as Mark's, which are more about "ways to change the system without becoming part of it." But Soufiane's vision is perhaps more in line with the majority of his generation, who are loath to rock the boat.

"My vision is not necessarily about reinventing anything," he tells me. "It's about the positive local actions that friends and neighbors already engage in, and looking into how those activities can be encouraged and promoted, whether that's shopping at a local business or learning how to ferment cabbage and sharing it with your neighbor who's canning green beans or pressing cider. It's about people taking back their own power. It's about empowering individuals, it's about empowering communities."

Soufiane feels so strongly about getting people involved on a local level that while he was still an undergraduate, he ran for county commissioner—and won. "I come from a family of union organizers and industrial workers," Soufiane tells me. And on my father's side, my grandfather and grandmother both fought for the revolution against the French in Algeria. I've heard stories about how my family were guerrilla fighters, living in extreme poverty, surviving on next to nothing. These are the stories of my heritage, of who I am." He has only visited his relatives in Algeria a few times, he tells me, because the rise of religious fundamentalism in the region has made it dangerous to travel there and, at times, is very stressful for his extended family. "I know I'm very privileged to be living in Ann Arbor—of all places—living this lifestyle of peace and comfort and opportunity. It's kind of amazing, if you think about it. My dad used to herd sheep. That's what he did for a living. His family were farmers; they didn't have much. Understanding what they worked and fought for implies a good deal of responsibility. I'm not saying I was enlightened and like, awesome, when I came to college, but my mind-set has definitely been shaped by what my parents and grandparents did for their country.

Soufiane's vision of local activism was formed very early on. "I vividly remember back in preschool, my teacher arranged for us to adopt a portion of a creek so that we would learn to be 'good stewards of nature.' That phrase stuck with me," he laughs. "I use it all the time now when I talk with people about local environmental activism. Every day we would go outside and check on our creek. We would pull out the trash, and study the water bugs, and just enjoy the environment. Then later, in elementary school, we took our stewardship a step further by creating the Buhr Park Children's Wet Meadow Project, which was an effort to further protect our creek from excessive run-off and pollution from driveways and parking lots. We restored wet meadows to a park in the creek shed by putting in native plants that hold water and filter it through the soil before it returns to the river. I kept up that work all through high school, and I still volunteer with the project to this day."

Soufiane's vision of localism combines the old-fashioned idea of sharing your extra tomatoes with your neighbor and the latest techniques in urban planning that incorporate ecological principles into each new piece of infrastructure. He explains that because both of these actions—the personal and the professional—always start small, without challenging the economic system head-on, they can be attractive to Millennials, especially those who are either apathetic about activism or overwhelmed with the difficulty of changing entire systems.

Soufiane is not such a dreamer that he believes progressives should all just go back to the grueling lifestyle of our rural forebears, nor does he imagine a romantic future of urban spaces transformed into sustainable family farms where everyone eats, wears, and trades only what they grow. While urban gardens are important to his vision, and small farms that do business locally must eventually replace the corporate megafarms that are so destructive of the environment, he acknowledges that rural life is not for everyone. "We do need to be manufacturing products," Soufiane explains, "but they should be things that people can actually use. If we're all just exchanging stocks for a living, we're building a false economy. But at the same time, whatever we manufacture can't be at the expense of the environment or at the expense of the worker, which so often happens in the capitalist economy, at least in the way it is currently structured. In my view, manufacturing doesn't have to be huge plants where you make thousands and thousands of gas-guzzling cars every day. Manufacturing can be, 'Let's make strawberry jam at my house and then sell it at the farmer's market.' You employ maybe five people. That's manufacturing too." Eventually, Soufiane believes, localism will outmaneuver globalization. When people take back their power from the giant corporations, their personal, everyday decisions, their influence on local politics, and their sheer numbers will create more livable and socially just communities.

Soufiane is convinced that people will take to the idea of localism because, deep down, everyone is aware that the earth needs help and that their lives are shallow without the community that caring for it can provide. And everyone, regardless of their politics, wants to change the world for the better. "Acting locally is a positive way, an on-the-ground way, a way to get your hands dirty, to feed into that local network, to feel that sense of place, because it empowers you as a person and it empowers your community as well," says Soufiane. "It doesn't matter if your small, everyday action fails to transform the world, because even if you fail, at least you're part of a real community, not a strip-mall community. You develop real relationships with your neighbors. You care for your little patch of the earth. And through your daily actions you feel you are contributing to the social good."

Soufiane came to his vision of localism out of a sense of frustration that bordered on depression during his second year in college. He had arrived on campus a few years into the Iraq war with a strong antimilitarism ethic, and with a couple of friends, he started Anti-War Action, a student group that could draw fifty or sixty people to demonstrations and events and had a mailing list of several hundred—a decent number for a progressive Millennial cause. But the following year, students were becoming more apathetic about the war, and so many dropped out that the group could no longer sustain itself. "At that point, I really started to lose heart," Soufiane says. "My idealism and my energy for activism were starting to dissipate. People didn't care anymore. So what was the point?"

Aimless and dispirited, Soufiane moved into a student co-op and was going through the motions, taking courses, trying not to think about the pressing need to work on global problems, trying not to feel guilty that he wasn't standing up for what he believed in, when a small event prompted a sudden shift in his thinking. It was February, a miserable month in Michigan, with gray skies and bone-chilling cold. "Everyone in the co-op was sort of seasonally depressed," says Soufiane. "But then, one of my housemates suggested that we build a raised bed and lay out a plan for a garden. We live on about an eighth of an acre, very small. But the idea touched everyone, and we got to work finding the lumber, building some smaller planters, and figuring out logistics."

Soufiane got caught up in the excitement, though he still worried that planting a garden would be "too much like slacking off and hanging out with my friends." He is an activist at heart, he tells me, and this little endeavor made him feel like he was avoiding the critical issues, not really getting anywhere.

"But as the season progressed and we actually finished building the raised beds and put the soil in them and planted the little seedlings, I was like, 'Wait! We've created more than a few radishes and string beans. We've done something together that's meaningful to all of us; we've built a sense of community that's entirely different from what we had before!' Suddenly I realized that very little thing you do is activism. Activism doesn't have to mean sit-ins and big demonstrations. Activism is also planting a little basil plant next to your house. And through this realization I gained more respect for my peers who used to make jokes when I'd go to antiwar demonstrations, or when I got arrested at a sit-in at the president's office. I used to think my friends were being apathetic because they weren't yelling in the streets. But now I realize that in their hearts, my peers want the same things I do. They all want to see change. They don't like war. They favor some sort of workers' rights. I don't think anybody's going to say that people should be abused in sweatshops. Even though we may not all agree on the specifics, I think there are several overarching principles we do agree on: social justice, racial equality, and environmental sustainability—those three at least. And the environment is the easiest one to start with; it's an almost deceptively critical issue that we can start work on personally, at home. I think that's the future of what our generation's activism is going to be. We may not be taking on the abstract issues or the biggest problems to be solved, but we can go out in the backyard and actually make a difference."

"Well, yes," I thought cynically, "we can each plant a few rows of beans. But meanwhile, the greedy people are winning." I asked Soufiane whether he really thought that localism was enough. Backyard gardening can make us feel good, I agreed, and it's true that the community we create is better than the lack of community we felt before, but does this mean we should shift our focus away from the larger issues of justice?

"Of course not," Soufiane replies. "Each of us should do what we're called to do. If you're working on global issues, or if you express your activism through teaching, that's great, that's fantastic. But not that many people are going to devote their lives to social justice work. Most people aren't doing anything, and if people are going to take back their power—which is critical, I think—*everyone* has to do something. For people of my generation, especially, the environmental issue is a great starting point. If people can grasp on to environmental sustainability as something they can participate in, something here and now, something noncontroversial that doesn't require them to argue or convince other people or even think very hard, it's a step in the right direction.

"Here's an example," Soufiane continues, acknowledging my skeptical look. "A lot of people who I never would have imagined would get involved in social activism are getting into recycling. And I mean, that's *small!* But they're starting to feel like their actions can actually make a difference on a very local level. My own friends won't come out to a demonstration, even when they believe strongly in a cause, because they feel they're not going to see any tangible results. Even a march on Washington is not going to make a dent in government priorities, much less make the nightly news. Look at what happened in the run-up to the Iraq war, when thousands of people in this town, myself included, were in the streets, and there were huge peace demonstrations in cities all across the country. President Bush thumbed his nose at us! Or was he even aware we were protesting? The major media outlets don't cover nonviolent demonstrations, and even when they do, they're looking for that one out-of-control individual who is going to smash a store window or yell obscenities at the cops. Now, I personally believe that it's important to demonstrate anyway, regardless of whether we make an impact or not. But most people of my generation don't think that way. If there's no quick, tangible result, they get frustrated." Apathy isn't inherent in people, Soufiane insists. "People are only apathetic when they don't have a venue to express their activism. They will be willing to be active if you find the right way for them to get involved. And since environmental sustainability is something everyone can basically agree on, it's a good stepping-off point."

Once Soufiane came to a new vision of how local activism could lead social change, he found an academic direction as well. Soon to be a graduating senior, he is pursuing a degree in Program in the Environment with a focus on integrating urban ecology into the design of urban spaces. "When you're planning a new road, for example, you can make sure that road incorporates rain gardens and native plants, which work to alleviate a lot of ecological problems related to water and soil quality, air pollution, and the heat effects of urban areas. So by adding back some of the natural systems that have been paved over by traditional urban development you're creating healthier communities and alleviating pressures on human infrastructure. At the same time, you're setting an example for the more traditional developers. That way, you *promote* these changes rather than mandate them, which would require political pressure, community education, and maybe more activism than people have the will for right now. But the overall effect is still a more sustainable urban ecology that benefits both humans and the environment."

"So you're saying that by building sustainable urban areas, we can revive our connection with nature and with our communities, which is a positive end in itself?"

"Well, no cities can be made completely sustainable right now," he answers. "Even the most advanced technology won't stop the negative effects of humans on the environment. But if we look at the way the environment was before we started disturbing it so much we can improve upon technology. And while we're talking about reenvisioning cities and communities, we need to start thinking about human interactions in a different way. Like I said, we don't actually have to reinvent or redo anything. Whether it's buying apples from a country store, or persuading your favorite restaurant to feature great local food, or volunteering in a food co-op, or setting up a rain barrel to direct the roof run-off into your garden rather than down the sewer, that's how we can create strong local communities that sustain and nurture themselves. The way I see it, all progressive issues are interrelated. You can't have an environmentally sustainable community if you don't have an economically just community."

"Interesting. How so?"

"Well, if you want to cut down on the CO2 emissions coming from cars, you need well-functioning, affordable public transportation to link people to their workplaces. If people buy locally, they won't be paying so much for packaging and shipping and fuel, which makes it easier on their budget while reducing their carbon footprint. Plus, they will be contributing to the resurgence of small, family farms, which employ more people than huge agribusinesses. And on a larger scale, if we stop diverting our resources to military adventures, we not only free up a lot of money for social programs, we're protecting the earth as well, since wars are horribly destructive to the environment. If people can grasp onto the environmental issue as something they care about and can do something about on a very small, very personal level, they are more likely to see the connections to larger issues. Planting a cabbage in your backyard may seem like a distraction, but I think it's a step in the right direction."

Soufiane tells me that he used to think that social change could only happen if a lot of people could be persuaded to take coordinated action, whether it was massive street protests, or signing online petitions, or just voting for a particular candidate or party. Now, the way he's thinking, "Anyone can do their own thing to the extent they're willing to, and as long as they feel everyone else has the potential to act, there's a feeling that we're all in this together, and we're all fighting for the same basic things. Then, as more people take individual action, people will begin talking to each other: 'I planted my raised bed, and now I'm going to come and talk to you about that raised bed,' and suddenly we build an interpersonal relationship, and eventually, we become part of a movement. So we can think of a whole slew of simple, personal actions as fruitful beginnings of both personal empowerment and the start of collective action. When I put a tin can into a recycling bin, when I volunteer with a group once a year to clean up the local river, when I walk over and talk to my neighbor about how she set up her rain barrel and how I might be able to do it too, all these small actions can grow into larger ones. So it's not about everybody getting out into the streets and holding a sign and saying 'Down with the president.' Maybe it's more about everybody changing the way they're living, and realizing that change is part of a larger context. This is the future of what our generation's activism is going to be. You go out into your backyard, and you actually make a difference. That's your space. Go ahead and do it!"

Soufiane envisions personal, individual activism as a way to awaken people's consciousness about local democracy and, eventually, to a deeper understanding of the underlying issues of equality that are central to a sustainable world. "People are remembering that the government is a body of individuals elected by the people," he says. "*We* are the government. Everybody who votes, everybody who participates, everyone who gets out there, whatever they're doing, they embody their local government. The national government is somewhat more disconnected. But on a local level, the individual who plants a raised bed could also make sure that their local government puts in a green roof on their next building, or that the city acts responsibly when it purchases its employees' apparel. And once you have your local government buying its uniforms from unionized factories, they're setting an example for other municipalities. These small actions are something everyone can do; something that's totally possible, totally do-able. So when you act locally, you're not getting discouraged and cynical the way you might if you're trying to act at a national or international level. If I'm trying to save the world and it doesn't happen, well, I'm going to get pretty disheartened. But if I try to get my local government to do something progressive, it's a lot easier. And in the end, if it doesn't work, it's not that big of a loss. You can just go back to your city council and try something else.

"It's like the concept of needing to find inner peace before you can work effectively for world peace," he explains. "You need to make your community a better place before you can make your state, or nation, or world a better place. Once we sustain a vibrant community where people know each other and interact with each other, where a friendly exchange of knowledge and goods and services can be fostered, then we can expand outward. And I think that at the heart of every interaction should be the belief that everyone has the same desire for basic rights and equalities. We're all human, and we're all in this together, and there's a sense of empowerment even in that."

* * * *

It is strange and wonderful that the visions of these young Millennials are so similar to that of the ninety-six-year-old Detroit activist and "movement elder," Grace Lee Boggs, even though, as these students tell me, they are not that familiar with her work. But maybe this is not such a coincidence after all. Born in 1915, Boggs is a member of the G.I. Generation, whose profile, according to Howe and Strauss, is strikingly similar to the Millennials. Both "comprise a 'Hero' archetype, the kind of generation that does great deeds, constructs nations and empires, and is afterward honored in memory and storied in myth."[5] Perceived at the time as "the best damn kids in the world,"[6] the G.I. Generation "cut trails and built dams during the Great Depression, landed on beachheads in Normandy and Iwo Jima, built Levittowns, conquered polio, built gleaming suburbs and interstate highways, landed astronauts on the moon, and held the White House for a record thirty-two years."[7]

Like the Millennials, Grace Lee Boggs's generation was seen as "special" from birth, "protected from harm, pressured to behave, prodded to achieve."[8] Like other "Hero" generations, the G.I. Generation arrived "just after an era of society-wide upheaval in values and culture,"[9] and became "the target of passionate adult efforts to encircle and protect the childhood world, to promote child achievement, and to attach a new sense of destiny to youth—to which it [responded] by meeting and beating adult expectations."[10] Popular children's literature of the day (*Pollyanna; Little Orphan Annie*) depicted the ideal child as "modest, cheerful, helpful, and deferential to adults,"[11] just like young Millennials. A new emphasis on conformity brought the first summer camps, where children rose early, saluted the flag, spent the day in healthy group activities, and drifted off to sleep to the sound of "Taps." The first Boy Scout and Girl Scout troops, Camp Fire Girls, and 4-H Clubs were formed then too, exhorting children to do their best and "be prepared" to "become productive citizens and give happiness to other people."[12] Like the Millennials, Boggs's generation thrived under all this molding and shaping, and it grew up markedly healthier, better educated, and more optimistic than their parents. Separated by a span of about sixty years,[13] both generations are passionate, energetic, idealistic, and socially progressive for their times. So perhaps we should not be surprised if we find similarities in their visions of a just society. "I have learned over the years that *when* you become a radical usually decides your politics," Boggs remarks.14

Born above her father's Chinese restaurant in Providence, Rhode Island, in 1915, Grace Lee Boggs has lived through the highs and lows of the twentieth century. In her recent book, *The Next American Revolution*, Boggs reminisces that during her lifetime, she has seen two world wars, the Great Depression, the rise and fall of Fascism, Nazism, and McCarthyism, the horrors of the Holocaust, the invention of atomic weaponry, and the protracted, bloody conflicts in Korea, Vietnam, Iraq, and Afghanistan. Yet during that same period, she has also participated in many of "the great humanizing movements of the past seventy years": the civil rights struggles of every group of color, the antiwar and antinuclear movements, the rise of black power, and the fight for labor rights, environmental justice, and women's liberation. 15 Each of these movements has been "a tremendously transformative experience" for her, expanding her understanding of "what it means to be both an American and a human being," while challenging her to deepen her thinking about how to bring about radical social change,16 especially in her hometown of Detroit, "the city that was once the national and international symbol of the miracle of industrialization and is now the national and international symbol of the devastation of deindustrialization."17

Grace Lee Boggs arrived in Detroit in the 1940s, a philosophy Ph.D. in hand, inspired by the labor struggles that were convulsing the city, and attracted to the intense intellectual discussions of black power and of a humanist version of Marxism that focused on the "spiritual as well as the physical misery of capitalism,"18 and envisioned the oppressed "not mainly as victims or objects, but as creative subjects."19 An activist for seven decades in the black community, Boggs has seen the rise and fall of Detroit's famed auto industry and the disappearance of factory work from the American scene through high-tech automation, outsourcing, and a "free market" foreign policy that puts profits before people the world over. She warns that "our heedless pursuit of material and technological growth has created a planetary emergency"[20] that can only be overcome if we are able to move beyond the hierarchal societies of the past that were built by domination of peoples and the destruction of the earth, and transform ourselves into global citizens who are loyal to mankind as a whole.

Like Soufiane, Boggs sees localism as the wave of the future. Faced with the ravaged city that Detroit has become, with its deserted factories and crumbling homes, stretches of vacant, overgrown land, and "food deserts"—neighborhoods where junk food and out-of-date canned goods are the only available nourishment—Boggs advocates "a whole new form of solidarity economics emphasizing sustainability, mutuality, and local self-reliance."[21] Always positive and enthusiastic in the face of immense challenges, Boggs notes that local environmental activism has already made headway amid the ruins of Detroit: "All over the city there are now thousands of family gardens, more than two hundred community gardens, and dozens of school gardens" as well as "garden cluster centers" where people share ideas, organize garden workdays, and exchange information about how to grow and sell organic, home-grown produce.[22] These kinds of local initiatives are not confined to Detroit, or even to U.S. inner cities, Boggs emphasizes. Initiatives such as the World Social Forum, a loose network of activists who are working on thousands of social justice issues worldwide, are inspiring local people to work out their own visions of decentralized, radically democratic, self-sustaining communities.[23]

Like her contemporary, Paulo Freire, Grace Lee Boggs envisions local activism and an expanded, more participatory democracy as great humanizing forces, creating "*more human* human beings and *more democratic* institutions."[24] Like Mark and so many other progressive Millennials I talked to, she stresses the importance of networking with people around the world, deep, authentic relationships with the community at home, the end of top-down, patriarchal philosophies and leadership models, and a move toward decentralized leadership, multiple alliances, and wide-ranging connections through the new technology.[25]

Activists in this "new American revolution" need to go beyond protest and negativity, says Boggs, and concentrate instead on "building community"—the buzz phrase, if there ever was one, of the Millennial generation. Like Justin, the Chinese American campus leader in chapter 7, Boggs believes it is time progressives of color move beyond victimization, identity struggles, and ethnic pride[26]—important as these ideas were in righting great wrongs and humanizing our society overall—and come together in deeply interconnected multicultural communities where "European Americans . . . embrace their new role as one among many minorities constituting the new multiethnic majority."[27] Like Soufiane, who believes so strongly in people's participation in government, Boggs affirms that local involvement is essential, both because it rebuilds communities that have been destroyed by global capitalism and because community engagement is an affirmation of the people's power. We have been pursuing our own individual interests, our own private happiness, acting like consumers instead of responsible citizens, she says. And in doing so, "we have left the job of governing to our elected representatives, even though we know that they serve corporate interests and therefore make decisions that threaten our biosphere and widen the gulf between the rich and poor both in our country and throughout the world."[28]

Like Soufiane and his Millennial peers, Boggs sees traditional protests as having limited value, even when they grow to a massive scale. "[Protests] may demonstrate we are on the right side politically, but they are not transformative enough," she says. They don't sufficiently address the crisis we face.[29] And like Mark, who is convinced that "people need someone to challenge them, someone to tell them, 'Hey, this is a problem and you need to be doing something about it,'" Boggs confirms—more eloquently—that "[each] of us needs to stop being a passive observer of the suffering that we know is going on in the world and start identifying with the sufferers."[30]

What joins these two generations historically, other than the similarities in their personalities, character, and vision? Is it simply that U.S. society cycles through a predictable set of experiences, parenting styles, and responses to stress and upheaval, as Howe and Strauss suggest? While it is intriguing that Hero archetypes have appeared once every four generations since the seventeenth century,[31] I think Boggs would find more meaning in the idea that her vision, and that of many progressive Millennials, does not just repeat progressive endeavors of the past, but chronicles an evolution of human society, each generation moving us a little closer toward radical equality and deeper, more human connection. While the "great deeds" of Bogg's "Hero Generation" chronicled by Howe and Strauss—raising the flag at Iwo Jima, building "gleaming suburbs" with their network of superhighways—may not seem like progress toward social justice goals from today's perspective, I believe those efforts have moved us further along that path. World War II, though immensely destructive of human life, built consensus for a universal declaration of human rights, more certainty that genocide is the world's business, and that wars of aggression and expansion should not be pursued or celebrated, even if we have yet to discover effective means of putting these convictions into practice. Although the gleaming suburban neighborhoods, generously subsidized by the federal government, were bastions of racial exclusion, they did provide comfort and a taste of luxury to countless working-class white families and set new goals and standards for the civil rights struggles to come. And for the most progressive of Boggs's generation, the energy of their pampered youth and their outrage at the injustices of the day created the impetus and drive for the great, "humanizing" social movements of her long lifetime.

Today's Millennial college students, whatever their politics, are building on past struggles in the same way. Though their sense of history may not be very deep or accurate, their understanding of injustice is shallow, and their focus is on living out their own special dreams, they take for granted what older generations found radical: a world where love knows no boundaries of race or gender, where skin color does not foretell a person's success, where global poverty is an atrocity requiring their immediate attention, and where ideally, at least, conflicts between human beings should not be solved by war.

Despite their egalitarianism and social justice leanings, most Millennial college students are not the traditional leftists of previous generations: they are less overtly political, less confrontational, less certain of what they want to change. Theirs is a humanist vision; they find it natural that all people, everywhere, have common needs and desires: fairness, human kindness, participation, and a sense of belonging. Unlike the radicals of Grace Lee Boggs's generation, many Millennial college graduates, even the most progressive among them, lack a lifelong commitment to work in the people's interest, for a life of indulgence is more available to this generation than it was to the progressives of the past. Millennials care about their environmental footprint, yet most do not believe so strongly in localism that they would sacrifice the chance to see the world, especially since their idea of travel goes way beyond the college road trip of previous generations: snowboarding in the Rockies, working for a few weeks on an organic farm in New Zealand or Patagonia, or buying a one-way ticket to Thailand just to see it, and stopping off in Nepal to "do Everest Base Camp" along the way.

With good teaching and significant opportunities for community engagement, independent exploration, and learning from their peers, Millennial college students do become aware of structural inequalities and the powerful interests that keep an unfair system in place. But as a generation, most Millennials have too much trust in their mainstream elders, too much faith in the perfectibility of the system to challenge it directly or to radically rethink how the world could work. While they may take up the leadership banner with confidence and flair, their vision is not so much an end point or a promised land as it is a process, a general direction, a style, a way of being and living that is flexible and open to change. On this point, I think Paulo Freire would approve: As humans, we have a restless curiosity, Freire says. "One of the best ways for us to work as human beings is not only to know we are uncompleted human beings, but to *assume* the uncompleteness. . . .We have to become inserted in a permanent process of searching."[32]

Notes

1. Anna Marie Murano, addressing the Board of Trustees at Evergreen College (*Cooper Point Journal,* 2011, May 12). While Murano's issue, divestment from Israel, is more radical and her methods more confrontational than most Millennials are comfortable with, her confident assertion of Millennial leadership is classic.
2. Friends of River Narmada, n.d.

3. Photos of these protests can be viewed at http://www.narmada.org/images/dharna2006/dharna.html.
4. For Roy's take on the Narmada Dam project, see Roy (1999, April), http://www.narmada.org/gcg/gcg.html.
5. Howe & Strauss, 2000, 326.
6. Ibid., 326.
7. Ibid., 325.
8. Ibid., 326.
9. Ibid.
10. Ibid., 328.
11. Ibid., 330.
12. http://www.usscouts.org/advance/boyscout/bsmotto.asp.
13. The G.I. Generation was born between 1901 and 1924; the Millennials came on the scene in 1982. Howe & Strauss, 327.
14. Boggs, 2011, 57.
15. Ibid., 29.
16. Ibid.
17. Ibid., 106.
18. Ibid., 60.
19. Ibid., 59.
20. Ibid., 32.
21. Ibid., 29.
22. Ibid., 125.
23. http://fsm2011.0rg/en.
24. Boggs, 2011, 51.
25. Ibid., 42.
26. Ibid.
27. Ibid., 30.
28. Ibid., 35.
29. Ibid., 36.
30. Ibid., 34.
31. Howe & Strauss, 326.
32. Horton & Freire, 1990, 11.

Chapter 10

The Soul of a Great University

In 1943, Mark Van Doren, Shakespearian scholar, English professor, literary editor of *The Nation*, and Pulitzer Prize–winning poet, was asked by the Association of American Colleges to write a treatise on liberal education. The end of the war was not yet in sight, and young men had been called to battle, so undergraduate education in the nation's colleges and universities had been almost completely suspended. This pause in the educational enterprise gave scholars the opportunity to reflect on the kind of education that might someday be restored in American colleges, as it was widely believed that they had strayed from their original mission, and improvement was long overdue.[1]

Van Doren's *Liberal Education* is written in the languid, expansive style of a man who is used to expounding on ideas in comfortable drawing rooms surrounded by other learned men who do not interrupt or argue with him.[2] He has taken a high, moral tone deliberately, he tells us, because "the mainspring of education is always somehow moral," and because he is interested in "what is good for men."[3] Despite his rambling exposition, replete with references to philosophers of the past, Van Doren's idea of a liberal education is not as vague as it might seem. It is a specific discipline, he says, with rules and an "inescapable content."[4] Its best practice harkens back to an earlier era, when students and teachers took the Classics more seriously, believing, as Van Doren does, that ancient literature is "the heart of what we need to know."[5] He laments the failure of his contemporaries to impart a love of Latin and Greek, whose study has "dwindled to a literary piddling." Schools seem to have forgotten the reason an educated man should read them fluently: these were the languages "that were used to give an account of the world, the clearest and the grandest that we have."[6]

In addition to the Classics, English literature and the humanities would have a central place in Van Doren's liberal curriculum, for "poetry, story, and speculation are more than pleasant to encounter; they are indispensible if we would know ourselves as men."[7] Science should not be neglected, he says, despite the narrow world it inhabits and the overweening importance it accords itself. The Greeks, after all, were scientists. But they were logicians and observers of natural phenomena, surely not technicians. "By science, of course, is not meant the technological religions which now fight one another for a following," Van Doren cautions. Science in its purest form is a method of thought that requires careful cultivation of the mind. It should therefore be included in the humanities, since "science is knowledge, and knowledge cannot be inhumane."[8]

Van Doren's conception of liberal education would not be complete without "training in the moral virtues," though he admits that this task is more difficult than it was in the days of the ancient Greeks, when "philosophers could count on a quick and natural understanding of what they meant by 'right reason'"—that is, "universal notions of right and wrong, good and bad, the becoming and the unbecoming."[9] At any rate, morality should not be taught deliberately, since "a consciously cultivated character is an intolerable thing";[10] rather, it should be allowed to arise naturally from rigorous intellectual training. Van Doren quotes Pascal: "Let us endeavor then to think well; this is the principle of morality";[11] and Whitehead: Education is an art that may convert "the knowledge of a boy into the power of a man."[12]

To these noble ends, Van Doren lists 110 "great books" that might comprise a liberal arts curriculum, as indeed they did at "one contemporary college whose entire effort is concentrated upon reading [them]": St. John's College in Maryland.[13] The list draws heavily on the ancient Greek tradition, though it also calls upon many later authors: Shakespeare, Chaucer, Montaigne, and Milton; the United States Constitution, Tolstoy's *War and Peace*, Darwin's *Origin of Species*, Marx's *Capital*, Freud's *Studies in Hysteria*, Mill's *On Liberty*, Bertrand Russell's *Principles of Mathematics*, and of course, the Bible, in its entirely. Such great works, Van Doren assures us, "are more essential to a college than its buildings and its bells, or even perhaps its teachers; for these books are teachers from which every wise and witty man has learned what he knows."[14] The common possession of the experience that the great books offer would "civilize any society,"[15] reason enough, in Van Doren's view, to place the Classics at the center of the college experience, especially at a time when America was emerging as a world power. But in order for students to study these books well, the faculty—all of them—should know them intimately, for in the ideal college there would be no departments or specialties; every professor would teach the seminars where the books are discussed. Ideally, students and faculty should also learn the languages in which these books were written: Greek, Latin, Italian, Spanish, French, German, and Russian, as well as the languages of science and mathematics, though such extensive study, Van Doren admits, would be so formidable as to be impractical. Fortunately, excellent translations are available. "The better a book," he assures us, "the more meaning it keeps in translation."[16] Such a curriculum, rigorously and sensitively applied, would mold students into cultivated men who would be ready with a quote at just the right moment in their conversations with other, similarly educated men, for "the great books are the source from which wit and humor come"; they are the "headwaters of sense, and the reference when we are wise."[17] And more than that: their study not only makes the man, it exalts him; he becomes a higher form of humanity, "more human than he was."[18] Such was the thinking about liberal education in 1943, the year I was born.

By the time I enrolled at the University of California in 1960, higher education had undergone a radical transformation. At Berkeley, Clark Kerr was presiding over what he called the "multiversity," a sprawling knowledge-producing complex where the ivy-shrouded undergraduate classroom that Van Doren so admired had been all but swallowed up by "institutes and ever more institutes," huge laboratories and research libraries, and ever-expanding numbers of departments, programs, and professional schools, each with their own aims, interests, courses, and specialized faculty. The multiversity was no longer a community of masters and students, directed by a single animating principle—"a soul of sorts," says Kerr; it had become radically decentralized, each part communicating only fleetingly, if at all, with the rest. The multiversity is not so much an organism as "a mechanism—a series of processes producing a series of results—a mechanism held together by administrative rules and powered by money."[19] Kerr does not take a position on this extraordinary transformation—he speaks of it dispassionately, neither regretting nor welcoming it. In the expressionless language of the technocrats at the center of his impressive institution, Kerr tells us that the transformation of the university is "regretted by some, accepted by many, gloried in, as yet, by few. But it should be understood by all."[20]

The mission of this new kind of university was to "serve the needs of society" by spearheading the discovery of new ideas, new products, new techniques and processes of the kind that had served the American military so well during the war, and now would not only help the nation maintain military superiority but also power it into the future. Rather than devoting more attention to the wisdom of the past, as Van Doren had proposed, the multiversity was now focusing its vast resources on "knowledge production." New, "useful" knowledge is the most important factor in a nation's economic and social growth, says Kerr. In fact, he implies, if universities fail to produce socially and economically useful new knowledge, they are not true universities.[21] But despite the celebration of scientific and technological progress and the intense focus on research professors and their coteries of graduate students, undergraduate education was still a priority in American colleges. The GI Bill of Rights had doubled admissions, thanks to generous government subsidies for tuition and living expenses for returning military personnel.[22] Within a few years after the war, two million veterans had returned to school, a million and a half to colleges and universities, permanently changing the nature and social makeup of higher education's student body.[23] Youth—now including more women, working-class, and first-generation college students—all needed to be educated, but the opportunities to decipher the great books in their original languages had all but disappeared. The new knowledge was expanding so rapidly, and the number of college students was so vast, that the intimate seminars Van Doren had so passionately advocated were now almost entirely replaced by huge, impersonal lectures, with no time for questions and few opportunities for undergraduates to work out their ideas in discussion or in writing.

I feel no nostalgia, obviously, for the cloistered male classrooms of the past. And I have felt no need for the "great books" (though I have enjoyed many of them) to instruct me in witty remarks for cultivated company. Yet the multiversity did not suit me well either. As a young student at Berkeley, I felt alienated—not only from the massive university system but also from my own mind and heart. My discomfort, in part, was with the banking system of education: the droning lectures that professors rarely changed from year to year, the tedious internalization of the facts and specialized vocabulary of the various disciplines—though I had discovered I had a decent memory and found a sort of aesthetic pleasure in hand-copying my lecture notes to fix the "received knowledge" in my mind. But the symptoms of my malaise were closer to what physicist Arthur Zajonc felt as an undergraduate at the University of Michigan during those same years: an "unsettling disorientation and longing" for meaning and connection.[24] Zajonc says that he was experiencing what later writers would term "the soullessness of the university that no longer views one of its tasks as offering their students an education in the meaning of life."[25] That may have been true of me as well. But the intense focus on meaning that had characterized Van Doren's sense of a liberal education was not the answer. The life lessons that were so brilliantly elaborated in classical literature could not explain a world that had so utterly changed. Long-established power relations were shifting. Civil rights movements were challenging the racial order; labor unions were demanding equality for the working class; colonies of the "great powers" were fighting, both violently and nonviolently, for their independence. Long-established certainties about whose knowledge was worthy of study by the Western elite were being challenged by those who had been trivialized and marginalized. Yet this larger conception of the world with its focus on equality among peoples and cultures, its connections between academic and real-world knowledge, and its stories of oppression and liberation had not yet entered the mind-set or practice of the multiversity, whose main concern was scientific and technological progress.

In class, my head was filled with questions I could not ask and that most professors were ill equipped to answer. Why did my *History of Art* textbook begin with the art and architecture of ancient Greece, when anyone who read *National Geographic* knew that the artistic traditions of India, China, the Middle East, and Africa were far older and at least as interesting? Why did my psychology professor take for granted that research on American male college students could illuminate universal truths about human nature? Why did historians treat oral cultures with such distain? I remember a professor who claimed that history began when people cared enough about their own past to write it down—all else was "mere anthropology." Observing my surroundings at Berkeley led to other questions: Why was the campus overwhelmingly white? Why did so many California streets and towns have Spanish names, when one so rarely heard Spanish on the street? Why were men and women represented in more or less equal numbers as undergraduates, but women were so seldom seen in the "knowledge industry" at the graduate level? Why didn't my course in abnormal psychology help me understand the emotional distress of the autistic children I volunteered to work with each week, or suggest any teaching techniques that might reach them? What wisdom would give me solace when the car carrying one of these children—the child sitting placidly on my lap—tumbled down an embankment, smashing the child's skull, while I suffered barely a scratch? Such questions were not considered appropriate in classrooms where students were expected to absorb and repeat whatever new knowledge had been discovered by eminent scholars, and where any deeper meaning or connection to one's own life were the province of one's family or religious tradition, or left to the confusion and turmoil of one's own mind.

Despite my agonizing questions, I found much to love about Berkeley: the riot of flowers blooming at Christmastime, the neighborhood dogs that arrived each morning to splash and bark in the campus fountain; the apparently serious attempt by someone to outfit the dogs with little pairs of shorts, an expression, in hilarious metaphor, of the prudery of the times; the long walks I would take alone in the silence of the hills above the campus; the candlelight vigils against the death penalty on the steps of Sproul Hall; my long philosophical conversations with street people—the antimaterialist, countercultural beat generation—about the nature of God, the perils of the cold war, and the reasons we should all question middle-class respectability. In one exceptional speech class that I signed up for only because I wanted to avoid the long lines for first-year English, we read and debated a short, controversial book each week—Machiavelli's *The Prince*, Freud's *The Future of an Illusion*. For reasons that were never clear to me, this seminar was open to anyone—seniors, graduate students, freshmen like me, even street people, who could be quite interested. We wrote a lot, I remember, and we each gave one speech of our own design. The graduate student in charge of the class did not instruct us in the meaning of the texts, or tell us that our ideas needed refinement, or test us on our memory of the authors' arguments. The purpose of the course was to hear unusual points of view, say whatever we thought, and puzzle over challenges to the standard platitudes that we found we had accepted without question. Oddly enough, our experience in this class resembled, in some sense, the Classical idea of a liberal education. As philosopher Martha Nussbaum explains, "Greek and Roman Stoic notions of an education that is 'liberal' [is one that] liberates the mind from the bondage of habit and custom, producing people who can function with sensitivity and alertness as citizens of the whole world."[26]

Such opportunities to liberate the mind within university walls were few. But outside the classroom, a nascent "free speech" movement was beginning to take shape. The animating principle at Berkeley in the early 1960s—the "soul" of the multiversity, though Kerr did not recognize it—was the atmosphere of spontaneous discussion and debate that had sprung up on the walkways that led into the campus. Impromptu speeches would begin when someone—usually a graduate student or a member of SLATE, the political party promoting free speech on campus—stepped up onto a bench and launched into a passionate discourse on some political topic. A crowd inevitably would gather. After a while, another speaker would replace the first, sometimes to elaborate on the original point, sometimes to veer off in another direction entirely. I remember a young woman dressed in a modest pair of shorts and halter top asking the crowd if we thought it was fair that the Oakland police had picked her up, dressed as she was, for indecent exposure, and had taken her to the station house and lectured her on morality. The police were harassing women to keep them in their place, she said, just like they were harassing blacks in the South, and both were unconscionable in a free society. Such speeches would go on for hours, challenging prevailing norms, analyzing political events, and calling for radical social change. However, this liberation of the mind, especially in a leftward direction, was eventually deemed so threatening to the prevailing order that the university attempted to ban all unauthorized political activities. In the face of massive student protests, sit-ins, and the arrest of more than 800 students, Ronald Reagan, the new state governor, directed the Board of Regents to dismiss President Clark Kerr for being "too soft" on student protesters. "Liberal education" had clearly gone too far. But the Berkeley free speech experiment sparked student activism on campuses across the nation that continued for the next thirty years, taking on issues that ranged from black power, to antinuclear action, to women's liberation, to antiwar activism and environmental justice.

What are the "uses of the university," as Kerr phrased it, as it is organized and led today? Do universities exist to create useful new knowledge that will make the nation more competitive in the global economy? Do they aim for prestige through their high-profile discoveries and "star" professors? Is their purpose to produce legions of good citizens who actively participate in public life—or at least come out to vote? Or is their tacit goal to enable their most dedicated and high-achieving students to pursue lucrative careers in their own interest? Do they aim to develop "the leaders and the best," as the Michigan fight song goes?

Or do they simply want to make undergraduates into better thinkers and more interesting human beings during an interlude in their lives that will never come again?[27] On the other hand, maybe higher education has abandoned its mission to educate undergraduates at all and, through an unspoken "disengagement compact" [28] between students and faculty, has made it easy for both to get by with as little work as possible. Or, as increasing numbers of critics claim, have university campuses evolved into training camps that turn out docile workers with specialized skills, rather than critical thinkers, social critics, and more evolved human beings?

Clearly, it is not easy to discover the true aims of higher education or to discern the myriad and conflicting purposes the multiversity has taken on, much less agree about what its mission should be today. But as Van Doren notes, "Perhaps no age has thought its education good enough. . . . Twenty-four centuries ago, in Athens itself, the mother city of our mind, Aristotle could record a prevailing uncertainty as to what education ought to be." Because all people do not agree about the upbringing of the next generation, Aristotle says, "We cannot determine with certainty to which men incline, whether to instruct a child in what will be useful to him in life, or what tends to virtue, or what is excellent; for all these things have their separate defenders."[29] So it is in the age of the Millennial Generation.

Perhaps the twenty-first-century multiversity is by its nature so loosely strung together that it can accommodate a variety of aims and purposes. The Ann Arbor campus certainly embodies all the styles and convictions and interests that have animated higher education in the past, as well as new ones that are emerging in response to the exigencies of the economy and the habits and preferences of Millennial students. Undergraduates can choose among 200 majors or create one of their own design. They can delve into Van Doren's "great books" in the university's Honors program or they can decipher "new age business models" and "supply chain management" in the business school. They can specialize in a field as worldly as Actuarial and Financial Mathematics or as ethereal as Jazz and Contemplative Studies. They can prepare themselves for a career in dentistry, or pick up a certificate in elementary education or nursing or sports management. They can intern with a researcher in neuroscience or complex systems in hopes of joining the knowledge industry, or they can choose a major that prepares them for no particular vocation—English, philosophy, Japanese, or political science. If they choose classes in economics or sociology that promote mainstream political views, they can learn to become "technicians of social control," as Aronowitz says, "providing the scientific legitimacy for social, education, military and other areas of policy."[30] Or, if they are persistent and thorough enough they can root out the courses where competing ideas are taught: feminist economics, Gramscian cultural theory, studies of the African Diaspora, labor organizing. If they choose service-learning courses or small seminars they can link social and economic theory to their experience of the world and reflect on their own place in it. Or they can sit in huge impersonal lectures, like I did at Berkeley, read expensive textbooks, cram for multiple-choice tests, and improve their memories.

In addition to academics, students at Michigan, as at other multiversities, can choose from a remarkable array of extracurricular activities that have sprung up in the competition for undergraduate tuition dollars. There are hundreds of study-abroad options, opportunities to volunteer or intern, sports and games of every variety, musical, dramatic, and literary clubs, religious organizations, political parties, and social justice causes. U-M's online "Maize Pages" lists 1,263 student organizations, ranging from Forty Days of Prayer, ("a student-led organization whose aim is to promote unity among Christians at the campus of the University of Michigan") to the Zombie Club, whose mission is "to study and examine zombie characteristics, actions, motivation, and weaknesses in order to better understand the species in preparation for a zombie apocalypse." No country boasts such an array of academic and extracurricular opportunities, says Harvard's Derek Bok. "From computers to gymnasia to huge catalogues stuffed with courses, American universities vie with each other to meet virtually every legitimate desire that able young people can express."[31]

Even the look of the twenty-first-century multiversity reflects its multiple purposes and ever-expanding range of possibilities. At Michigan, ivy still covers the walls of the older buildings, whose tiny dorm rooms and funky basement classrooms still exude a certain charm. Next to them are the eye-catching structures that house the business school and its luxurious accommodations for international visitors. Further on is the law school, with soaring oak trees shading a sober quadrangle, and beyond that, the squat, concrete administration buildings, rumored to still house underground bunkers where officials can protect themselves from any student demonstrators, should the need arise. Across campus are the colossal science and medical complexes, with lavishly funded, state-of-the-art laboratories concealed within their featureless exteriors. The "institutes and ever more institutes" described by Kerr in the 1960s have proliferated even further; they are everywhere now: institutes for social research, for transportation, gerontology, nanotechnology, entrepreneurial studies, women and gender, global sustainable enterprise, and hundreds more, often with the names of their successful alumni benefactors prominently displayed above their doorways.

Spiraling undergraduate tuition seems to fund much of the multiversity enterprise. "Many have long suspected that the research universities may in fact subsidize their graduate research operations with undergraduate tuition," says Jennifer Washburn in *University Inc.*[32] At Michigan, "tuition now accounts for 70% of the university budget."[33] According to a report from the National Center for Public Policy and Higher Education, college tuition and fees increased 439 percent from 1982 to 2007 while median family income rose 147 percent.[34] Though parents fund their students' education when they can, most Millennials are obliged to borrow heavily, making them "the first generation of young people to embark on adulthood in debt."[35] As the costs of a residential education become more prohibitive, universities are putting more of their courses online, and, according to *The Chronicle Research Services Report on the College of 2020*, "the conversion to more convenience for students will multiply over the next decade." Students will be accessing their course material, their class discussions, their study groups, and even their professors from their cell phones and other computing devices.[36]

The newest and perhaps most troubling feature of the multiversity is its intimate relationship with the private sector. "Universities share one characteristic with compulsive gamblers and exiled royalty," says Harvard's Derek Bok. "There is never enough money to satisfy their desires."[37] After the collapse of the Soviet Union at the end of the 1980s, when Congress drastically cut government funds for academic "knowledge production" that helped the United States maintain military superiority, university presidents aggressively began to seek corporate investment. Today, there is no longer any clear boundary separating academia from commerce, says Washburn:

> Market forces are dictating what is happening in the world of higher education as never before, causing universities to engage in commercial activities unheard of in academia a mere generation ago. Universities now routinely operate complex patenting and licensing operations to market their faculty's inventions (extracting royalty income and other profits and fees in return). They invest their endowment money in risky start-up firms founded by their professors. They run their own industrial parks, venture capital funds, and for-profit companies. . . . The question of who owns academic research has grown increasingly contentious, as the openness and sharing that once characterized university life has given way to a new proprietary culture more akin to the business world.[38]

One might think this move toward the commercialization of higher education, as Bok puts it,[39] would have little impact on the lives of undergraduates, whose living, learning, and social activities take place far from the corporate board rooms and academic offices where these relationships are forged. But undergraduate education suffers from these new arrangements in countless ways. Since the days of Kerr's multiversity, when cold war research had become so highly valued, professors in science and business—and, increasingly, in tenure-track positions in any department—not only have been generously compensated but also have been relieved of any expectations to teach undergraduates or to teach them well. Between 1963, when Kerr first described the multiversity, and 1994, when he reflected on his tenure as president, the teaching hours of the research faculty had decreased by about half[40] while their pay had increased dramatically. The highest prestige is now accorded to full professors who snag the largest grants, publish the most papers, and forge the strongest connections with industry. Young tenure-track faculty devote their days and nights to research and writing—standard requirements for advancement—while excellence in teaching is seen as irrelevant or even as a liability. When teaching is neither fully recognized nor appropriately rewarded, there is little incentive for faculty to improve it. "How to escape the cruel paradox that a superior faculty results in an inferior concern for undergraduate teaching is one of our more pressing problems," said Kerr in 1963.[41] That issue has become only more critical today.

Administrators, too, have allowed universities to "drift away from an undergraduate instructional focus," replacing full-time professors with part-time instructors, and diverting resources toward nonacademic functions, including their own salaries.[42] "Cost containment" provides the rationale for devaluing undergraduate education. "The application of accounting principles to academic employment and planning is perhaps the most blatant indication that higher education is going corporate," says Aronowitz. Although graduate student instructors and non-tenure-track faculty often make highly effective and inspiring teachers, according to both student and administrator evaluations, they are poorly compensated (at Michigan, they often earn less than local high school teachers), and endure job instability and continual cutbacks in benefits, despite the ever-increasing undergraduate tuition. In addition, the traditional mainstays of liberal education—philosophy, languages, literature, and the social sciences—are declining while fields that make money, study money, or attract money are flourishing.[43] The result, say education critics Andrew Hacker and Claudia Dreifus, is that "higher education has lost track of its original and enduring purpose: to challenge the minds and imaginations of this nation's young people, to expand their understanding of the world, and thus of themselves....Campuses have become preserves for adult careers," and professors, administrators, and even presidents "have used ostensible centers of learning to pursue their own interests and enjoyments."[44]

Some critics go even further, charging that American higher education is now characterized by "limited or no learning for a large proportion of students."[45] According to a study of the data collected on more than 2,300 students across a wide array of campuses who participated in the Collegiate Learning Assessment, a "state of the art" measure of student learning, three semesters of college have a "barely noticeable impact" on students' critical thinking, analytical reasoning, problem solving, and writing,[46] skills that are highly valued among the nation's employers. Today's students are studying dramatically less, yet their reduced effort has "little impact on their grade point averages,"[47] and this, say the authors, has grave consequences for U.S. standing in the global economy. Even if one does not think that the purpose of higher education should be about maintaining world dominance, the meager intellectual gains many students make after four or five years of college can still be disappointing. Learning, says Stanley Aronowitz in *The Knowledge Factory*, "is the process by which a student is motivated to participate in, even challenge, established intellectual authority." The problem is not that U.S. students have lost their edge in science and mathematics; by allowing the university to turn into a "knowledge factory" we have declined the opportunity to creatively rethink the social and economic systems that produce inequality. "Possibilities for genuine social and cultural as much as scientific innovation depend, not on following others," Aronowitz says, "but on the formation of an autonomous self, capable of finding its own voice."[48]

All these criticisms suggest we should look closely at the essential purpose of higher education today, especially at the nation's multiversities. Should their mission simply comprise the vague conglomeration of interests, specialties, "client services," and opportunities for profit that the university enterprise has become? While this would at least be an honest statement of the status quo, it does not reflect the kind of commitment to education and intellectual discovery that we should expect from a great institution. To be sure, it is hard to rein in the complex "mechanism" that has characterized higher education since it began changing so drastically in the mid-twentieth century. The multiversity, Kerr said in 1963, "has demonstrated how adaptive it can be to new opportunities for creativity; how responsive to money; how eagerly it can play a new and useful role; how fast it can change while pretending that nothing has happened at all; how fast it can neglect some of its ancient virtues."[49] This disturbing statement, which has become an even more accurate description of higher education today, suggests we should consider revisiting the idea of an animating principle that might hold the sprawling complex together and infuse it with meaning.

There is nothing inherently wrong with universities serving multiple purposes. "Knowledge production" can be tremendously exciting and animating, and connecting undergraduate and graduate students with the exploration of new and difficult intellectual questions at the highest levels can set standards for superior achievement as well as help support inventions and creative ideas that might truly benefit society. For those who come to college for a wider-ranging intellectual exploration under the guidance of devoted faculty and advisors, the multiversity can provide an outstanding "liberal education" in the arts and humanities. And since so many students from modest backgrounds aspire to a college degree—a virtual requirement for any job that can support a family these days—many students and their parents prefer specialized training that leads straight to a respectable career; they may not see the value of challenging authority or becoming an autonomous intellect or a "citizen of the whole world" when such nebulous goals do not connect students directly with the job market.

The problem is not that all these functions have become housed in the nation's universities; rather, it is that the sheer size of multiversities and their unruly competition for prestige and profit have resulted in the exploitation of students, the lowering of educational standards, and the diversion of research and development from "serving the public good" to serving the interests of the privileged few. Without a way to hold the institution together, or to remind it of its potential as a collection of human intelligence and talent that could elevate rather than exploit society, the problems will only increase in the years ahead.

When Kerr first described the multiversity, he noted this lack of "glue" as a major difference from the small, sheltered communities of masters and students of the past. "A community should have a soul, a single animating principle,"[50] he says, but the multiversity can only be held together by its president, who is not always up to the task. Kerr described the role of the head of a multiversity as a "mediator," although the term seemed to confuse people, since it suggested "unprincipled compromise."[51] "I wish I had used a different word with different public connotations," Kerr said, "political leader, or community leader, or campus statesman, or unifier, or peacekeeper, or chief persuader, or crisis manager, or agent of integration—anything but mediator."[52] The term had led to no end of trouble, both with the activist students who felt Kerr was conceding too much to the demands of the state, and with the administration and the governor, who thought the opposite.

In his reflection written in 1972, Kerr elaborates on his own sense of the word "mediator" and the need for that role in balancing the competing aims of the multiversity's various constituents: "The tone should have been conveyed of active leadership, of statesmanlike solutions, of holding the campus together against internal and external attacks, of keeping the peace as against disruption, of using ideas and principles to bind the ties, of relying on persuasion rather than on force, of seeking consent rather than governing by fiat, of being the guardian of reason in debate, decency in human relations and sanity in action, of meshing together the discordant elements into a productive entity."[53]

As Kerr struggles to convey the skills needed to keep the multiversity under some semblance of control, he compares his role with that of the Clerk of a Quaker Meeting: "The person who keeps the business moving, draws forth ideas, seeks 'the sense of the Meeting.'"[54] But Kerr, himself a Quaker, does not explain what "the sense of the Meeting" means, or where it comes from, or what seeking it does for the body as a whole. In fact, Kerr doesn't mention the most distinguishing feature of the Religious Society of Friends, which is that meetings, either for worship, or for conducting the business of the institution, or for committee work, are all held together by a single animating principle, that there is 'that of God'—or that of the spirit, or the light—in every human being. By concentrating on that spirit, on the humanness of each individual, one is able, ideally, to hear conflicting ideas and opinions without rancor, and to make humane decisions in concert. In Quaker Meetings, as in Quakerism generally, there are no rules, no beliefs that members must attest to, no formal hierarchy, no pastor or preacher or any other "head" that can be called upon to settle disputes quickly and firmly. As a Quaker myself, and as a committee convener and activist member, I can attest that Quaker decision making and dispute resolution can be frustrating and time consuming and can call upon all of one's reserves of patience. But the successful practice of discerning the group's common feeling, spiritual insight, and intellectual position—"the sense of the Meeting"—allows Quaker Meetings to bring together the most intellectually diverse and independent-minded individuals to make deeply considered decisions despite their differences. Without that connection between people, without the conscious and continual practice of spiritual insight and clarity, Quaker Meetings could not function—or perhaps they would turn into a town hall meeting, or a session of Congress, or, indeed, a multiversity: a collection of individual ideas, interests, and political positions, all tugging at each other, "students versus faculty, humanists versus scientists, younger versus older faculty members . . . a Tower of Babel partially falling apart rather than being held loosely together."[55] As Kerr said of his university during the turmoil of the 1960s, "a narrow barrier of tolerance stood between peace and war . . . and when tolerance was gone, what had been unbroken peace became intermittent warfare."[56]

Obviously, the multiversity is not a religious institution, nor do I believe it should become one. But I do think it can be animated by a unifying principle that calls on the highest human aspirations and capabilities of all its members. Because of my experience with Quaker process, I believe it is possible for a multiversity to retain its hugely diverse and dynamic character, yet find a soul or animating principle that helps clarify its priorities and infuse its research and teaching with a larger purpose. Mission statements of large research institutions often mention that one of their primary responsibilities is to "serve society," or "promote the public welfare," or that the institution was established "for the benefit of mankind." But what if the university were to ask itself, "Which society are we serving? How much of society? How far does 'society' extend? Who benefits, and who suffers from our leadership, from our advanced knowledge, and from the ideas and inventions that we produce, preserve, and convey to the world?"

As human society advances, by fits and starts, toward respect for multiple forms of knowledge and equitable, dignified sharing among all people, the multiversity should aspire to lead in this direction rather than resist and lag behind. But such leadership would require us to know "who and what we are for, and who and what we are against," as Freire says. We would need to take a stand in favor of all the world's peoples, not just the ones who are most "like us," whether they be white Protestant males, as in Van Doren's day, or "the people who care enough about their own history to write it down," or the people whose creative genius has made them wealthy at the expense of the most vulnerable, or whose life of privilege has blinded them to suffering.

Once the university knew who and what it was for, and who and what it was against, its priorities would fall more naturally into place. With the mission of undoing inequality, oppression, exclusion, and injustice animating the soul of the university, its research, theory building, teaching, even its fund-raising and profit-making activities would incline more naturally toward a broader conception of the public good. We could not continue to pretend that the university excels in teaching while the majority of its undergraduates still sit in huge, impersonal lectures given by underpaid, undervalued faculty. We would consider small classes of the utmost importance for students at all levels, since it is there that they are most likely to engage deeply with ideas, explore complex social problems, question their own assumptions and prejudices, and find their own voice. We would consider a thorough understanding of race and class dynamics to be essential knowledge for all our students, whatever their majors or professional aspirations. We would foreground history from the point of view of the oppressed and excluded, and expect this history to be a vital component of our students' understanding of social and economic inequality. We would do more, consciously and programmatically, to bring the "periphery" of Millennial students who "care about humans in the abstract" into the smaller "core" who are beginning to understand structural forms of injustice and develop their own visions of a fairer world. We would provide students with significant intellectual, social, and cultural training in how to interact "in dialogue, hope, humility and sympathy" with people in oppressed communities before we send them out into the world. We would offer ample opportunities for them to disconnect from their personal technology, read and write with patience and care, ask themselves difficult questions, and reflect on the meaning of human suffering, including their own. In the end, the multiversity would agree with Van Doren that "the mainspring of education is always somehow moral" and that with deeply considered, critical education, students are capable of becoming "more fully human": wiser, more generous, more compassionate, more inclined to cooperate peacefully as equals, more able to withstand the storms of their inner life. As Paulo Freire, I am sure, would agree, a multiversity unified by a deep concern for social justice would prepare our Millennial students for their highest vocation: to work for a world of greater equality between peoples, a more just order among nations, "a world in which it will be easier to love."

Notes

1. Van Doren, 1943, vii.
2. Indeed, Van Doren mentions that he discussed these ideas in conversations with such luminaries as Mortimer Adler, Jacques Barzun, Joseph Wood Krutch, Lionel Trilling, and many others (ix).
3. Van Doren, vii.
4. Ibid., viii.
5. Ibid., 44.
6. Ibid.
7. Ibid., 51.
8. Ibid., 54.
9. Ibid., 59.
10. Ibid., 61.
11. Ibid., 63.
12. Ibid., 66.
13. Ibid., 149–50.
14. Ibid., 148. Van Doren acknowledges that the list is not necessarily complete and that it will need to be revised frequently.
15. Ibid.
16. Ibid., 153–54.
17. Ibid., 156.
18. Ibid., 17.
19. Kerr, 15.
20. Ibid., 1. In "Reconsiderations after the Revolts," written in 1972, Kerr complains that his message had been misunderstood; he was only describing and analyzing the multiversity, not approving or defending it (111).
21. Aronowitz, 2000, 30.
22. Returning servicemen and women of color, however, benefitted little from this kind of affirmative action, since most colleges in the 1940s did not accept racial minorities on principle (Katznelson, 2006).

23. Aronowitz, 27–28.
24. Palmer & Zajonc, 2010, 53.
25. Ibid., 54.
26. Nussbaum, 1997, 8–9.
27. Hacker & Dreifus, 2010, 239.
28. Arum & Roksa, quoting Kuh, 2011, 5.
29. Van Doren, 2–3.
30. Aronowitz, 4.
31. Bok, 2003, 23.
32. Washburn, 2005, 207.
33. LEO Matters, 2011.
34. Lewin, 2008.
35. Hacker & Dreifus, 238.
36. Chronicle Research Services, 2011.
37. Ibid., 9.
38. Washburn, xi–xii.
39. Bok, 2003, 3.
40. Kerr, 142.
41. Ibid., 49.
42. Arum & Roksa, 11–12.
43. Engell & Dangerfield, 1998.
44. Hacker & Dreifus, 8–9.
45. Arum & Roksa, 30.
46. Ibid., 35.
47. Ibid., 3–4.
48. Ibid., 144.
49. Kerr, 34.
50. Ibid., 15.
51. Ibid., 107.
52. Ibid., 108.
53. Ibid.
54. Ibid., 29.
55. Ibid., 98.
56. Ibid.

References

Addams, J. (2002). *Peace and bread in time of war*. Urbana: University of Illinois Press.
Andreas, J. (2002). *Addicted to war*. Oakland, CA: A.K. Press.
Aronowitz, S. (2000). *The knowledge factory*. Boston: Beacon Press.
Arum, R., & Roksa, J. (2011). *Academically adrift: Limited learning on college campuses*. Chicago: University of Chicago Press.
Atran, S. (2007, August 24). Sacred barriers to conflict resolution. *Science, 317*, 1039–40.
Boggs, G. L. (2011). *The next American revolution: Sustainable activism for the twenty-first century*. Berkeley: University of California Press.
Boggs, G. L. (2010, May 9–15). Living for change: We who believe in freedom cannot rest. *Living for Change Newsletter*. Detroit: The Boggs Center.
Bok, D. (2003). *Universities in the marketplace: The commercialization of higher education*. Princeton, NJ: Princeton University Press.
Bok, D. (2007). *Our underachieving colleges: A candid look at how much students learn and why they should be learning more*. Princeton, NJ: Princeton University Press.
Brecher, B. (ed.) (2010). *The new order of war*. Amsterdam; NY: Editions Rodopi.
Brindley, L. (2009, January 25). We're in danger of losing our memories. *guardian.co.uk*. http://www.guardian.co.uk/technology/2009/jan/25/internet-heritage.
Brodkin, K. (1998). *How Jews became white folks and what that says about race in America*. New Brunswick, NJ: Rutgers University Press.
Cellular-News. (2009, April 7). Survey finds Smartphones transforming mobile lifestyles of college students. http://www.cellular-news.com/story/36898.php.
Chacham, R. (2003). *Breaking ranks: Refusing to serve in the West Bank and Gaza Strip*. New York: Other Press.

Chandler, D. (1983). *A history of Cambodia.* Boulder, CO: Westview Press.

Chappell, P. K. (2009). *Will war ever end? A soldier's vision of peace for the 21st century.* Weston, CT: Easton Studio Press.

Chappell, P. K. (2010). *The end of war.* Westport, CT: Easton Studio Press.

Chronicle Research Services. (2011). Executive Summary. *The College of 2020: Students.* http://etcjournal.files.wordpress.com/2009/06/thecollegeof2020.pdf.

Collier, P. (2007). *The bottom billion: Why the poorest countries are failing and what can be done about it.* London: Oxford University Press.

Cooper Point Journal. (2011, May 12). Board of Trustees told to divest. http://cooperpointjournal.com/news/board-trustees-told-divest.

Democracy Now. (2010, June 24). 3 US soldiers speak out on McChrystal's firing, Petraeus as replacement, and the unending war in Afghanistan. http://www.democracynow.org/2010/6/24/3_us_soldiers_speak_out_on.

Democracy Now. (2010, July 16). The food bubble: How Wall Street starved millions and got away with it. http://www.democracynow.org/2010/7/16/the_food_bubble_how_wall_street.

Dennis, R. M. (1995, Summer). Social Darwinism, scientific racism, and the metaphysics of race. *Journal of Negro Education.* http://findarticles.com/p/articles/mi_qa3626/is_199507/ai_n8730395/?tag=content;c011.

Dobrin, S. I. (1997). Race and the public intellectual: A conversation with Michael Eric Dyson. *JAC: A Journal of Composition Theory. 17*(2), 143–81.

Dwyer, R. E. (2007). Expanding homes and increasing inequalities: U.S. housing development and the residential segregation of the affluent. *Social Problems, 54*(1), 23–46.

Easterly, W. (2006). *White man's burden.* New York: Penguin Press.

Einfeld, A., & Collins, D. (2008, March–April). The relationship between service-learning, social justice multicultural competence, and civic engagement. *Journal of College Student Development,* (49), 2.

Engell, J., & Dangerfield, A. (1998, May–June). The market model university: Humanities in the age of money. *Harvard Magazine.* http://harvardmagazine.com/1998/05/forum.html.

Farley, R., Danziger, S., & Holzer, H. J. (2000). *Detroit divided.* New York: Russell Sage Foundation.

Fenty, J. (1997). Knowing your students better: A key to involving first year students. Center for Research on Learning and Teaching Occasional Paper #9. University of Michigan.

Fiddler, M., & Marienau, C. (2008, Summer). Developing habits of reflection for meaningful learning. *New Directions for Adult and Continuing Education, 118,* 75–85.

Fischer, M. J. (2008). Does campus diversity promote friendship diversity?: A look at interracial friendships in college. *Social Science Quarterly, 89*(3), 631–655.

Fox, C. (Forthcoming). *Three worlds of relief: Race, immigration, and the American welfare state from the Progressive Era to the New Deal.* Princeton, NJ: Princeton University Press.

Fox, H. (2009). *When race breaks out: Conversations about race and racism in college classrooms.* Rev. ed. New York: Peter Lang.

Freire, P. (1981). *Education for critical consciousness.* New York: Continuum.

Freire, P. (1986). *Pedagogy of the oppressed.* New York: Continuum.

Freire, P. (1989). *Learning to question*. New York: Continuum.

Freire, P. (1998). *Pedagogy of freedom*. Lanham, MD: Rowman & Littlefield.

Freire, P. (2007 [1997]). *Pedagogy of the heart*. New York: Continuum.

Freire, P., & Macedo, D. (1987). *Literacy: Reading the word and the world*. New York: Routledge.

Freyberg-Inan, A. (2003) *What moves man: The realist theory of international relations and its judgment of human nature*. Albany: State University of New York Press.

Friends of River Narmada. (n.d.). http://www.narmada.org/index.html (accessed May 17, 2011).

Fry, D. (2006). *The human potential for peace*. Oxford, UK: Oxford University Press.

Gabriel, S. (2010, December 19). Mental health needs seen growing at colleges. *New York Times*. http://www.nytimes.com/2010/12/20/health/20campus.html?emc=eta1.

Galen Productions. (1996). *Chicano! The history of the Mexican American civil rights movement*. Los Angeles: NLCC Educational Media.

Gish, A. G. (2001). *Hebron Journal: Stories of nonviolent peacemaking*. Scottdale, PA: Herald Press.

Grossman, D. (2009). *On killing*. Rev. ed. Boston: Back Bay Books.

Guardian UK. (2011, April 6). Is Duke Nukem forever a throwback to gaming's sexist past? http://www.guardian.co.uk/technology/gamesblog/2011/apr/06/duke-nukem-forever-capture-the-babe.

Guglielmo, T. (2003). *White on arrival: Italians, race, color and power in Chicago, 1890–1945*. New York: Oxford University Press.

Hacker, A., & Dreifus, C. (2010). *Higher education?* New York: Times Books.

Hafner, K. (2009, May 26). Texting may be taking a toll. *New York Times*. D1. http://www.nytimes.com/2009/05/26/health/26teen.html.

Hampton, H. (2006). *Eyes on the prize*. Alexandria, VA: PBS Video.

Harris, G. (2010, July 9). Caustic government report deals blow to diabetes drug. *New York Times*. http://www.nytimes.com/2010/07/10/health/10diabetes.html?emc=tnt&tntemail0=y.

Harvey, D. (2005). *A brief history of neoliberalism*. New York: Oxford University Press.

Hayes, E., & Cuban, S. (1997, Fall). Border pedagogy: A critical framework for service learning. *Michigan Journal of Community Service Learning*, 72–80.

Hedges, C. (2002). *War is a force that gives us meaning*. New York: Public Affairs.

Hochschild, A. (1999). *King Leopold's ghost*. New York: Mariner Books.

Holt, J. (1994 [1964]). *How children fail*. Cambridge, MA: Da Capo Press.

Horton, M. (1999). *The long haul*. New York: Teachers College Press.

Horton, M., & Freire, P. (1990). *We make the road by walking*. Philadelphia: Temple University Press.

Howe, N., & Strauss, W. (2000). *Millennials rising: The next great generation*. New York: Vintage Books.

Huffington Post. (2009, April 16). 10 most offensive Tea Party signs and extensive photo coverage from Tax Day protests. http://www.huffingtonpost.com/2009/04/16/10-most-offensive-tea-par_n_187554.html.

Illich, I. (2000 [1971]). *Deschooling society*. London: Marion Boyars Publishers Ltd.

Iran Contra Coverup. YouTube. http://www.youtube.com/watch?v=35KcYgMPiIM.

Irvine, M. (2004–2009). "The Postmodern," "Postmodernism," "Postmodernity": Approaches to Po-Mo. http://www9.georgetown.edu/faculty/irvinem/theory/pomo.html.

Jones, J. W. (2006, April). Why does religion turn violent? A psychoanalytical exploration of religious terrorism. *Psychoanalytic Review, 93*(2), 167–190.

Kansas State University. (2010, January 13). People's racial biases can skew perceptions of how much help victims need. *ScienceDaily*. http://www.sciencedaily.com/releases/2010/01/100112121948.htm (accessed July 24, 2010).

Katznelson, I. (2006). *When affirmative action was white: An untold history of racial inequality in twentieth-century America.* New York: W.W. Norton.

Kaufman, F. (2010, July). The food bubble: How Wall Street starved millions and got away with it. *Harper's Magazine*, 27–34.

Kerr, C. (2001 [1963]). *The uses of the university*. 5th ed. Cambridge, MA: Harvard University Press.

King, M. E. (2007). *A quiet revolution: The first Palestinian Intifada and nonviolent resistance.* New York: Nation Books.

Koopman, S. (2008). Imperialism within: Can the master's tools bring down empire? *Acme: An International E-Journal for Critical Geographies, 7*(2), 283–307.

Kozol, J. (1967). *Death at an early age.* Boston: Houghton Mifflin.

Kurlansky, M. (2008). *Nonviolence: The history of a dangerous idea.* New York: Modern Library.

Lamont, S. (2001, December 3). Alabama students protest racist depiction of blacks. *Militant*. http://www.themilitant.com/2001/6546/654654.html.

LEO Matters. (2011, May). *The Fair Compensation Issue, 14.* www.leounion.org.

Lewin, T. (2008, December 3). College may become unaffordable for most in U.S. *New York Times*. http://www.nytimes.com/2008/12/03/education/03college.html.

Loewen, J. (2007). *Lies my teacher told me.* Clearwater, FL: Touchstone Books.

Lovetoknow. (n.d.). Texting shorthand. http://cellphones.lovetoknow.com/Texting_Shorthand (accessed May 25, 2010).

Madland, D., & Teixeira, R. (2009, May 13). New Progressive America: The Millennial generation. *Center for American Progress*. http://www.americanprogress.org/issues/2009/05/millennial_generation.html.

Mahony, L., & Eguren, L. E. (1997). *Unarmed bodyguards.* West Hartford, CT: Kumarian Press.

Marullo, S. (1999). Sociology's essential role: Promoting critical analysis in service learning. In J. Ostrow, G. Hesser, & S. Enos (eds.), *Cultivating the sociological imagination: Concepts and models for service-learning in sociology*, 11–27. Washington, DC: American Association of Higher Education.

Michigan Civil Rights Commission. (2010, March). A report on the conditions of migrant and seasonal farmworkers in Michigan. http://www.michigan.gov/documents/mdcr/MSFW-Conditions2010_318275_7.pdf.

Mitchell, T. D. (2008, Spring). Traditional vs. critical service-learning: Engaging the literature to differentiate two models. *Michigan Journal of Community Service Learning*, 50–65.

Mokhtari, S. (2009). *After Abu Ghraib: Exploring human rights in America and the Middle East.* Cambridge, MA: Cambridge University Press.

Morton, K. (1995, Fall). The irony of service. *Michigan Journal of Community Service Learning,* 19–32.

National and Community Service. (2006, October 16). Report finds sharp increase in college student volunteering. http://www.nationalservice.gov/about/newsroom/releases_detail.asp?tbl_pr_id=489.

Nauert, R. (2010, April 23). College students "addicted" to social media, study finds. LiveScience. http://www.livescience.com/culture/addicted-social-media-100423.html.

Nelson, R. (1991). *Roots in water.* New York: Broadway Play Publishing.

New Politics Institute. (2007). The progressive politics of the Millennial Generation. http://www.newpolitics.net/node/360?full_report=1.

Nussbaum, M. (1997). *Cultivating humanity: A Classical defense of reform in liberal education.* Cambridge, MA: Harvard University Press.

Orfield, G., & Lee, C. (2007). Historic reversals, accelerating segregation, and the need for new integration strategies. *The Civil Rights Project,* UCLA. http://www.civilrightsproject.ucla.edu/research/deseg/reversals_reseg_need.pdf.

Palmer, P., & Zajonc, A. (2010). *The heart of higher education.* San Francisco: Jossey-Bass.

PBS Frontline. (2010, February 20). Digital Nation: Interview Sherry Turkle. http://www.pbs.org/wgbh/pages/frontline/digitalnation/interviews/turkle.htm.

Peace and Justice Studies Association & the International Peace Research Association Foundation. (2006). *Global directory of Peace Studies and Conflict Resolution programs.* 7th ed. Fairfax, VA: COPRED.

Peace Pledge Union. (n.d.). Genocide. http://www.ppu.org.uk/genocide/g_cambodia1.html (accessed September 20, 2010).

Pew Research Center. (2010a, February). Millennials: A portrait of Generation Next. http://pewsocialtrends.org/assets/pdf/millennials-confident-connected-open-to-change.pdf.

Pew Research Center. (2010b, February). Almost all Millennials accept interracial dating and marriage. http://pewresearch.org/pubs/1480/millennials-accept-iinterracial-dating-marriage-friends-different-race-generations.

Phenix, L. M. (1985). *You got to move: Stories of change in the South.* http://www.milestonefilms.com/movie.php/ygtm/.

Ponchaud, F. (1978). *Cambodia: Year Zero.* New York: Henry Holt & Co.

Power, S. (2002). *A problem from hell: America and the Age of Genocide.* New York: Basic Books.

Pryor, J. S., Hurtado, S., DeAngelo, L., Palucki Blake, L., & Tran, S. (2010). *The American Freshman: National Norms. Fall, 2010.* Los Angeles: Higher Education Research Institute at UCLA.

Ravitch, D. (2010). *The death and life of the great American school system.* New York: Basic Books.

Reardon, B. A. (1996). *Sexism and the war system.* Syracuse, NY: Syracuse University Press.

Reeves, J. (2010, April 22). Kappa Alpha Fraternity, inspired by Robert E. Lee, bans

Confederate Rebel uniforms. *Al.com: Breaking News from the Birmingham News*. http://blog.al.com/spotnews/2010/04/kappa_alpha_fraternity_inspire.html

Roy, A. (2010). *Poverty capital: Microfinance and the making of development*. New York: Routledge.

Roy, A. (2009). *Field notes on democracy*. Chicago: Haymarket Books.

Roy, A. (1999, April). The greater common good. Friends of River Narmada. http://www.narmada.org/gcg/gcg.html.

Schorn, D. (2010, April 26). Popping pills a popular way to boost brain power. http://www.cbsnews.com/stories/2010/04/22/60minutes/main6422159.shtml.

Science Daily. (2008, September 2). http://www.sciencedaily.com/

Sharp, B. (n.d.). Counting hell. Mekong.net. http://www.mekong.net/cambodia/deaths.htm (accessed September 6, 2010).

Sharp, G. (1973). The methods of nonviolent action. In Sharp, Part 2, *The politics of nonviolent action, 109–902*. Boston: Porter Sargent Publishers.

Shaw, R. (2008, November 11). Origins of the Obama machine. *In These Times*. http://www.inthesetimes.com/article/4037/origins_of_the_obama_machine/.

Stearns, E., Buchmann, C., & Bonneau, K. (2009, April). Interracial friendships in the transition to college: Do birds of a feather flock together once they leave the nest? *Sociology of Education, 82*, 173–95.

Strain, C. R. (2006, November). Moving like a starfish: Beyond a unilinear model of student transformation in service learning classes. *Journal of College and Character, 8*(1), 1–12.

Stramer, J. (2010). The language of war: George W. Bush's discursive practices in securitizing the Western value system in the "War on Terror." In Brecher, B., *The new order of war*, 35–48. Amsterdam: Rodopi.

Sugrue, T. J. (1996). *The origins of the urban crisis: Race and inequality in postwar Detroit*. Princeton, NJ: Princeton University Press.

Tanaka, Y., & Young, M. B. (eds.). (2009). *Bombing civilians: A twentieth-century history*. New York: The New Press.

Thetalkingdrum.com. (n.d.). Dead Prez and their thoughts on revolution. http://www.thetalkingdrum.com/rbg.html (accessed July 18, 2010).

Thomas, C. A. (2006). *At hell's gate: A soldier's journey from war to peace*. Boston: Shambhala Publications.

Tinker, B. (2006, April). Language to open hearts and minds. *The Portland Alliance*. http://www.theportlandalliance.org/2006/apr/openhearts.htm (accessed October 4, 2010).

Tolstoy, I. (2008 [1914]). *Reminiscences of Tolstoy*. Sioux Falls, SD: NuVision Publications.

Tormey, S. (2004). *Anti-capitalism: A beginner's guide*. Oxford, UK: Oneworld Publications.

Torres, C. A. (1998). *Education, power, and personal biography: Dialogues with critical educators*. New York: Routledge.

Tufts University. (2009, December 18). Nonverbal communication of race bias on TV influences viewers' own bias. *ScienceDaily*. http://www.sciencedaily.com/releases/2009/12/091217141310.htm (accessed July 24, 2010).

United Students Against Sweatshops. (n.d.). http://usas.org/ (accessed August 21, 2010).

United Students Against Sweatshops. (2010, June 7). Young workers plan the future of the union movement. http://usas.org/2010/06/07/young-workers-summit/.

University of Illinois at Urbana-Champaign. (2010, April 21). Color-blind racial ideology linked to racism, both online and offline. *ScienceDaily.* http://www.sciencedaily.com/releases/2010/04/100421162611.htm (accessed July 24, 2010).

University of Michigan. (2009a). 2009 University of Michigan Entering Student Factbook. http://www.umich.edu/~rsa/factbook.html.

University of Michigan. (2009b). Undergraduate Profile, 2009. http://provost.umich.edu/college_portrait/2009/.

University of Michigan. (2010, May 27). Podcast: Why empathy is declining among college students. RecordUpdate. http://www.ns.umich.edu/podcast/audio.php?id=1244.

University Record. (2010, February 1). National study provides snapshot of U-M incoming class of 2009. http://ur.umich.edu/0910/Feb01_10/711-national-study-provides-snapshot-of-u-m-incoming-class-of-2009.

Van Doren, M. (1943). *Liberal education.* New York: Henry Holt and Company.

Washburn, J. (2005). *University, Inc.: The corporate corruption of higher education.* New York: Basic Books.

Weiss, T. G. (2007). *Humanitarian intervention.* Cambridge, UK: Polity Press.

Werner, D., & Bower, B. (1982). *Helping health workers learn: A book of methods, aids, and ideas for instructors at the village level.* Berkeley, CA: Hesperian Foundation. http://www.hesperian.org/.

Wikipedia. (n.d.). List of emoticons. http://en.wikipedia.org/w/index.php?title=List_of_emoticons&direction=prev&oldid=364361575 (accessed May 26, 2010).

Wilkinson, R., & Pickett, K. (2009). *The spirit level: Why greater equality makes societies stronger.* New York: Bloomsbury Press.

Winant, H. (2001). *The world is a ghetto: Race and democracy since World War II.* New York: Basic Books.

Wolff, S. (2006). *Ethnic conflict: A global perspective.* Oxford; New York: Oxford University Press.

Workable Peace. (n.d.). Project Information. http://www.workablepeace.org/project.html (accessed September 20, 2010).

York, S. (1999). *A force more powerful.* Films for the Humanities and Sciences. http://www.aforcemorepowerful.org/films/index.php.

York University. (2009, January 9). Surprisingly high tolerance for racism revealed. *ScienceDaily.* http://www.sciencedaily.com/releases/2009/01/090108144747.htm (accessed July 24, 2010).

Zinn, H. (2003). *A people's history of the United States.* New York: Harper Perennial.

Zinn, H. (2006, September 2). War is not a solution for terrorism. *Boston Globe.* http://www.boston.com/news/globe/editorial_opinion/oped/articles/2006/09/02/war_is_not_a_solution_for_terrorism/